Myth and Politics in Ancient Near Eastern Historiography

Statue of Idri-Mi
Courtesy of the British Museum

Myth and Politics in Ancient Near Eastern Historiography

MARIO LIVERANI

Edited and Introduced by
Zainab Bahrani and Marc Van De Mieroop

Cornell University Press
Ithaca, New York

First published 2004 by Cornell University Press

First printing Cornell Paperbacks, 2007

Library of Congress Cataloging-in-Publication Data

Liverani, Mario.
    Myth and politics in ancient Near Eastern historiography / Mario Liverani;
edited and introduced by Zainab Bahrani and Marc Van De Mieroop
        p. cm.
    Includes bibliographical references and index.
    ISBN 13: 978-8014-4333-6 (cloth : alk. paper)
    ISBN 13: 978-8014-7358-6 (pbk : alk. paper)
    1. Middle East–History–To 622–Historiography. 2. Middle East–History–
Sources. I. Bahrani, Zainab, 1962- II. Van De Mieroop, Marc. III. Title.

DS62.2.L58 201
939'.4–dc22   2004050091

Paperback printing   10   9   8   7   6   5   4   3   2   1

Contents

Editors' Introduction[*]

Myth and Politics in Ancient Near Eastern Historiography brings together, for the first time, a series of essays by the leading historian of the ancient Near East, Mario Liverani. These essays have all appeared previously in scholarly journals, mostly in the Italian language (one in French). Because their original language is not widely read outside Italy, they have been ignored to a great extent by non-Italian scholars, despite their often fundamental rereading of ancient texts that are the basis of many of our historical reconstructions. Their presentation here is thus aimed at giving them the audience they deserve. The intention of this edition is also to provide more than a translation into English of earlier essays: the collection has the unifying theme that all the chapters are fundamentally concerned with the question of historiography. Although they cover a wide range of historical and chronological subjects, they are all rigorous investigations of how the historian makes meaning of an ancient document. In other words, they address the historian's craft as an intellectual enterprise. This focus on the work of the historian has implications for history as a practice in general, not only for the ancient Near East.

At the same time, this is also a collection of essays that allows the reader to see the development of Liverani's work from the early 1970s until the 1980s. The papers retain a great validity more than twenty years later because they were revolutionary in character and their concerns have only recently come to be shared by other scholars in ancient Near Eastern studies. They continue to stand as a paradigm of historical criticism of ancient Near Eastern textual sources.

[*] The essays published here were originally translated from the Italian and French by Mario Liverani himself, who also removed some philological discussions. They were sent to John Baines for publication in the Equinox series. Baines asked us to edit them for their English style. We decided also to provide short introductions that are intended to contextualise the material discussed in the essays. We do not aim to update the bibliography and discussion, except when easily accessible recent English translations are available. John Baines went over our work several times, and Mario Liverani read and commented on the final version. We have attempted to turn Liverani's elegant Italian style into acceptable English academic writing, but must acknowledge that this has on occasion done a disservice to his original. Since the content of these contributions is so important, we have persevered, even if we may not always have succeeded in rendering the form.

Liverani's scholarly and methodological concerns were developed in relation to literary and anthropological scholarship of the time when he wrote the essays. In retrospect, from the point of view of twenty to thirty years on, we can see that the work arose out of an intellectual climate of the late 1960s and early 1970s, when structuralism and post-structuralism was being developed in Continental Europe. Liverani's questions and concerns, his insistence upon the nature of the processes of reading historical documents, emerged within this climate.

One of Liverani's methodological innovations is his utilisation of a structural analysis of myth for Mesopotamian material. In 'Adapa, guest of the gods' (chapter one), rather than adhering to a standard reading on the level of the narrative myth, he takes an anthropological approach, inspired by Claude Lévi-Strauss, that considers the rituals of hospitality. The dyads of food and drink, clothing and bathing are aspects of treating guests according to obligatory rules of behaviour. Anu's startling offer of immortality is understood in the context of these rules, and Adapa's rejection saves the god from having to change the destiny of mankind. Liverani intersects a structuralist approach of mythical narrative with anthropological discussions of rituals of hospitality (deriving notably from Julian Pitt-Rivers), and with the more standard philological criticism of the ancient historian.

In chapter two, 'Telipinu, or: on solidarity', Liverani explicitly takes his colleagues to task. He points out that the 'lazy historian' reads the ancient text at face value, and considers it to be an accurate narrative that only needs to be adjusted with additions or minor corrections from other sources. Liverani insists on the point that sources are always historical reconstructions in themselves and that they do not have a 'pure historical aim'. Instead, their aim is political, moral, theological, and so on. We have to analyse their ideology in order to come closer to the original intent of the text and the historical reality. In the case of the edict of Telipinu, a structural analysis reveals a binary pattern of good and bad reigns that succeed one another, with Telipinu's presenting a culmination of the positive development. To accept this as an accurate reflection of what happened in Old Kingdom Hittite history is naive, and the text of the Edict has to be seen as providing information about Telipinu rather than about the reigns of his predecessors.

The above points may seem obvious to the theoretically aware reader today. However, at the time of the essay's publication in 1977, historians generally did not think about these methodological issues. It also needs to be stressed that Liverani, as a historian of the ancient Near East, was not simply following methodological trends established in other areas of the discipline of history. In fact, he addressed these historiographic issues at the same time as historians such as Hayden White were beginning to write more directly about historical criticism. Hayden White's work in the 1970s and 80s is best known for employing the critiques of literary narrative, rhetoric, and so on, in the study of historical texts that had been traditionally considered transparent documents (see, for example, the papers collected in Hayden White, *The Content of the Form*, Baltimore: The Johns Hopkins University Press, 1987). Parallel to that body of work, Liverani already in the early 1970s insisted on considering the historical document as a written source, with qualities that require the same kind of reading as other written texts. Thus, Liverani's work should not be seen as influenced by these changes, but rather as participating in them at the forefront, in relation to sources from antiquity. Part of the reason why his theoretical commentaries on history have been less known than those of his contemporaries is no doubt that work in ancient Near Eastern studies is not widely read by other historians, who consider the field to be peripheral, if a historical discipline at all. An important aim of this edition of Liverani's writings is to present the development of his thinking about historical criticism to a wider audience by contextualising and historicising it within the broader framework of academic theories that emerged in both the humanities and social sciences in Continental Europe while he was composing them.

Take, for example, the third chapter, 'Shunashura, or: on reciprocity' (first published in 1973). Here Liverani discusses a document that is neither a historical narrative of events nor an annal, but a single document – a treaty. He analyses it as a literary text, focusing on the use of symmetry in its formation, and correlating that duality or mirroring to the importance of exchange and binary parity in certain events. The symmetry in the text is only apparent, however, and disguises a lack of equality in the political reality: the equality is not between the king of Hatti and Shunashura, king of Kizzuwatna, but between the former and the king of Mitanni, the intended but only indirectly implied audience of the treaty. Without a literary and structural semiotic analysis, such an understanding could not have been achieved.

From his earliest work Liverani has been concerned with the idea that history is a realist genre. In terms of narrative, or rather of the relationship between historical narrative and realism, we can look at the essay on Idrimi, 'Leaving by chariot for the desert' (chapter four). Liverani argues that the story told about Idrimi is true, but that the narrative follows the format of a fairy tale and can be analysed with the techniques developed by Vladimir Propp. The elements of the young hero who has obstacles to overcome, and sets out by himself into the desert, can be also found in other ancient Near Eastern texts, where they need equally to be seen as literary devices rather than factual data. The details in these stories are emphasised or concealed according to the function of a specific remark in the framework of the entire narrative. This emphasis on details is what Roland Barthes called 'the Reality Effect' (e.g., in *The Rustle of Language*, R. Howard, translator, New York: Hill and Wang, 1968, pp. 141–54): the historical narrative provides an image that is excessively detailed in order to convince the audience that it is real.

Chapters five and six, on the Syrian rulers Rib-Adda and Aziru, deal with the self-construction of their authors in letters to the Egyptian Pharaoh. They use literary devices to present their case: Rib-Adda is like a righteous sufferer, who has been abandoned by his god, the Pharaoh; Aziru uses a language that expresses exactly the opposite of what he ostensibly states. The analyses of these letters are consequently not unlike those of the descriptions of Idrimi and of Joash. In 'The story of Joash' (chapter seven), a similar approach of deconstructing an account according to narrative formulae and logic is applied to a Biblical account. The story is an apologia to justify why Joash ended up on the throne of Judah, and shares the literary elements of other such political documents found elsewhere and in other periods in the ancient Near East. In all of these cases Liverani uses a deconstructive approach in order to read against the grain of the narrative as it is constructed in the texts. He strips the text of its ideology, de-mystifies it, and unmasks its aims, which are always out of reach of a surface reading of the text. In other words, his concern is with ideology.

Liverani's critique of ideology is of an Althusserian, or structuralist-Marxist, bent, and his was the first true concern with ideology to enter ancient Near Eastern Studies. After the late 1970s, it had a tremendous impact on the rest of the field, where the concept of ideology was taken up by art historians and philologists alike, especially by those working on the Assyrian empire (e.g., Irene Winter, 'Royal Rhetoric and the Development of Historical Narrative in Neo-Assyrian Reliefs', *Studies in Visual Communication* 7 [1981], pp. 2–38). By the 1980s 'ideology' had become a standard approach to the definition of the material, although some of those who adhered to this approach missed Liverani's original methodological insights, often taking ideology to mean simply coercive propaganda. In the meantime, Liverani's own work became more and more complex, moving from structuralism to psychoanalytic and gendered readings of historical texts.

For example, in Liverani's rereading of the biblical book of Judges 19–21 (chapter eight), published in 1979, he focused on the human body as the medium of a message before such a reading had become fashionable in history and cultural studies, where the literature is now enormous (e.g., Caroline Walker Bynum, *Fragmentation and Redemption: Essays on Gender and the Human Body in Medieval Religion*, New York: Zone Books, 1992). Moreover, Liverani introduced questions of gender theory when feminist studies of the Bible had barely begun. The relationships of women, hospitality, and exchange were, of course, issues central to Marcel Mauss's study of exchange (*The Gift*, London: Routledge and Kegan Paul, 1969) and in the structuralist anthropology of Claude Lévi-Strauss (notably *The Elementary Structures of Kinship*, London: Eyre and Spottiswoode, 1969), but

Liverani took these anthropological discussions much further by considering them in relation to the historical text.

In more recent years, Liverani has taken the critique of historiography and directed it inward, in a self-reflexive turn towards his own field. This work is not represented in the present collection, but it is more accessible since it includes several articles in English. Such self-reflexivity is now widely acknowledged as a hallmark of postmodernism, and in this too Liverani's work has been groundbreaking, despite his stance against postmodern scholarly scepticism (*Orientalia* 69 [2000]: pp. 331–32). In his critique of ideology he extends his perspective into our own day, reminding us that in this era of globalisation, we would be mistaken to consider ourselves outside of ideology. Ideology must still be addressed, not only in the ancient texts themselves, but also in the way that we, as students of antiquity, mediate those texts into scholarship. The writing of history, even ancient history, far from being an innocent didactic exercise, is inevitably influenced by changing political needs, religious, political and ideological biases, and so on. For instance, Liverani's historiography of studies on Mesopotamian urbanism ('The Ancient Near Eastern City and Modern Ideologies', in G. Wilhelm [ed.], *Die orientalische Stadt: Kontinuität, Wandel, Bruch*, Saarbrücken: Saarbrücker Verlag, 1997, pp. 85–108) connects views of the city to the contemporary situations of the scholars who express them: Orientalism, colonialism, neo-capitalism, and others. A study of the interplay between archaeology and history in modern scholarship reveals how the (counterproductive) antagonism between the two disciplines has been very much tied to general ideological trends of the eras in which scholars worked and continue to work ('History and Archaeology in the Ancient Near East: 150 Years of a Difficult Relationship', in H. Kühne *et al.* [eds], *Fluchtpunkt Uruk. Archäologische Einheit aus methodischer Vielfalt. Schriften für Hans Jörg Nissen*, Rahden/Westf.: Leidorf, 1999, pp. 1–11). In addition to critiques of ideology, these recent essays present epistemological reflections on the discipline of ancient Near Eastern studies in general.

Liverani's scholarly output continues to be so prolific and so innovative that one could all too easily overlook his earlier works. That would, however, be a grave mistake; his early articles are as relevant today as when they were first published. We hope that the present selection will not only make more students of history aware of the insights on periods and texts Liverani provides, but will also inspire them to follow his path. A more rigorous examination both of the ancient record and of modern influences on the scholar can only help the study of the ancient Near East to find its rightful place in the discipline of history as a whole.

Zainab Bahrani
Marc Van De Mieroop

Acknowledgements

Chapter 1 was originally published in Italian in *Religioni e Civiltà*, Bari, 1982.

Chapter 2 was originally published in Italian in *Oriens Antiquus* 16, 1977.

Chapter 3 was originally published in Italian in *Oriens Antiquus* 12, 1973.

Chapter 4 was originally published in Italian in *Annali dell'Istituto Universitario Orientale di Napoli* 22, 1972.

Chapter 5 was originally published in Italian in *Altorientalische Forschungen* 1, 1974.

Chapter 6 was originally published in Italian in *Studi Orientalistici in Ricordo di Franco Pintore*, GJES Edizioni, Pavia, 1983.

Chapter 7 was originally published in French in *Vetus Testamentum* 24, 1974.

Chapter 8 was originally published in Italian in *Studi Storico-Religiosi* 3, 1979.

Abbreviations

AHw   W. von Soden, *Akkadisches Handwörterbuch* (3 vols). Wiesbaden: Harrassowitz, 1959–1981

ARAB   D. D. Luckenbill, *Ancient Records of Assyria and Babylonia* (2 vols). Chicago: The University of Chicago Press, 1926–27

ARE   J. H. Breasted, *Ancient Records of Egypt* (5 vols). Chicago: The University of Chicago Press, 1906–1907

ARM   *Archives royales de Mari* (26 vols). Paris: Imprimerie Nationale; Editions Recherche sur les Civilisations, 1950–88

CAD   *The (Chicago) Assyrian Dictionary*. Chicago: The Oriental Institute; Glückstadt: Augustin, 1956 ff.

EA   el-Amarna tablets, quoted from Knudtzon 1907 and Rainey 1970

KBo   *Keilschrifttexte aus Boghazköi* (41 vols). Leipzig: Hinrichs; Berlin: Gebr. Mann Verlag, 1916–1999

KUB   *Keilschrifturkunden aus Boghazköi* (60 vols). Berlin: Vorderasiatische Abteilung der Staatlichen Museen; Akademie Verlag, 1922–1990

THAT   E. Jenni and C. Westermann (eds), *Theologisches Handwörterbuch zum Alten Testament* (2 vols). Munich: Chr. Kaiser Verlag; Zürich: Theologischer Verlag, 1971–1976

TWAT   G. J. Botterweck and H. Ringgren (eds), *Theologisches Wörterbuch zum Alten Testament* (10 vols). Stuttgart: W. Kohlhammer, 1963–2000

Urk IV   K. Sethe and W. Helck (eds), *Urkunden des ägyptischen Altertums. IV: Urkunden der 18. Dynastie* (22 vols). Leipzig: Hinrichs; Berlin: Akademie Verlag, 1906–1958

'I segni formano una lingua, ma non quella che credi conoscere'

Italo Calvino, *Le città invisibili*: Le città e i segni, 4

(Signs form a language, but not the one you think you know)

PART ONE

Mesopotamia

1

*Adapa, guest of the gods**

INTRODUCTION

One of the handful of Akkadian literary texts found at the Egyptian capital of Amarna is the short story of Adapa. By the fourteenth century, the composition was thus known outside Babylonia, which must be its region of origin. We do not have any manuscripts from Mesopotamia proper until the seventh century library of Ashurbanipal, however. Altogether only four fragmentary manuscripts are known so far, but they do allow us to reconstruct the outlines of the story at the beginning of this chapter.

The main character, Adapa, was one of the seven antediluvian sages who brought civilisation to humankind. In this story he appears as the priest of the god Ea in the city of Eridu near the Persian Gulf, and is responsible for the care and feeding of his god, having to procure fish for the offerings. In the course of his duties he disturbs the natural order, and is invited by the god Anu in heaven to justify himself. There he misses the opportunity to gain immortality by refusing the food and drink offered him. The chapter here analyses the story as a foundational myth to explain human mortality.

The poem was recently fully re-edited by Izre'el 2001. Recent English translations have appeared in Dalley 1989: 182–7; Foster 1993: 429–34; Foster 1995: 97–101.

★ ★ ★ ★

1 THE NARRATIVE LOGIC

1.1 THE STORY AND ITS 'CONTRADICTIONS'

The Babylonian myth of Adapa – a short text, whose basic plot is fortunately preserved in four surviving fragments[1] – is one of the numerous myths that

---

* Originally published as 'Adapa ospite degli dei,' in *Religioni e civiltà* (Bari, 1982), 293–319.

[1] Fragment B (the largest) is from the Amarna archive of the mid-second millennium; fragments A, C, D are from the seventh century library of Ashurbanipal at Nineveh. The diffusion of the tale in space and its persistence through time are thus certain. The translations normally used are those

explain the mortality of man, from the ancient Near East and elsewhere. More specifically the text narrates (as do other myths) the vicissitudes of a mythical figure, endowed with archetypal responsibilities,[2] who had access to immortality, and yet ultimately let it slip from his hands.

The myth is well known, but a summary of the events is in order. The boat of Adapa, 'son' of the god Ea and his priest in Eridu, was capsized by the South Wind (*šūtu*) in a sudden storm, while he was fishing in the open sea to provide food for the god's table. In anger, Adapa cursed Shutu, and his words effectively broke the wings of the wind, which thereupon subsided. The supreme god Anu noticed this disturbance in the natural order, was told of its cause, and summoned Adapa. But Ea – here, as elsewhere, the helpful god of wisdom and cunning – gave Adapa two instructions in order to avoid the expected punishment by Anu. He first instructed Adapa to dress as if he were in mourning, and to tell the gods he would find at Anu's door, Tammuz and Gizzida, that he was dressed this way because they had disappeared from earth. This way he would gain their goodwill and assistance. Ea's second instruction was that Adapa should refuse the food of death (*a-ka-la ša mu-ti*) and the water of death (*me-e mu-u-ti*) that would be offered to him. But he should accept the clothing and the oil for anointing. Armed with these instructions, Adapa set out. As foreseen he obtained the help of Tammuz and Gizzida, was introduced into the presence of Anu, was interrogated, and was able to explain his reasons. At this point Anu, struck by the extraordinary wisdom and cleverness of Adapa (the evident gifts of Ea), decided not to be mean-spirited and to offer the food and water of life (*a-ka-al ba-la- ṭi, me-e ba-la- ṭi*) to the hero. Adapa, certain that these were the deadly victuals against which Ea had warned him, refused them, and accepted only the clothing and oil. At the end of the mythical narrative Anu explained that his chance to gain life had been lost:

> Anu looked at him and laughed: 'Come here, Adapa: why did you not eat and drink? (Now) you will not live!' ... 'Let him be taken away and brought back to his land!'
>
> (B 66–70)

In the fourth fragment (D), a kind of appendix (badly preserved and probably 'secondary' in character)[3] shows that the myth could be used as a spell, perhaps

---

by Speiser in Pritchard 1969: 101–3 and by Labat 1970: 290–4. The long article by Furlani 1929 contains a complete bibliography up to that date; I will therefore quote only later studies, and only when they are relevant to the arguments of this chapter.

2 Adapa is explicitly labelled (A 6) *riddum*, i.e. '(model) to be followed, imitated' by all mankind. On this term see *AHw*, 981; *CAD* R, 324. The archetypal-foundational value of the mythical story and its protagonist need no longer be demonstrated, although some scholars still maintain that Adapa could obtain life for himself only.

3 The secondary character of fragment D has been noticed many times, especially by Jacobsen 1929–30: 201–3 (but see Michalowski 1980 for a different opinion). In defining its use as an incantation

against diseases linked to the south wind, against which Adapa's intervention must have been considered particularly effective.

The many interpreters of the myth have dwelt insistently on a presumed logical (and psychological) inconsistency and a presumed narrative 'contradiction'. The question is: How is it possible that Ea gave to his favourite, Adapa, instructions that turned out to be detrimental, although he is the god of wisdom, and in particular of predictions? How is it possible that he foresaw the offering of the food and water of death, while those of life were in fact offered? Various scholars have proposed every conceivable answer. Some suggested that Ea willingly deceived Adapa in order to prevent him from becoming immortal (either to keep the correct relationship between man and the divine world, or more practically, to keep Adapa's priestly services), or in order to punish him for an offence that was too serious to forgive. Conversely, others suggested that Ea gave advice that he honestly considered to be good, but that his evaluation of the situation was undermined by the change in the behaviour of Anu, who, instead of punishing Adapa, decided to reward him. The story of the various interpretations has been told many times (Furlani 1929: 159–61; Roux 1961: 27 and 30; Castellino 1967: 129–30; Buccellati 1973: 62; Xella 1973: 259–60), and I need not repeat it here. Let me just add that the most recently proposed solution – that divine victuals are by their very nature deadly to men, so that the food of death (in Ea's terminology) and the food of life (in Anu's terminology) are the same [4] – is in clear contradiction with what the narrative in fact says. Such an interpretation is more on the level of our historical-religious perception than on the level of a proper understanding of this specific Babylonian text.

1.2 NARRATIVE CONVENTIONS IN MYTHS AND FAIRY TALES

Generally speaking, the procedures used hitherto in analysing the myth of Adapa act as if it were a realistic novel. The behaviour and psychology of the characters are supposed to fit the requirements of plausibility and consistency – or else they require a development that must be coherently justified from a psychological point of view. Otherwise a novel does not 'stand'. I argue here that, on the contrary, we have to analyse the myth of Adapa according to the 'rules' of mythical narratives (but do I need to state such an obvious principle?), and more generally

---

as 'secondary', I wish to emphasise that the myth's aim is to explain much more than a remedy against a certain disease. In other cases, however, the relation between myth and incantation can be more fundamental.

[4] The suggestion by Böhl 1959: 429, that divine victuals (nectar and ambrosia) are deadly to men, has been taken up again by Buccellati 1973: 63 and makes up the substance of the article by Xella 1973: 257–66. See also Kienast 1973: 234–9.

of traditional stories (especially fairy tales), with which myths share many formal procedures and narrative devices.

In my opinion – and here I simplify to the maximum – two characteristics must be emphasised. The first characteristic is that in realistic narratives every single act performed by a character must find a motivation in the character himself (including even the unreasonable conduct of the mentally insane or the erratic behaviour of the absentminded). In myths or fairy tales, on the other hand, any single act can be unmotivated and unreasonable in itself, provided it is effective in setting up the explanation of the ensuing acts. The characters accomplish (or undergo) without any surprise the most improbable and strange things, which are impossible to predict or justify. But there is a coherent line that runs throughout the narrative and culminates at its conclusion.[5] The explanation of behaviour is therefore to be understood after the fact: the behaviour that leads to the desired conclusion is coherent. Naturally, the more complex the cultural reality the myth aims to provide with a foundational explanation, the more complex becomes the way in which an organic resolution of all the elements is reached. As we shall see, the cultural reality that the myth of Adapa seeks to explain is rather complex, and sufficiently 'contradictory' (contradictions are always stimuli to understanding) to require that different lines in the development of the narrative plot should coexist. But to ask whether Ea 'tricks' Adapa or is tricked by Anu, whether he foresees the outcome or is surprised by it, why Tammuz and Gizzida stand at Anu's gate, or why Anu waits 'seven' days before asking about the south wind, is devoid of meaning in the framework of the narrative logic of myth and fairy tale. Such problems should trouble us only – to use V. Šklovsky's words (1976: 58) – 'as much as a chess-player is troubled by the question why the knight cannot move in a straight line'.

The second element in the narrative logic of myths and fairy tales to be considered here is that it proceeds through oppositions and reduplications of a somewhat algebraic character. The positive or negative qualities of the single elements are always clear-cut, and are set in contrast on paradigmatic and syntagmatic axes, in order to obtain a maximum of distinctness. In this purely formal sense (we shall see its substantive relevance later on) the opposition of effective and ineffective advice is realised both through an opposition of the pair food + drink and the pair clothing + oil, and through an opposition of Ea's foresight and Anu's behaviour. Here is a tentative summary of the situation, by means of a diagram that is indeed algebraic:

---

5   Cf. the similar considerations (yet different in terminology and in the frame of a more complex methodology) by Lévi-Strauss 1964: 119.

	Ea's foresight	Ea's remedy	result according to Ea	Anu's offer	Adapa's behaviour	real result
food+drink	−	−	+	+	−	−
clothing+oil	+	+	+	+	+	+

The procedure is algebraic in the sense that the result (third and sixth columns) is positive if it comes from two equal premises, either both positive (lower line) or both negative (upper line, first and second columns). The result is negative if it comes from two premises of opposite value (upper line, fourth and fifth columns). The algebra of the Adapa myth is satisfactory; the myth 'works' well on the formal level, because all the possible combinations are present, and build up an organic system.[6]

Now, in order to explain fully the system of oppositions upon which the Adapa myth is based, we have to consider both the paradigmatic opposition between food + drink and clothing + oil (an opposition mostly ignored by previous studies), and the syntagmatic opposition between Ea's prediction and the actual course of events. In the case of the pair food + drink, the development is a reversal. In the case of the pair clothing + oil, there is an unchanged repetition. But the unchanged repetition is not useless or merely ornamental; it is not even a simple emphasis (by contrast) of the reversal affecting the other pair.[7] It is an essential point that in Ea's prediction the results are homogeneous (both positive), while in reality they are different. The myth – as is shown already by a purely formal analysis – therefore provides a foundation for a reality that is ambiguous and contradictory, and *must* be so (indeed it is founded as such). I shall examine this point below (§3.1); but I may anticipate here by saying that if the myth had to explain only human mortality, then the entire part dealing with clothing and oil would be practically meaningless.

1.3 PARADIGMATIC VS. SYNTAGMATIC ARRANGEMENT

In fact, all the scholars who have dealt with the myth, with the partial exception of Giorgio Buccellati, have paid little or no attention to the pair clothing + oil.[8] They consider it to be 'neutral' (the term was used by Furlani 1929: 171), that is,

---

6 Also the sequence - + - is implicitly taken into account. It is what Ea wants to avoid, namely the offering of deadly food, its acceptance by the unsuspecting Adapa, and his death.

7 On this point also I refer to Lévi-Strauss 1973: 79: 'a sequence which the old mythography would have interpreted as a semantic redundance and a rhetorical device must, like the myth as a whole, be taken absolutely *seriously*.'

8 The pair clothing + oil was especially noticed by Jacobsen (1929–30, who announced the point in his title), but without establishing any meaningful opposition to the other pair, food + drink.

not affecting the opposition 'life vs. death', and irrelevant to the development of the plot, since there is no contradiction between Ea's foresight and Anu's proposal. On the contrary, I think that the pair clothing + oil has an essential role in the inner balance of the myth, and that the acceptance of these 'external' gifts is as meaningful as the refusal of the 'internal' gifts (food + drink).[9] I shall consider all this in my analysis of the technological and cultural setting. In the formal analysis here we can start by observing, with Buccellati (1973: 64), that the clothing and the oil for the anointing of Adapa are intended to remedy the dirtiness and mourning which he assumed while approaching Anu's gate. If we carry this observation further, the entire situation makes more sense:

(1) Ea foresees (correctly) that the 'good' behaviour of Adapa towards Tammuz and Gizzida would bring him 'good' clothing and oil (= access to Anu's house).

(2) Ea foresees (incorrectly) that the 'bad' behaviour of Adapa towards Shutu would be punished by means of 'bad' food and drink.

In accordance with his forecasts, Ea tries to remedy two problems *in parallel*: the support of Tammuz and Gizzida should lead to the introduction of Adapa into Anu's presence; the refusal of the victuals should lead to avoiding the punishment. But the two problems are set *in sequence*, and the positive passing of the 'first test' changes the algebraic starting-point of the 'second test' from negative to positive.[10] Ea's mistake was to consider in a paradigmatic relation two elements that he should have considered in a syntagmatic relation. The two following charts set out what I mean in visual form:

(1) Ea's forecast (two problems in parallel)

problem	starting situation	Adapa's behaviour	result
admittance to Anu's presence	good behaviour towards Tammuz and Gizzida	accepting of clothing + oil	
	+	+	+
absolution from guilt	bad behaviour towards Shutu	refusal of food + drink	
	−	−	+

---

[9] On the appropriateness of characterising the two pairs of elements as 'external' and 'internal' cf. §2.1, §3.1 below.

[10] On the problematic nature of hospitality, see Pitt-Rivers 1977, chap. 5 ('The Law of Hospitality'). The stranger is submitted to a preliminary 'test' or 'incorporating ritual': if he passes it, he becomes a guest, otherwise (if he turns out to be inadequate) he can even be put to death (pp. 95–6). This indeed happens to Adapa, who passes the first test but not the second one, and therefore will die. In particular by refusing the food offered to him, he breaks a specific rule of hospitality (pp. 109–10). Anu has therefore no second thoughts, and just decides according to the results of the tests (before which the guest's standing is undecided).

(2) Real development (two problems in sequence)

good behaviour towards T.&G.	accepting of cloth + oil	result of first test	Anu's attitude	refusal of food+drink	final result
+	+	+	+	-	-

It could be objected here that the two pairs of products, the external ones (clothing + oil) and the internal ones (food + drink) are not offered in sequence but simultaneously. It is my opinion, however, that the logical sequence is more important than the chronological sequence for an understanding of the myth's narrative structure. (If only we had more variants of the myth, we could work on the plot with more assurance.) Now, on the logical plane (as we shall see better later on), the acts of cleaning and dressing, the 'external' acts, mark physical admittance. Naturally they precede the act of participating in a meal, which marks social admittance. These hints introduce us to the technological and cultural analysis of the myth. Suffice it now to emphasise that the pair clothing + oil plays a relevant and not a 'neutral' role in the 'narrative logic'. In trying to understand what the myth is really trying to explain, the acceptance of the external gifts (related to the opposition 'inside / outside') must be evaluated at the same level as the refusal of the internal gifts (related to the opposition 'life / death').

2 THE TECHNOLOGICAL AND CULTURAL SETTING

2.1 THE BASIC REQUIREMENTS OF LIFE

The four services offered by the gods to Adapa (clothing, oil, food, and drink) are not a casual collection, to which an element can be added or subtracted; they build up a structured cluster. The structure is obtained through the intersection of the two oppositions, 'solid / liquid' and 'internal / external', resulting in the following scheme:

	internal use	external use
solid	food	clothing
liquid	drink	oil

The four elements constitute the minimal necessities of life: if we are clothed and cleansed, fed and refreshed, we survive; otherwise we die. The opposition 'solid / liquid' seems only classificatory in function. By contrast, the opposition 'internal /

external' is heavy with meaningful implications. Indeed, the two internal elements are indispensable for all physical life, not only for humans but also for animals. When Enkidu, the man created by the gods to challenge Gilgamesh in the Epic of Gilgamesh, lived as an animal, he ate and drank,[11] but he entered civilisation by dressing and anointing himself. Both external elements have a similar physical function (by dressing we protect ourselves from the natural elements; by washing and anointing we keep the skin free from disease and dryness); but above all they have a cultural function: they let people live as civilised beings. Therefore, in the case of admission into civilised society (as it takes place when granting hospitality), the sequence of services is: (1) external ones, (2) internal ones. In other words, the theoretical urgency and essentiality (to eat and drink certainly come first in a physical evaluation) is reversed, in accordance with an evident cultural perspective. First, we have to admit into our circle (we have to supply the characteristics that are human and 'ours'), and then we take care of physical needs (we should not do that for someone who was not admitted as 'one among us').[12] Granting the external services has only an introductory effect (it lets one pass from the 'outside' to the 'inside'). The internal services, the really vital ones, engage people who participate in the same elements in order to belong to the same group, to share a common destiny, and to abstain from mutual hostility.

The four services do not work as a cluster only in the cases of hospitality or accepting a newcomer, cases that are relatively rare, even if they are delicate and significant. We encounter the four also within groups that already exist and live together: both the family and the 'great organisations' (temple, palace) have to supply their members with the means of survival. The documentation is most abundant for the 'great organisations'. The ration system, as standardised in Mesopotamia and in surrounding countries, supplied these four elements (and nothing else) for the survival of the individual members of the productive units. Anything else that was available in the technology of that time (from pots to looms, from agricultural implements to weapons) is not a product but a means of production. As such, all tools were the property not of individual members, but of the 'household' considered as an impersonal unit, and they were managed by the ruling members – the father of the household for the family, the officials in charge for the great organisations (see Liverani 1976b, esp. 97).

The cluster of four basic services is amply attested in Mesopotamia and throughout the entire Near East in all periods. The four elements were not

---

11 He did not eat bread or drink beer, but grass and milk, victuals that do not require a cultural treatment (cooking, fermentation, etc.). Shifting from natural victuals (grass, milk) to cultural ones (bread, beer), has the same meaning as shifting from the dirty + naked state to the anointed + dressed one.

12 On the oppositions inside / outside, extraneous / guest (or possible guest) see chapter 8.

always listed together, because the documents had a purely practical purpose. If water, rather than beer or wine, was used as drink, it did not need to be quoted in the administrative texts that record the distribution of rations from the store-houses. Water was neither scarce nor expensive, and could be drawn directly from wells or rivers. Clothing, on the other hand, was usually supplied annually, and was not recorded in monthly summaries. The standard system of Mesopotamian rations, studied in detail by I. J. Gelb (1965),[13] was structured around three commodities: food + clothing + oil. (Water was irrelevant for the administration and beer was produced from the same barley that was the basis of solid food.)

Sumerian		Akkadian	
šc-ba	síg-ba	*iprum*	*lubuštum*
–	ì-ba	–	*piššatum*

The complete cluster of all four elements can be found in culturally paradigmatic texts, such as literary ones. It is impossible and useless to quote all the data here; a few examples will suffice. In the Epic of Gilgamesh, Enkidu's shift to human (civilised) life takes place through these four elements: bread and beer, clothing and oil (Labat 1970: 159: II tablet, iii 95–106; see n.11 above). When he refuses Ishtar's offer of marriage, Gilgamesh lists the same four elements as constituting the supplies that a husband (head of the household) has to provide to his wife. He also points out that these would turn out to be ridiculous in their case, given the goddess's different needs and self-sufficiency (Labat 1970: 182: VI tablet, 25–28). In other genres of texts too the same fourfold cluster is found. For instance, in a request for oracular response, the postulant asks the god not to take into account his possible faults: dirty clothing, unclean food, drink, and oil (*ibid.*, 279). In curses the fourfold cluster of essential goods is overturned in its component elements, but keeps its structure. Therefore, in Assyrian treaties the transgressors are predicted to get

---

[13] See also the abundant Old Babylonian material quoted in *CAD* L, 237 (3 a–b). The system was still in use in later periods. See – to quote just a few examples – for the Middle Babylonian period, Wiseman 1968: 179 (TR 3005), with improvements by Postgate 1971: 468 (food, clothing, and oil for the guard corps), or §A 36 in the Assyrian Laws (the case of a woman left by her husband without oil, wood, clothing, or food). For the Neo-Babylonian period, see the sequence *ipru-piššatu-lubuštu* in *CAD* L, 235 (2 b). The same sequence appears in the lexical series, see Landsberger 1937: pl. 3: iii 47–90 ('to his nurse, for three years, he provided food, oil, and clothing'; cf. also the Laws of Eshnunna, §32); 1957: i 22–4.

Dust as their food,
asphalt as their ointment,
ass urine as their drink,
papyrus as their clothing
    (Weidner 1932–33: 20–21: Rs. iv 14–16; see Wiseman 1958: 65–6: vi 490–492)

or else, not mentioning water, as in the ration system:

the food in your mouth,
the cloth on your body,
the oil of your anointing,
may they go bad!
    (Pettinato 1975: 152 and 154: iv 16'–17')

A famous Neo-Assyrian letter depicts the ideal reign as follows:

the hungry ones are sated,
the parched ones are anointed,
the naked ones are dressed
    (Parpola 1970: n.121: Rev. 1–3; see Fales 1974)

In the neighbouring countries of Mesopotamia-Egypt, Syria-Palestine, Anatolia – the same fourfold cluster of essential goods is documented as well. It is a recurrent pattern in a large region that was quite homogeneous from the technological and economic point of view, notwithstanding local differences (such as barley / emmer wheat, wool / linen, beer / wine, etc.). Egyptian funerary offerings mostly deal with the problem of provisioning (life / death), and usually contain only the pair bread + beer, but sometimes the external elements are also included (see Morenz 1969: 50):

        bread   (linen)

        beer   (oil)

The goods considered to be essential for the dead are obviously the same that were necessary for the living. The stereotypical boast of Rekhmire can be quoted as an example of a system of centralised rations, which he issued paternalistically as his ethical duty:

I gave bread to the hungry one, water to the thirsty, meat, oil and clothing to the
unprovided   (Gardiner 1925: 70)[14]

---

[14] Cf. similar claims in Zayed 1964: 200 ('I gave bread to the hungry one, water to the thirsty one,

Conversely, when the central redistributive system failed, the artisans of Deir el-Medina protested:

> There is no cloth, no oil for anointing, no fish, no vegetables!
>
> (Edgerton 1951: 140)[15]

In this and other Egyptian texts drink is not mentioned, because in the form of water it is not a costly item, as we have seen for Mesopotamia:

> Who ate my food…
> who dressed with my linen…
> who anointed with my myrrh… (Amenemhat's teachings, Bresciani 1969: 144)

> Fill his stomach,
> put clothing on his back,
> ointment is a remedy for his body (Maxims of Ptahhotep, *ibid.*, 40)

The complete cluster is attested in the Ramessid scribal miscellanies:

> (Writing) is more pleasant than bread and beer,
> than clothing and ointment (Caminos 1954: 374: P Lansing 2: 2–3).

For Syria and Palestine, it will suffice to quote two biblical texts as examples. One is the list of goods in Hosea 2:7, where, for stylistic reasons, the cluster is expanded into six elements: bread and water, wool and linen, oil and drink. The other is the ideal behaviour as depicted in Ecclesiastes:

> eat your bread in joy,
> drink your wine in good spirit
> ………….
> be always dressed in white clothes,
> and let oil never be absent from your body! (Ecclesiastes 9:7–8)

The obligation/boast of the good ruler to provide the needy with the essential means of sustenance is encountered also in Anatolia, in terms not dissimilar from those already seen for Egypt (and from those to be found later in the New Testament):

---

clothing to the naked one') and in Bresciani 1969: 425 ('those who were hungry are happily sated now, those who were thirsty go drunk now, those who were naked are dressed now in fine linen').

[15] In practice the Ramessid system of rations (see Janssen 1975: 455–93) was more varied. Different solid foods (fish, dates, vegetables, etc.) were in use besides the basic cereals, and water was also supplied, albeit not costly (the administration had only to maintain water-carriers, as it did woodcutters for fires). Finally, supplies of oil and clothing are poorly attested.

Give bread to the hungry one,
give oil to the [...],
give clothing to the naked one   (Otten 1961: 371; Goetze 1957a: 90)

2.2 RULES OF HOSPITALITY

The examples I have quoted are representative of a much larger corpus that seems to supply an adequate technological and cultural framework for the four-fold cluster of goods in the Adapa myth. The cluster is in no way a literary device of symmetry, but a system deeply embedded in the basic necessities of the life of the time. Some texts dealing with the treatment reserved for guests are even more relevant here. The customary norm that Adapa had within his grasp (so to speak) is clearly evident: we cannot let the guest, with whom we have eaten and drunk, die. One passage in a Hittite text, in particular, seems expressly meant to provide us with the 'key' to the Adapa myth:

> The guarantee in the Hatti land is such: if we give bread and drink to somebody, then we do not harm him in any way.
>
> (Sommer 1932: 10–11; *KUB* XIV 3: ii 63–64)

A passage of the Elisha cycle in 2 Kings is equally clear. Through the trick of temporarily blinding, the prophet is able to seize some Aramaeans who are besieging Samaria. The king would like to kill them, but Elisha replies:

> Do not kill them! Even those you seized by your sword or by your bow, do not kill them! Give them (instead) bread and water, in order that they eat and drink, and (then) let them go back to their lord.   (2 Kings 6:22; cf. 2 Chronicles 28:5–15)

Transformed from prisoners into guests, the Aramaean soldiers are allowed to survive and are sent back unhurt to their comrades, who will be forced in their turn – given the reciprocal character of the law of hospitality – to stop the siege and renounce any hostile action against Israel.

To eat bread and drink water together is an explicit symbol of an alliance, of the willingness not to kill one another. A Hittite text concerning the Kashkeans states:

> If an enemy flees, you must not welcome him into your city as if you were allied with him. You must not give him bread and water. You must not send him back (unhurt) to his city.   (von Schuler 1965a: 122, §32': 77–78)

In the bilingual testament of King Hattushili I the opposition is clearly and repeatedly made between 'to eat bread and drink water' and to 'die':

If you will listen to my royal words, you will eat bread and drink water… But if you will not listen to the royal words, you will not live, you will be destroyed!

(Sommer 1938: 12–3: iii 33–37; cf. also iii 29 and 48)

In the practice of international relations, the obvious 'guest' is the messenger/ ambassador, who should be seriously worried if he is not admitted to share food and drink with the host-king. Therefore the Babylonian king reassures the Egyptian Amenophis IV:

Since the day the messenger of my brother arrived here, I have not been well, and (for this reason only) his messenger did not eat food or drink water in my presence.

(EA 7: 8–10)[16]

Correct and incorrect behaviours in participating in a meal are explicitly opposed in another letter, also of Babylonian origin:

When you gave a great party, you did not send your messenger (saying): 'Come, eat and drink', and you did not send the gifts for the festival… Look (instead) at what I did: I gave a big party in my house, and your messengers saw it, and I stood at the entrance of my house and said: 'Come, eat and drink with me! ' I did not do as you did!   (EA 3: 18–20 and 23–29)

In the same Amarna archive there is much information on the hospitality given to messengers, who never have to fear for their personal safety, notwithstanding the shifting political alliances between their kings. If political relations become strained, messengers can be retained for months and years, even until their natural death, in a state of formal hospitality that comes to resemble captivity.[17]

As we have seen in the Elisha episode, the law of hospitality is reciprocal. Not only is the host required to respect the people to whom he supplied the symbolic services of hospitality, but the guest is prohibited from harming his host and he even has to reward him. When the two 'angels' decide to destroy Sodom, they take care to keep Lot and his entire family alive. They were the hosts from whom they had received shelter and washing, food and presumably also drink. Therefore all the Sodomites died, with the exception of Lot in his capacity as host

---

16 For a different case, where the host refuses to eat and drink with the messenger/guest see Oppenheim 1967: 179 (1240: 16–11').

17 On the hospitality provided to messengers, see Zaccagnini 1973: 51–8; Lynn Holmes 1975: 376–81; in particular EA 161: 22 (food and drink), 287: 44 (food, clothing, oil). On earlier (Old Babylonian) procedures, see Munn-Rankin 1956: 96–108. On messengers kept until their death, see EA 16: 43–51; Oppenheim 1967: 145 (*KBo* I 10: Rs. 34–7); and the Egyptian tale of Wen-Amun (Wilson in Pritchard 1969: 28; Lichtheim 1973–80: II, 228).

who had shared food with the 'angels' (Gen. 19:1–29).[18] Similarly, when Joshua decreed the total destruction of Jericho, the harlot Rahab with all her relatives went free, because she had hosted the Israelite scouts and saved them from the king of Jericho (Josh. 2 and 6:22–25).[19] In the Assyrian Weidner chronicle, the beerseller Ku-Baba is rewarded with kingship for having hosted and given food and drink to the fishermen of the Esagila sanctuary, who were pursued by the officials of the king of Akshak.[20]

Yet another observation can be made on the data so far reviewed: the two pairs of goods and services have quite different functions. The pair I labelled as 'external' (clothing and oil) marks a shift in social status or in spatial location. It marks the end of a trip or admittance into a house, but also entrance into matrimonial status or royal investiture.[21] In its absence (dirt, mourning) it marks retreat, and even (in the form of nakedness) exclusion from civilised society. The 'internal' pair (food and drink), by contrast, has a direct bearing on the problem of life, of sustenance. Only the members – be they permanent or temporary – of a household are properly entitled to receive the victuals, both in the nuclear family and in the great organisation of temple or palace, whose officials are charged with maintaining all the people who are part of the household.

If one leaves aside these and other possible differences among traditions that are not relevant to the present discussion, the core of the institution is that the guest, who is in some way assimilated with members of the host household, cannot be injured, and certainly cannot be killed. It is even usual to give him gifts and to initiate a relationship of reciprocity. After Adapa has arrived at Anu's gate as a defendant, he is able (thanks to Ea's first instruction) to enter as an 'external' guest. He is attended to with goodwill, and is offered the external services, which he has no problem accepting. At this point the mechanics of the hospitality gift and a kind of prestige competition between Anu and Ea interfere. Ea gave wisdom to Adapa, so what should Anu give him that is more important? This leads Anu to offer Adapa life (B: 57–61). And the way Adapa can get this 'gift' is the

---

18 Because of the theme 'destruction of the inhospitable city', the Sodom episode is strictly similar to the one in Judges 19–21 (on which see Chapter 8).

19 The customary rule of hospitality is here reworked in terms of an explicit 'covenant' (but this is the specific ideological framework of the editor).

20 Grayson 1975: 147–8: 38–45. C. Grottanelli reminded me in this context of the episode between Jesus and the Samaritan woman (John 4:5–15). In the context of hospitality offered by a mortal being to a god, the possibility is presented of a reciprocal exchange of water that quenches only temporarily for water 'of eternal life'.

21 Kutsch 1963: 27–33, 36–66 (this work makes abundant use of data generally relevant to our topic); also Zaccagnini 1973: 32–40 (especially *KBo* I 14: 'It is custom that, when kings rise to kingship, the kings their peers send them fitting gifts: a royal cloth and pure oil for anointing'); Kümmel 1967: 10–11 (the 'substitute king' is anointed with 'oil of kingship' and dressed with 'cloth of kingship').

very continuation of the procedure of hospitality, its deepening to the 'internal' level: he is offered drink and food. If Adapa had eaten and drunk, he would have become the guest who ate with the immortal gods: he would have become immortal too, because the gods – like men – could not permit someone to whom they had given bread and water to die. Adapa, by accepting the external elements but refusing the internal ones, does not become a partaker of the divine destiny: he is not punished, but he does not receive the gift of immortality. Anu is relieved ('he smiled'; B: 66)[22] for not having been obliged by the strict rules of hospitality to change the mortal fate of humankind.

3 THE FOUNDATIONAL FUNCTION

3.1 THE MORTALITY OF PRIESTS

Only at a primary and very crude level of analysis could it be said that the basic function of the Adapa myth is the foundation of human nature as mortal. As an archetypal representative, Adapa lost for all in his category what he lost for himself, and would have gained for all in his category what he would have gained for himself. But Adapa is not the archetype of the common man, just as other famous seekers after immortality (Gilgamesh and, probably, Etana) are not. The latter were kings, and Adapa was a priest.[23] The model heroes of these privileged categories came close to immortality, while common humankind is not even involved in such a problem. The king, Gilgamesh, and the priest, Adapa, had the opportunity to obtain immortality. While coming close to immortality, they even got something instead. The sole remaining episode of the short epic of Adapa is extremely similar from this point of view to one of the many episodes in the long tale of Gilgamesh. When he approaches Ut-napishtim, Gilgamesh has a miserable appearance, one proper for mourning. This is exactly as Adapa is when he approaches Anu's gate in the same conditions. The miserable appearance stimulates (so to speak) the hosts to provide the guests with the 'external' services of hospitality, the services that, in fact, relate to that appearance. Both Gilgamesh and Adapa are cleansed and refreshed through clothing and anointing. And at the same time, according to the logic of hospitality, they are also admitted into the house, thus becoming 'external' guests. At this point they have the opportunity

---

[22] This 'smiling/laughing' (*ṣâḫu*) of Anu, which is so obvious and appropriate at this point, has been subject to various interpretations that I need not discuss here.

[23] This fact – so evident in the text – has not been taken into due account until now, except by Kirk 1970: 122–5 (pages not without misunderstandings), who concludes 'Just as the Gilgamesh myth has as one of its themes the insistence that even a king must suffer death, so the Adapa myth may emphasise that even the greatest scrupulousness in carrying out the temple rituals cannot be expected to carry so unnatural a reward as immortality.'

also to become 'internal' guests, through partaking in food. In a chronological sequence for Gilgamesh, and only a logical one for Adapa, they are offered food. But they are unable to take advantage of the opportunity, they do not take the food: Adapa because he follows Ea's advice, Gilgamesh because he is overcome with an insuperable drowsiness (Labat 1970: 219). Had Gilgamesh not slept but eaten the bread put next to him by Ut-napishtim, he would have attained immortality, as the 'internal' guest who had eaten with immortal Ut-napishtim.[24]

The opportunity Adapa lost – like the one Gilgamesh lost – is not one of general immortality. And even after he lost this opportunity, Adapa was not denied privileges. The myth provides a foundation to the specific condition of priesthood, not the generic mortality of humankind. Adapa is mortal, yet he is an 'external' guest of the gods. In order to understand the problem of the myth, we have to change the order in which its themes are considered: how is it that Adapa (= the priest) is mortal, although he was a guest of the gods? How is it that the priest does not partake in the gods' fate, although he is 'at home' in the temple, the abode of the immortal gods? Consequently, the Adapa myth (as already seen in the formal analysis, §1.2 above) explains at the same time two apparently contradictory features of priesthood: the priest is 'at home' among the gods, yet he is mortal. According to the myth the reason for this is that Adapa was a guest of the gods only for the 'external' goods, and not for the 'internal' ones. He was admitted into the house of the gods, but he was not their commensal partner, he did not partake of their nature and their fate. We could say that he is like a servant (this is in fact the priest's function in the god's house) who lives in the house, but has no right to inherit the patrimony.

Adapa's priesthood is explicitly indicated at the beginning of the text, where he is described as a model priest, one who excels in diligence, especially in providing fish and other foods for the god's table. It must be borne in mind that the care given by Adapa to the gods (in fact to their images in the temple) is similar to what he was offered when he was the guest of Anu. The reciprocal nature of hospitality explains the correspondence between the two. In the introduction to the text it is stressed that Adapa's main activity is to give 'food and drink' (A 12) to the gods, while his priestly title *pašišu* 'anointed',[25] underlines his own purity and does not refer to the 'external' service of anointing the gods' images (a service that is attested in texts). From Mesopotamian texts in general we know that the priestly function was not limited to feeding the gods with solid and liquid victuals

---

[24] Ut-napishtim, a man but immortal, is isolated on a remote island, as if in 'quarantine'. Gilgamesh would have become immortal too, if he had not fallen asleep and had partaken of the bread of Ut-napishtim. One could say that immortality is a kind of contagious disease for men, transmitted through food.

[25] See Renger 1969: 143–72. The habit of anointing divine statues is well attested (*AHw*, 843, s.v. *pašišu* G 3; and more in general Kutsch 1963: 4).

(a most important function, because it needed to be done daily), but extended to anointing and clothing the divine images in the inner cella of the temple.[26] The standard fourfold cluster of services is therefore in regular use in the interactions between priesthood and the gods. The 'foundational' myth of Adapa points us in one direction; the reality of the daily cult points in the opposite direction.

The myth thus provides a foundation both for the mortality of priests and for their free access to the gods' houses. As is well known, Mesopotamian temples had large spaces (mostly external courtyards) which were open to common people on the occasion of festivals or the like. But the inner cellae, where the divine images were placed, fed, and cared for, were accessible only to the cult officials, as is indicated by the small dimensions of these rooms.[27] So the myth explains how one category of people is admitted where others are excluded, and how this category – although so much 'at home' in the divine world – has the strictly human characteristic of mortality.

3.2 PRIESTHOOD AND ITS LIMITS

It could be pointed out that there is a contradiction between the description of Adapa's priesthood as already perfect from the beginning of the story and the fact that such perfection is explained by the story itself. Two observations can be made in this connection. First, in dealing with a mythical account it is out of place to see an absolute correspondence between the chronological sequence of events and the logic of the problem these events elucidate (cf. § 1.3 above). The myth as a whole provides a foundation for the idea of a model priesthood. This development took place 'a long time ago' (cf. A 5, A 16), and the audience should not be surprised to find from the beginning of the story a description of the prototypical priest, who has already reached the final stage. He is perfectly wise and perfectly scrupulous in his care and feeding of the gods. Second, in strictly literary terms the beginning of the story is a kind of static/descriptive premise, and the true narrative begins only at line A 19. Lines 1–18 can thus be viewed as an anticipation of the final resolution.

A closer scrutiny of this contradiction, however, reveals that it is not so uninteresting. In fact, before the events narrated in the myth, Adapa cannot really be

---

[26] See the penetrating pages of Oppenheim 1964: 183–94 ('The Care and Feeding of the Gods'), who correctly began by lamenting the lack of valuable Assyriological studies on this subject.

[27] As far as I know, there are no comprehensive studies on the relevant archaeological data, but the general picture is clear. A possible encounter of the divine image with common people took place by bringing it out of its cella (on the occasion of processions or external rituals). Any neat generalisation is out of place, however, in view of the wide range in time and space of the evidence.

defined as a model of perfection. With respect to wisdom he seems to be imperfect, because he lacks sufficient wisdom. With respect to efficiency he seems to be imperfect, because he goes for excess. Adapa's cursing of the South Wind was an inconsiderate and negative act, indeed the divine tribunal considered it to be a 'sin'. It is only in the course of the events described in the myth that Adapa becomes completely wise and moderate, thanks to the direct intervention of Ea, who teaches him how to behave in this difficult situation. Moreover, it is Ea who leads Adapa to the exemplary condition of the model priest, through balancing the acceptance of the external goods and the refusal of the internal goods.

The contradiction and the 'balance' have further implications. In a manner that is secondary and accessory, when compared to the basic problem of mortality/admission, the myth also explains other elements that make up good priesthood. Those elements do not pertain so much to the relationship between priests and gods, but rather to that between priests and the common people, who are the audience of the myth itself. A first element is that the care of gods – in Adapa's case procuring fish – should not go against the interests of the population at large. The gods themselves do not want that, and consider infraction of that rule to be a serious offence. By breaking the wings of the South Wind, Adapa caused a serious malfunction in the atmospheric cycle, which had negative consequences for the basic agricultural (or agro-pastoral) economy of Mesopotamia.[28] The 'disappearance' of Tammuz and Gizzida, gods connected with the growing cycle of vegetation, is the symbolic expression of the agricultural crisis that follows on Adapa's inconsiderate action. That action remains inconsiderate, even if it was part of his divine service. A good priest must not exaggerate in his zeal for feeding the gods, to the point of damaging the basic production intended for the entire community's sustenance. In this sense, the myth reassures the common people that the priesthood does not, and must not, surpass certain limits by being overly zealous, or the like.

A second ancillary element is that Adapa does not eat the food of the gods, he only provides it. His main function is in fact that of providing food, of preparing it in the best way possible, and of ensuring that all the rules of purity are respected. He is the person who deals with the sector of 'divine food', yet he does not touch this food nor does he make use of it.[29] Naturally the priest will eat

---

28 This is the basic thesis of the article by Roux 1961. According to him (p. 21), Tammuz and Gizzida are standing at Anu's gate because of the problems in the natural cycle, which they usually guarantee. For arguments against this interpretation, see Xella 1976: 47–59.

29 See Oppenheim 1964: 191: 'There is no trace in Mesopotamia of that *communio* between the deity and his worshipers that finds expression in the several forms of commensality observed in the sacrificial practices of circum-Mediterranean civilizations… The image is the heart and the hub of the entire system. His attendant worshipers lived from the god's table, but they did not sit down with him.'

some food (also produced by the community), but he will not try to become assimilated to the gods themselves. The food surplus the community reserves for the feeding of the gods should end up with the gods, not with the priests.[30] In its entirety, the Adapa myth explains the priestly function in all its basic character-istics. Adapa (and the others who will follow him in the priestly function) is admitted to the divine house, but remains a normal man, a mortal man. He takes care of the gods with great regularity and zeal and so provides the country with a positive attitude on the part of the divine world. In doing so, Adapa has to display great wisdom and balance. He cannot exaggerate his function at the expense of others that may be lower but are equally important. The priesthood cannot ruin the economy of the country, nor can it appropriate for its own use privileges that remain divine.

Appendix: Adapa and Adam

The comparison between the myths of Adapa and of Adam in the Garden of Eden (Genesis 3) was such a great concern of early studies that it led to distor-tions in the analysis of the Adapa myth itself. Later, a quite justified and positive reaction took place against such an aberrant direction of inquiry.[31] By now it is commonly accepted that the Babylonian text should be studied for its own mean-ing and without preconceptions brought in from the outside. Yet, this principle must not become a kind of 'complex', preventing us from comparing anew the two myths, which are without doubt very similar – the more so now that we are better prepared for this task. Moreover, most of the proposals in the older studies have turned out, after closer scrutiny, to be devoid of value.[32]

I think that both myths not only deal with the same problem, that of human mortality, but that they are also arranged along the same structural axis. The correspondence of the specific elements has not been pointed out until now, because it has not been noticed that the Adam myth insists mainly on the first segment of the sequence, and restricts the second segment (upon which the Adapa myth insists) to just one statement of Yahweh (moreover, out of its proper place): 'Behold, man has become as one of us in recognising good and evil. Now,

---

[30] At this point we could introduce the problem of ideology as 'false consciousness', or at least the problem of the relationship between 'authors' and 'audience' in a myth like that of Adapa, which is so clearly generated by the priestly side.

[31] Furlani's 1929 study deserves (not secondary) praise for marking this 'secular' turn in inter-pretation.

[32] Let us just consider the attempts to read the name Adapa to make it like Adam, or the impossible comparison between the Mesopotamian city of Eridu and biblical Paradise, etc. I have to disagree with the equation Ea = Yahweh, as suggested in the study of Buccellati 1973: 64–5. On the other hand, I think that the structural correspondences between Ea and the snake, and Anu and Yahweh, are quite obvious.

may he not stretch out his hand to pick up also from the tree of life, may he not eat and live forever!' (Gen. 3:22).[33] My proposal is to compare the two myths according to the following sequence:

(1) By intervention of Ea/of the snake, Adapa/Adam acquires wisdom (about heaven + earth / good + evil).
(2) If Adapa/Adam, as a 'guest' of the gods, accepts the food and drink of life / if he eats from the tree of life, he will become immortal like the gods.
(3) In order to forestall Adam's immortality, Yahweh immediately drives him out of paradise and sends him to earth / Anu offers an opportunity to Adapa, but the latter's refusal allows Anu to drive him back to earth.[34]
(4) Nevertheless, the protagonists do get something. On this point the differences are linked to the fact that Adapa is the prototype of priesthood (as Gilgamesh is of kingship), while Adam is the prototype of humankind. Adapa, even after having been driven back to 'his' earth and his mortal condition, obtains privileges related to his priestly function and his 'cosmic' wisdom ('heaven and earth'). He gains admittance into the divine house, daily contact with the gods, knowledge of rituals and of rules of purity, and the exorcising power of his words (the effectiveness of his curse against the South Wind is to be connected to the priestly exorcisms dealt with in fragment D). Gilgamesh, as is proper for a king, obtains a kind of permanence in time which is linked to his 'name', that is, the eternal fame that belongs to someone who accomplishes memorable feats. Adam, as the prototype of common humankind, obtains *in the form of 'curses'* the perpetuation of species, therefore immortality, not of the individual person but of the human community. The 'curse' of women consists of the pains of childbirth and the 'curse' of men consists of the hard work of getting food. Now, childbirth and food, generation and nourishment, are the ways in which humankind sur-

33 In stating that the statement is 'displaced', I mean that the expulsion that immediately and correctly follows (Gen. 3:23) is already presupposed by the 'curses' that precede it (Gen. 3:16–19). The entire passage of Gen. 3:20–24 is a secondary conclusion, poorly attached to the preceding plot.

34 Both Adapa and Adam are expelled from the divine abode because they broke the rules to be followed by guests (see Pitt-Rivers 1977: 109–10), the former since he refused the food offered to him, the latter since he took a forbidden food. Because both heroes have to acquire the fruit of the first trial (wisdom) and not that of the second trial (life), the permutation (in Lévi-Straussian terms) in value between the attainment of wisdom by Adapa (positive value) and Adam (negative value) brings about the fact that the myth of the former deals especially with the second trial, and the myth of the latter deals especially with the first trial. Both cases deal thus with the 'missed' trial. This permutation is also connected to the value of the donor, who is positive in the first case (Ea is a god) and negative in the second (the 'tempting' snake). Therefore the permutation is connected in origin to the adaptation of Adam's story to monotheism (which is an imperfect adaptation).

vives.[35] It is a 'cursed' way, yet it is a real way. Both were unavailable to Adam and Eve when they were not yet cursed but still ignorant. At that time they shared some aspects of animal nature and of divine nature, but not at all of human nature. The well known sexual symbolism of the pair 'snake and apple' makes it quite certain that the kind of knowledge acquired by eating the fruit of the 'tree of the knowledge of good and evil' was the knowledge of sexual acts, through which not the single individual, but humankind, survives through time.

[35] Also in Mesopotamia survival is always entrusted to the 'seed' (*zēru*), i.e. to the generation of sons, besides being entrusted to the 'name' (*šumu*) in some cases. On the 'name' as 'fame' (therefore a means for enduring through time), see Kraus 1960. Naturally, sons too provide a continuation of the 'name' (see already Kraus 1960: 130: 'Name → Namensträger → Sohn'); but to translate the hendiadys *šumu u zēru* as 'sons and descendants' (as is done in *CAD* Z, s.v. *zēru*), eliminates completely the opposition between the ideological element and the physical one.

PART TWO
Hittite Anatolia

2

Telipinu, or: on solidarity*

INTRODUCTION

In the seventeenth and sixteenth centuries, the Hittites created a centralised state in Anatolia often referred to as the Hittite Old Kingdom. Later historical tradition from the second half of the second millennium remembered this period as one where a number of strong and powerful kings, the ancestors of the Hittite royal house, were succeeded by a confused set of weak ones. Of the powerful ones, Hattushili I was regarded as the creator of the state, while his successor, Murshili I, was the great conqueror of Aleppo in northern Syria and of Babylon in southern Mesopotamia. Upon his return home, the latter was assassinated and the state fell into disarray from which it did not recover for some two centuries. In that long period of weakness only one king stands out, Telipinu, who was the author of an Edict, ostensibly trying to reverse the situation by regulating succession to the throne.

The writing of Hittite Old Kingdom history has been plagued by the fact that very few, if any, records from the period itself survive. On the other hand in the late second millennium court at Hattusha were kept a number of copies of texts likely composed under some of the early rulers. Most prominent among them, and well preserved, are the 'Annals of Hattushili I', 'Hattushili's Testament', and the 'Edict of Telipinu' (for lengthy English quotations of these texts, see Kuhrt 1995: 238–50). The last one seems to have the advantage for the modern historian that it contains a lengthy introduction, surveying the history of the state from a king called Labarna to Telipinu's days. The use of this document as a source for Old Kingdom history and an analysis of its function within Telipinu's reign are the subject of this chapter.

The sources allow us to draw up the following king list where the dates of the rulers are very tentative:

Hattushili I	1650–1620
Murshili I	1620–1590
Hantili I	1590–1560

* Originally published as 'Storiografia politica Hittita – II. Tepilinu, ovvero: della solidarietà', *Oriens Antiquus* 16 (1977), 105–31.

Zidanta I	]	
Ammuna	}	1560–1525
Huzziya I	]	
Telipinu		1525–1500 (Bryce 1998: xiii)

The Edict of Telipinu was fully re-edited by Hoffman (1984). Van den Hout recently translated it into English (1997). For a recent English translation of the Hittite Laws referred to in this chapter, see Hoffner (1997).

The dream discharges the unconscious excitation, serves it as a safety valve and at the same time preserves the sleep of the preconscious in return for a small expenditure of waking activity.   Freud (1955: 579)

1 TELIPINU'S EDICT AS 'READY MADE' HISTORY, OR AS HISTORY 'TO BE CONSTRUCTED'

Laziness is common among historians. When they find a continuous account of events for a certain period in an 'ancient' source, one that is not necessarily contemporaneous with the events, they readily adopt it. They limit their work to paraphrasing the source, or, if needed, to rationalisation. No one would recommend such a procedure on a theoretical level, but nonetheless it continues to be used, especially in fields where awareness of the methodology and aims of history is not great. It is only too easy to object – and it can never be repeated often enough – that such 'ancient' historical narratives are generally separated by decades or centuries from the events they narrate. Therefore they are not to be considered as primary sources, but as historical reconstructions in themselves. And it is only too easy to recall – this too can never be repeated often enough – that such historical narratives do not have a 'pure' historical aim, if such an aim could ever exist. Their aim is political, moral, theological, or whatever else it may be, and therefore they view events from a particular perspective. All these objections can be subsumed under a single point: history is not something that already exists or is already reconstructed, and that can be accepted without question. On the contrary, it is an active engagement, which the ancient authors took up in relation to their own needs, not to ours. In fact, the 'lazy' historian fails twice: first by refusing to take an active role, and then by preserving the active role of the ancient source without even recognizing the fact. Instead, we need to take an active role with respect to the passive 'material' source. In order to make the ancient documents passive, we need to dismantle them and strip them of their specific ideology. First of all it is necessary to understand them truly – a task not always as easy and automatic as some seem to believe, and a task in need of proper analytical techniques.

A striking example of the historians' laziness can be pointed out in the treatment of Old Kingdom Hittite history. Until recently, sources actually dating back to that period were very rare. But the Telipinu Edict, one of those continuous historical narratives that are so easy to accept as accurate, made up for this lack.[1] The temptation was too great: from this Edict one could not only gather 'information' about specific events, but even explanations of these events, their sequence, and the overall development of the early Hittite state. Currently, the treatment of the Old Kingdom in the leading handbooks on Hittite history is written as a straightforward paraphrase of the historical introduction to the Edict.[2]

The first detailed presentation of Hittite political history in the Old Kingdom, published by Hardy in 1941, is typical of this trend. The three reigns of Labarna, Hattushili, and Murshili are presented strictly following the respective passages of the Edict, with here and there the insertion of passages from other texts, such as the 'Palace chronicles' (Güterbock 1938: 100–101) and the 'Testament' (Sommer 1938) of Hattushili I. All of those are juxtaposed without question, as if they were all 'pieces of information', equally reliable and equally important (Hardy 1941). The reigns following these three are all evaluated in negative terms, in imitation of the Edict. Moral judgements are included in the sentences marking the transition from one reign to the next: 'Although the Hittite kingdom had indeed experienced bad times during the reign of Hantili, more evil was to befall it after his death'; 'Misfortune for the royal family and for the state continued, more trouble beset Ammuna than had come to his predecessors'; or 'When Ammuna died, conspiracy in the royal family and among the nobles began anew' (Hardy 1941: 207–8). It is informative to compare how the reign of Ammuna is narrated by Telipinu and by Hardy in a synoptic table. The comparison underlines how direct quotations and paraphrases are used without much change:

Ammuna became king, but the gods claimed the blood of his father Zidanta. They did not allow him to prosper, and in his hands they did not allow the orchards, the vineyards, the cattle and the sheep to prosper. The country then made war on him… Galmiya, Adaniya, the Arzawa land, Sallapa, Parduwatta and Ahhula; but everywhere his army goes to battle, it does not come back victorious. (B ii 1–3, A ii 1–4; §§20–21)	When the seasons were unfriendly and fought against Ammuna, famine came to the land, for 'The grain, the orchards, the vineyards, the cattle, and the sheep [did] not [prosper] in his hands'. Countries and cities which had remained loyal in the time of Hantili now revolted, namely the cities… -las, Galmiyas, Sallapas, Parduwatas and Ahhulas, and the lands of Adaniyas and Arzawas. When Ammuna went forth with his army to bring the rebellious lands back to his control, he was unsuccessful (Hardy 1941: 208).

---

1 Laroche 1971: no.19. The division of this text into paragraphs, used in the present study, goes back to the edition by Forrer 1926: no.23. It is also found in the transcriptions and translations by Friedrich 1925–26: 21 ff. and by Sturtevant and Bechtel 1935: 183–93.

2 For instance, the description of Labarna's reign provided by Goetze 1928: 16 can be compared with the corresponding passage in the Edict, quoted in the present study at p. 31.

The picture drawn in the Edict is literally accepted, and only some (useless) rationalisations and explanations are added.

The detailed historical presentation by O. R. Gurney in the *Cambridge Ancient History* is, unquestionably, characterised by a markedly critical attitude and by various and important new insights (which I will discuss below). But his presentation does not manage to overcome the habit of using the Edict as its basic structure and its guide in the evaluation of the historical situation. The introductory passage is symptomatic of this contradiction, which is not sufficiently recognised:

> The texts relating to the Old Kingdom are few in number and for the most part badly mutilated, and historians of this period have always taken as basis the well preserved constitutional decree of Telepinush, one of the last kings of the Old Kingdom, which contains a long historical preamble contrasting the firm and orderly government of former kings with the anarchy into which the kingdom had subsequently sunk, and thus giving in effect the outline of Hittite history down to the author's time (Gurney 1962: 9).

It is not necessary to add examples. Even the most synthetic treatments refer back to the Edict, or quote long passages from it. This is the case, for instance, with H. Otten (1961: 338, 344), in line with the conscious styling of his exposition as an 'anthology'. A long direct quotation is not a bad solution, after all: the ancient text has a very effective, albeit elementary, stylistic tension. At least the misunderstanding of a paraphrase is avoided. That only apparently proposes a 'new' historical reconstruction, while really it does no more than make a banalisation of the ancient source. But both solutions (the direct quotation and the paraphrase) confirm the idea that history was 'already reconstructed' once and for all, and can be obtained by putting the old chronicles in sequence.

The Telipinu Edict cannot be considered a 'neutral' source, since it is a political document, largely aimed at proving its own assumptions. It is fully bound up with the apology of the new king, and embedded in a specific political and legal situation. A passive acknowledgement of that situation is not enough. We must also prepare the necessary analytical tools to bypass it. We have to extract from the Edict not only the features of a historiographical tradition about past events, but also a more complex and credible understanding of the present – that is of the situation that led Telipinu to promulgate the Edict.

We must bear in mind from the outset that the Telipinu Edict makes use of a simple, yet effective, pattern: 'good → evil → good'. This is often found in political addresses of an apologetic or propagandistic nature. Its aim is to convince the audience that the normal and optimal situation of the archetypal past was destroyed by negative acts in the recent past, which everyone experienced. But it was about to be restored by the new king, or had just been restored – that is the

'Good News' (cf. in general Liverani 1973a, esp. 187–8; for specific applications cf. chapter 3 and Liverani 1974a). On the basis of an independent analysis of documents of the time, modern historians can decide that there had been in fact a period of political and military prosperity under the first kings, then a period of decay and internal troubles, until order and prosperity were finally restored by Telipinu. But modern historians would show an unparalleled simple-mindedness if they managed to extract this development from the Edict (where it has a precise persuasive function), without even realizing that they are taking over not facts, but a biased historiographic theory. A preliminary comparison with historical data from the period in question is necessary in order to evaluate how genuine the Edict is – a 'ready made' history which has until now been followed too uncritically as an unquestionable guideline for a history that is 'to be constructed'.

2 PROSPERITY, DECAY, RESTORATION

The optimal state of political, military, and economic prosperity of the Hittite kingdom is described at the very beginning of the text, without a preamble. It is set in Labarna's reign:

> In olden days Labarna was a great king, and his sons, his brothers, his relatives, his kinsmen and his troops were united. The country was small, but wherever he went to war, he subjected the enemies' lands by force. He devastated the lands, he deprived the lands of (their) power, and he made them the borders of the sea. When he came back from an expedition, every son of his went to one of the (conquered) lands: to Hupishna, to Tuwanuwa, to Nenasha, to Landa, to Zallara, to Parshuhanta, to Lusna. They governed the lands, and large towns were founded.   (A I 2–12; §§1–4)

The extreme stylisation of the picture is underscored by the fact that, immediately afterwards, the reigns of Hattushili and Murshili are described repeating the same phraseology. We are thus dealing with a true and proper model of the prosperous and well-governed kingdom. The 'recipe' for prosperity is clear-cut. It consists of internal harmony in the royal house and in the ruling class, and of military activity directed toward the outside world. Exactly when this state existed is vaguely defined. Labarna is placed 'in olden days' (*karû*), from which fact it has been deduced that he was the first Hittite king. Hattushili's reign is introduced by 'eventually' (EGIR-*pa*), from which it has been deduced that he was Labarna's successor. In fact, neither of these positions is necessarily implied by the text. The placing of Labarna at the beginning in particular is due more to his providing an original model, a recently built and therefore still intact archetype, than a precise 'date'.

A decisive step toward understanding the archetypal function of Labarna's reign is taken when we realise that there is no trace of him in contemporary documents.[3] We have only historiographical projections, among which that of Telipinu is the most complete, but not the only one.[4] In an older document, the 'Testament' of Hattushili, the name or title of Labarna is used to refer to three different persons: to Hattushili himself, to an appointed and subsequently disinherited heir of his, and to 'his grandfather's son'.[5] It has been proposed that the 'Labarna I' of Telipinu's Edict is to be identified with Hattushili's 'grandfather's son' (Riemschneider 1971: 98–9). This identification is quite unlikely, however, if we bear in mind what the Testament itself states:

> My grandfather had appointed his son Labarna in Shanahuitta, but then his servants
> and his great ones despised his words and put on the throne m[y father] Papahdilmah.
> Now, how many years have elapsed, and how many of them have escaped their fate?
> The great houses, where have they gone? Are not they in ruin?
> (Sommer 1938: 12–15: iii 41–5; the restoration 'my father' is by Bin Nun 1975: 8–9,
> 55, 240)

This Labarna therefore neither reigned – he was perhaps installed as a local petty king in the town of Shanahuitta (cf. Riemschneider 1971: 99) – nor could he function as a memorable model and 'founder' of Hittite kingship and state. On the contrary, it must be emphasised that a Labarna immediately preceding Hattushili is the protagonist of an episode that can be seen as a negative model of disintegration. The royal decision was not respected, 'servants' rebelled, the ruling class was divided, and sanctions were the result. Thus, in Hattushili's testament we find no trace of an important model reign that immediately preceded his own. The term Labarna, used as a title rather than as a personal name, refers to a confused circle of designated and actual rulers. It is easy to hypothesise that a specific Labarna, that is, a historical person by that name, never existed. In that case his archetypal function in the Telipinu Edict would turn out to be even neater and

3   The historical realisation of this fact (already implicit in the position of Macqueen 1959) is to be
    credited to Gurney 1962: 10, 12. Otten 1966: 113–14 saw the reigns of Labarna and Hattushili as
    originally one, but eventually uncoupled by later historiographic tradition. Riemschneider 1971:
    81 n.10 and Kammenhuber 1970: 282, 284 argue against this idea. Bin Nun 1975: 60–1 trusts the
    'ancient' source. Otten 1968: 104 stresses that a comparison of the 'king-lists' (cf. the table on his
    p. 122) shows Labarna and Hattushili to be two names of the same king, uncoupled by the
    compiler of Telipinu's edict.
4   Cf. Labarna in the Alakshandu treaty (Friedrich 1926–30: II, 50–51: i 3). In *KUB* XXI 29: ii 3–5
    'Labarna (and) Hattushili' are matched, with a verb in the plural (von Schuler 1965a: 19 n.1).
5   Sommer 1938: 20–9, 31–2, 209, 251. If we interpret it as a title only (Macqueen 1959), the
    'son/small Labarna' (TUR-*la-an la-ba-ar-na-an* in ii 2-3; *la-ba-ar-na-an* DUMU-*sa-an* in iii 41–2)
    should be the 'crown-prince'.

uncontaminated by conflation with a precise historical reality, a reality that could not have been archetypal. We should also reject the idea that the personal name of the first king Labarna became a royal title T/Labarna.[6] Rather, I suggest that it was an opposite process. The name of this non-existent, archetypal king was derived from a royal title, which was unquestionably very old and had no linguistic meaning in Hittite.[7] In other words: 'There was once a king, whose name was Majesty'.

The reign of Hattushili was, of course, truly historical. It can, however, be questioned whether its reconstruction as supplied by the Edict is exact. The atmosphere of exemplary concord and unity painted by Telipinu as something to be admired and imitated is clearly contradicted by a contemporaneous and unimpeachable document, the 'Testament' of Hattushili, mentioned above. In appointing his adoptive son,[8] Murshili, as heir to the throne, Hattushili openly revealed the atmosphere of ferocious competition inside the royal family. That antagonism went back to the time of his grandfather, as I have already pointed out. Under Hattushili alone several rebellions took place: by his sons Huzziya and Hakkapili, by his daughter, and by his grandson, Labarna (Sommer 1938: *passim*; cf. Bin Nun 1975: 22–5). Other texts of the same period, while fragmentary, confirm the picture, and add interesting details.[9] The author of Telipinu's Edict was well aware of the situation, and could not pretend to ignore it. Indeed he inserted, between the descriptions of the exemplary reign of Hattushili and the equally exemplary one of Murshili, a paragraph that makes reference to the start of the internal troubles (§7). The evident incompatibility between what is stated in §7[10] and what is stated in the previous and subsequent paragraphs cannot but underline how the ideal history presented in the Edict contradicted what was well

---

6   On the variants Labarna and Tabarna and their uses, the work by Sommer (1938: 20–29) remains fundamental, but its conclusions cannot be followed. See now Bin Nun 1975: 32. It should be noticed that the personal name Tabarna in the early version of the Zalpa text (*KBo* XXII 2 Rs. 11), was reinterpreted as a royal title in its late copy (*KBo* III 38 Rs. 28'; cf. Otten 1973: 12, 50).

7   Cf. already Macqueen 1959, esp. 180–4 on the title Labarna, and 184–8 on the parallel feminine title Tawananna. In Macqueen's study the criticism of the historical value of Labarna 'I' is quite noteworthy. It should be noted that the common opinion on the historicity of Labarna I (and of a Tawananna I) brings about a double semantic shift (title → proper name → title): see e.g. Riemschneider 1971: 99–100 n.106, and Kammenhuber 1968: 30; 1969: 432.

8   Here I follow Sommer 1938: 67, on the basis of the Talmi-Sharruma treaty (*KBo* I 6 Vs. 13), which is late, but preferable as a *lectio difficilior* (notwithstanding Riemschneider 1971: 82: 'Schreibfehler oder falsche Tradition', criticised by Bin Nun 1975: 240–1).

9   On the conspiracies and rebellions in the time of Hattushili, and on his Edict (Forrer 1926: no.10), which in a sense is a prelude to Telipinu's, see Hardy 1941: 201–2, attributing it to Murshili; Bin Nun 1975: 240–1.

10 In compositional terms also §7 seems to be an insertion that disturbs the consistent pattern: A1 = Labarna, internal concord (§§1-2); A2 = Labarna, external successes (§§3-4); B1 = Hattushili, internal concord (§5); B2 = Hattushili, external successes (§6); C1 = Murshili, internal concord (§8); C2 = Murshili, external successes (§9).

known in the Hittite court – as it is to us – about the internal situation under Hattushili. In particular, §7 blames the beginning of the troubles on 'servants', which means that the trouble affected only lower social strata, and, as such, was tolerable. The ruling class was at first either not involved or only a victim. But this detail too contradicts Hattushili's testament, where it is the ruling class, the royal family itself, which was torn apart by struggle between factions.

The thesis implicit in the first part of the Edict, that the military power of the kingdom was the result of inner concord, cannot be maintained. Precisely at the height of Hittite military power, when Hattushili passed on the kingdom to Murshili, internal rivalries and struggles were also at their height. The Edict would make us believe that behind the conquest of Aleppo and the destruction of Babylon there was a united court, when in reality there was ferocious strife. Furthermore, the military situation itself was not as unequivocal as it is depicted in the Edict. Hattushili's 'Annals' record that in his third year, when the king was engaged against the western Anatolian state Arzawa, the Hurrians raided all over the country. Only the capital city Hattusha remained undamaged (Otten 1958: 78). We shall see that Telipinu used the same invasion by the Hurrians in order to portray a phase of disintegration of the kingdom immediately before his reign. But a similar invasion already took place, perhaps for the first time, during the model reign of Hattushili. That reign was thus neither harmonious nor unaffected by external threats.

It is less easy to check the explanation given in the Edict for subsequent events, because there are no texts from the reigns of Hantili to Huzziya. From the Edict we gain the impression that Hantili's reign was rather long, and that the king was militarily engaged in Syria and on the Euphrates. It can hardly be doubted that either during, or immediately after, Hantili's reign, Hittite control over Syria came to an end. But it is questionable whether this was a consequence of internal events in Hattusha. On the international scene this was, after all, the time when political reorganisation in Syria and Upper Mesopotamia culminated in the formation of the Mitanni kingdom, made possible by the defeat of Yamhad by Murshili (cf. Kammenhuber 1968: 62–87). The process of political consolidation of the Hurrian people was so important that by itself it could account for the regression of Hittite power. Similarly, the fortifications built by Hantili in Hattusha and elsewhere were not a symptom of 'weakness', but a reaction to new pressure by the Kashka people from northern Anatolia.[11] We see

---

11 Von Schuler (1965a: 22–5, followed by Haas 1970: 6) critically studied the references to a Kashkean invasion in Hantili's time that occur in later texts of Hattushili III and Tudhaliya IV, and concluded that they were anachronistic. Von Schuler is probably correct, as he uses a proper historical methodology (while Bin Nun 1975: 90–1 tries at all costs to preserve the reliability of the later sources, believing them to refer to Hantili II). I can only suggest that the lack of any

quite clearly that the difference between the military fortunes of Hattushili and Murshili, and the misfortunes of their successors, was not related so much to inner cohesion (always rather precarious), but to the international situation as a whole, to the capacity of neighbouring peoples to resist and react to Hittite expansion (Gurney 1966: 4).

Ammuna's reign was a disaster because of a famine. Immediately afterwards came Telipinu's reign, on which the Edict is obviously our main source. There are great differences between using it as a source for the events preceding its promulgation, for the promulgation itself, and for the events following promulgation, and especially its outcome. The text is certainly a good source on how Telipinu took possession of the throne, and on the – probably irrelevant – military events at the beginning of his reign. But that is not the point. The Edict is an excellent source for understanding the Edict itself and the situation that determined its promulgation. I think that up till now it has never been used explicitly enough in this way. Most frequently it has been used as a source on what happened after its promulgation, and that is an incautious and paradoxical use! The Edict certainly deals with what should happen afterwards, but these are programmatic and normative indications, related to the future. To use such projections as if they were news about events implies that every decision had been implemented (Hardy 1941: 209), and that the Edict had been effective. But the Edict cannot inform us about that, and subsequent events point to a very different outcome.

Telipinu is credited especially with re-establishing internal order. He is thought to have reformed the system of succession to the throne, but the impact of that action was quite modest, as we shall see. He is also thought to have revitalised the *pankuš* assembly, but that ceased to be active after his reign (cf. Gurney 1966: 10). So the opposite conclusion needs to be drawn: the most serious crisis of the Hittite state took place immediately after Telipinu. Royal succession was not more orderly than before the Edict, and unpredictable persons competed for, and gained access to, the throne.[12] Telipinu is also credited with great power on the international scene. But at exactly this time Ishputahshu, king of Kizzuwatna, assumed the title of 'Great King', and removed south-east Anatolia from Hittite control.[13] More specifically, Telipinu's reign is credited with

---

references to the Kashka in Telipinu's Edict, where the Hurrians are mentioned as invaders, is probably an allusion to the situation under Telipinu himself (see below).

[12] The various reconstructions (cf. Gurney 1966: 13–16) have been set in question by the discovery of a king called Tahurwaili (Otten 1971), to be dated around the time of Tudhaliya(-Nikkalmati). In any case, the following facts remain evident: Telipinu's successor, Alluwamna, was an ephemeral ruler, the Hittite state was weak until a strong reaction by Tudhaliya 'II' (on whose role, see Houwink ten Cate 1970: 57–62). Otten describes correctly (1968: 115) the state of internal strife after Telipinu.

[13] Hardy (1941: 209 n.125) tried tendentiously to save the pattern 'decadence → restoration', by

unique importance in administrative and juridical matters, because of what is stated in the Edict. Until the 1960s, there was a tendency to credit him also with the Hittite law code, without any specific reason beyond his seeming to be the most 'qualified' person.[14] New analyses of the ductus of the manuscripts and the diachronic study of the Hittite language have established that some manuscripts of the code are earlier than Telipinu. The source for every misunderstanding and for every preconceived theory is the hypothesis – which is stated as if it were obvious and not even perceived to be a hypothesis – that the Edict did achieve its intended effect. Even behind this presumption is the conviction that the intention of the Edict was necessarily to achieve the effect it proclaims. It is therefore necessary to concentrate our analysis on these two points: efficacy and purpose.

3 THE SYSTEM OF SUCCESSION TO THE THRONE

Since the Telipinu Edict was largely meant to be a reform of the system of succession to the throne, it is wise to begin with this point. The general and rather clear meaning of the Edict is that a direct link existed between solidarity in the ruling class and the fortunes of the country, and between legitimacy of kingship and divine favour. Moreover, the methods that had been used in the recent past to gain access to the throne produced such abuse that it was necessary to change the rules of succession, or at least to define them better in order to redress the situation.

We are not told how the ideal kings at the beginning of Hittite history ascended the throne. Labarna was king 'in olden times', and Hattushili and Murshili became kings 'later on', but the Edict does not go into detail. On the one hand, we could say that their kingship was too abstract and too perfect to imagine that they were not kings before becoming such, that there could have been problems of choice or of competition, or that their enthronement was a historical, human event. On the other hand, we cannot avoid the suspicion that the author of the text would have had difficulty maintaining the pattern of an optimal model, if he had chosen to go into detail. It was wiser for him to leave details out of the picture. We cannot state this for Hattushili's succession to Labarna, simply because we have seen that Labarna was a fictitious person. Yet I suspect that when Hattushili moved from Kushara to Hattusha, he was inspired

---

dating Ishputahshu's bulla before Telipinu. But the parity treaty between Isputahshu and Telipinu shows clearly that the previous situation was maintained.

[14] Cf. e.g., Goetze 1928: 21; more cautious in 1957a: 111 n.4. Imparati 1964: 6–8 still tended to accept Telipinu as the author, despite her knowledge of early studies by O. Carruba on the 'early ductus' (see her p. 6 n.7).

by political needs, related to difficulties in his rise to power, rather than by triumphalist motives (which could have been advanced only after Hattusha became a splendid capital city). Above all, the episode of Labarna and Papahdilmah suggests an atmosphere of armed conflict and pitiless repression. The fact that Hattushili's 'grandfather' reigned (Sommer 1938: 12) and that Hattushili defined himself as 'son of the Tawananna's brother' (Otten 1958: 78) does not imply that he was the only legitimate heir to the throne. The coalescence of the two definitions (both of them 'authentic') simply shows that his legal position was not uncontested, rather than proving a concurrence of patrilineal and matrilineal systems. The same Hattushili, who had to declare Murshili his 'son' in order to make him his heir, was unable to call himself the 'son' of a previous king.[15]

As for the passage from Hattushili to Murshili, we know, thanks to Hattushili's 'Testament' that the transmission of power had been problematic. There were conflicts, factions, and conspiracies inside the royal family during the succession, and rebellions and repressions afterwards. The succession was far from 'normal', even if it was made 'legal' through the Testament, which deliberately regularised and propagandised it. It was not the normal succession for which everyone was hoping. The Testament was written at a juncture when Hattushili 'had become old' and had 'begun to die', in the words the author of Telipinu's Edict used (C ii 8–9, §18; cf. Kammenhuber 1955: 46–7), when he wanted to underscore a forced succession. The old king, who lacked independent will and sufficient energy, was in the power of pretenders. Among those the most energetic and unprejudiced were to prevail, after eliminating or marginalising the earlier and more legitimate candidates.[16] But the author of Telipinu's Edict did not want to give this succession a negative connotation. He made no reference to the features that we perceive in Hattushili's Testament, where they are given a positive connotation for Murshili's benefit. To sum up, if we consider things objectively, we cannot see a great difference between the enthronement of the exemplary king Murshili and those of his wicked successors.

The author of the Edict presented the subsequent phase in very negative terms. He also made explicit judgements, although not without ambiguities and omissions. The reconstruction of events is roughly as follows:

---

15 Bin Nun maintains (1975: 56, on the basis of Forrer 1926: no.10, 28–31), that Hattushili's father reigned: but it could have been an adoptive relationship. As to her restoration of Sommer 1938: iii 44 (cf. n.12 above), first, it is a simple conjecture, and second the passage refers to the appointment of a local king in Shanahuitta.

16 I mean that Murshili is to be considered as the real 'author' of Hattushili's Testament, and that the disinheriting of the previously appointed heir may be considered to be an arbitrary act. Hattushili's charges against him are quite generic and inconsistent. The reconstruction by Bin Nun 1975: 71–2 seems rather fanciful.

(a) Hantili, brother-in-law[17] of Murshili, kills him (Zidanta being a conniver) and succeeds him on the throne.[18]

(b) Zidanta, son-in-law[19] of Hantili, kills the legitimate heir, Kasheni son of Hantili, in order to take his place.

(c) Ammuna, son of Zidanta, kills his father, either to speed up the succession or to decide it to his own advantage.

(d) Huzziya becomes king by taking advantage of two murders; that of Tittiya (presumably the legitimate heir) and his family, executed by Tarushhu, and that of Hantili (II,[20] another possible heir), executed by Tahurwaili on behalf of Zuru (another pretender?).

(e) Telipinu, brother-in-law of Huzziya, has Huzziya executed by Tanuwa, in order to take the throne.

Not all the responsibilities are openly stated, certainly not those concerning Telipinu! I shall return to this point later. What matters at this point is that such a list of cases cannot constitute something like a 'system of succession to the throne', for two reasons. First, each case was different (murders of the father-in-law, the brother-in-law, the father, and of someone who is not a relative) and did not repeat one another. They constituted a parade of horrors rather than a fixed procedure. Second, these were clearly not applications of a juridical and moral norm, but violations of such a norm. Beneath the sequence of criminal episodes we can grasp a glimpse of the norm: there were legitimate heirs, sons, queen-mothers, single persons, or entire families that had to be eliminated in order to make space in a theoretical line of 'legitimate pretenders'.[21] To sum up, there were rules of succession, which were not explicitly described because they were well known but rather complicated. These certainly did not include the rule (an oedipal behaviour, displaced one generation) that one had to marry the former king's daughter and kill his son in order to succeed him!

---

17 On the problem of the reading DAM or NIN! cf. Riemschneider 1971: 85–7 n.33; Bin Nun 1975: 87–8 n.129–30.

18 Riemschneider 1971: 87–8 noticed that Hantili is never explicitly called king, and thought that he only acted as a regent for his son Kasheni, who, as son of Murshili's sister, was the legitimate heir according to the matrilineal system. Yet Hantili's wife is called queen (as accepted by Riemschneider 1971: 87 n.38), and Hantili never left the throne to Kasheni even when the latter was an adult. He kept reigning until his old age (as accepted by Riemschneider 1971: 89). The absence of the title of king can be considered as a matter of chance. See also Bin Nun 1975: 90.

19 On the basis of an obvious and generally accepted restoration of a broken passage, see Riemschneider 1971: 90 n.57.

20 This is the current opinion (cf. Riemschneider 1971: 89 n.50); Cornelius 1956: 302–4; 1958: 103 n.16 argued against this on the basis of a shorter chronology.

21 It is useless and incorrect to postulate relationships of descent not stated in the Edict (e.g., that Hantili 'II' was the son of Ammuna's son). Such proposals are biased, in that they favour patrilineal over matrilineal succession, or the long over the short chronology, or vice versa.

If we want to reconstruct a 'system of succession to the throne'[22] in the historical section of Telipinu's Edict, we have to do so 'in the negative', not 'in the positive'. We have to consider who was eliminated rather than who succeeded, and the position of the victims rather than that of the instigators of the crimes. In particular, it is biased to consider as meaningless the actual patrilineal successions Hantili–Kasheni and Zidanta–Ammuna,[23] and as meaningful the 'matrilineal' successions, all of them obtained through criminal acts, all in support of a theory that the successor was the sister's son.

At the least we have to recognise that the Edict, as well as Hattushili's Testament (and Hittite evidence in general), was thought out and written down in a patrilineal way. An heir was designated as 'son'; the new king sat on 'his father's throne' (even if that was not exactly true);[24] and in order to eradicate completely a line of rivals to the throne, one had to eliminate 'So-and-so, with all his sons', and not (rather paradoxically!) 'So-and-so with all his sister's sons'...

In any event, Telipinu did not describe a norm he wanted to replace with another, more appropriate, one. Instead, he wanted (or rather he states that he wanted) a strict application of the norm, in order to get rid of the chaos, which resulted from the fact that everyone broke the norm. In practical terms, however, given a situation (as the Edict presents it) in which sons-in-law and brothers-in-law had tried to take the throne by killing the king's sons, the norm proposed by the 'reformer' Telipinu was quite improper, paradoxical, and suicidal. Telipinu decided:

> A first male prince has to become king. In the case that there is no first male prince, a second male prince has to become king. In the case that there is no male prince (at all), give a husband to the first daughter, and he has to become king
>
> (A ii 36–39; cf. Goetze 1930b: 158).

In essence he said to his sons-in-law that, if they wanted to inherit his throne, they had to eliminate his sons first. If that was the purpose of the 'reform' in the

---

[22] Today it is widely accepted that Telipinu's edict changed a customary rule of matrilineal descent to a 'patrilineal' one, see especially the analytical study of Riemschneider 1971. The basic contributions in this direction (after Macqueen 1959) were provided by the studies of Dovgjalo, quoted by Riemschneider 1971: 80 n.5. See also Haas 1970: 315–8, and finally Bin Nun 1975, *passim*, esp. 213–7.

[23] As was done by Riemschneider 1971: 91. The proposal by Bin Nun 1975: 93–4, that Ammuna killed his father Zidanta because he would have appointed his sister's son as heir, seems to me equally biased (in the sense defined in n.21 above).

[24] Riemschneider 1971: 94–7 always took the expression 'father's throne' literally, and therefore considered Telipinu as the son of Ammuna. On the commonly accepted opinion, see his p. 94 with n.78–81; Bin Nun 1975: 17–21, 221.

system of succession, and it was intended to remedy the situation described above, is was quite inappropriate and counter-effective.[25]

But I do not think that there was, or could have been, any reform. First, the system of succession to the throne was strictly linked to the general system of inheritance, which was valid for every family and not subject to arbitrary change (cf. Bin Nun 1975: 15, 229–30 on the link between access to the throne and the inheritance system). The king was a father who left his inheritance, his material goods, and his role in society. That inheritance was not different from any other, except in its size and in the fact that it could not be divided. Second, as Hattushili's testament and Telipinu's edict make clear, the legitimacy of kingship was an important issue. It was too much linked to widespread acceptance and appreciation by the entire population to be artfully created against time-honoured customs. Telipinu did not replace the old powers of the nobility to designate a *primus inter pares* with an absolute king (a thesis that was supported especially by A. Goetze, and influenced by the modern 'mythology' on the Indo-European origin of the Hittites). A system of elected kingship is never attested, not even under Hattushili I.[26] Telipinu did not substitute a patrilineal system for a matrilineal one (matrilineal features did exist in the Old Kingdom, but such features tended toward self-extinction; cf. Gurney 1966: 11–12). Telipinu did not substitute a rigid casuistry for a free designation. There was always what could be called 'designation within a norm'. The only thing that Telipinu could do was to confirm existing norms. Those were probably similar to the general rules of inheritance that asserted the primacy of direct heirs over acquired ones. Such norms present an unavoidable incentive to crime when the inheritance could not be divided, as was the case with the throne (cf. Bin Nun 1975: 91–9 on the conservative and negative effects of Telipinu's measures).

Telipinu could not and did not want to change these rules; he could only confirm them in an innovative and resolute tone. He could not invent anything on a technical-juridical level, but had to show a new political will to ensure the norms were respected.[27] He did not confront a new and better law with an old and inadequate one. He opposed a renewed application of the law to an earlier situation of illegality. His decisions and his words, endowed with the solemnity

---

25 A strict line of legitimate pretenders to the throne was a stronger incentive for murder than designation by the previous king. Compare the interesting hypotheses by Goetze 1957b: 57 and by Bin-Nun 1975: 235, linking the Edict with Telipinu's personal problems.

26 Cf. Sommer 1938: 210: 'im Punkt der Thronfolge der König allein bestimmt'; see in general Gurney 1966: 10–11; Pugliese Carratelli 1958–59: 100–105.

27 The issue is not to understand whether Telipinu wanted to innovate or just to codify an already existing procedure (cf. e.g., Gurney, 1966: 10; Riemschneider 1971: 79; Bin Nun 1975: 230; Pugliese Carratelli 1958–59: 105–106). The Edict was more propagandistic than normative in character and purpose.

of a verdict, even of an oracle, brought chaos to an end, and let the reign of order start again, not so much because of the Edict's technical effectiveness, but because of the absolute value of its proponent.

4 THE BLOODY DEEDS

The promulgation of the Edict was preceded and inspired by the protest of a delegation of 'men of the gods', who came into the presence of the king to tell him:

> Behold, blood has become widespread in Hattusha. (A ii 33)

The king immediately summoned the tribunal (*tuliya*), explained his reasons, issued his measures, and promulgated the 'new' rules of succession to the throne. That was the context of the Edict, one in which the king evidently had difficulties, as he was recently enthroned after various criminal events. Public opinion, or at least that of the members of the court and the inhabitants of the capital, contested Telipinu. At the very least, the people were confused, so they organised themselves, and formalised their unhappiness through a delegation of 'men of the gods', that is people considered most fitting for the serious task of confronting a king.[28]

Telipinu was able to take advantage of his position as judge. He responded by turning himself from someone accused to an accuser, from someone charged with a crime to one who moralises. In order to accomplish this, he placed his case in a sequence of earlier similar cases. Then he tried to divert the ire of public opinion toward the previous cases, removing himself by appearing not as the last in a negative sequence, but as the first in a new, positive, one. Telipinu probably succeeded with respect to the general population, or at least a part of it (we shall see that he addressed the sector he needed to win over more attentively). But, at the same time, he made it possible for us, later historians, to get a glimpse of his crimes, which we come to know only from the Edict.

Let us see what charges were made against him, even if only at the level of insinuation and suspicion. First is the charge that he had exiled king Huzziya and his five brothers and taken away their royal status; then that Huzziya and his brothers were all murdered; finally, that queen Ishtapariya and prince Ammuna also died. Telipinu's responsibility for these events is implied by two sets of facts. First, it seems clear that public opinion considered him to be responsible. He was accused by the delegation, which pushed Telipinu into self-defence by means of

---

[28] The procedure of presenting an issue to the king through a delegation was usual in the Hittite world: cf. *KUB* XL 62 + XIII 9: i 1–12 (von Schuler 1959: 446–9), and §55 of the Hittite Laws.

the Edict. He even quoted the charges and admitted at least some collusion. Second, it is significant that Telipinu included his own case in a sequence of cases that were clearly considered to be alike, and at the same time he had no difficulty in admitting the guilt of earlier kings. In those earlier cases the kings had been in a position quite similar to Telipinu's, the case that was actually under discussion.

Telipinu's defence was as follows: it is true, I have demoted Huzziya and I sent him into exile, but I had to do so, or he would have killed me. Therefore I accomplished a 'preventive retaliation' against Huzziya, having caught him on the point of committing a crime against me. Moreover, Huzziya would certainly have killed me, yet I only demoted him, so I was generous:

> Let them go and stay (there), let them eat and drink, let no one injure them. And I repeat: these people injured me, while I will not injure them.   (A ii 13–15, §23)[29]

The charge of having taken the throne illegally was turned around into a boast of generosity, good will, and tolerance. But in fact, Huzziya and his brothers were killed somewhat later,[30] so that Telipinu's defence became meaningless to an unbiased observer.

Telipinu's defence regarding the later developments was that he was absent and busy defending the country. He did not know what was happening. The instigation and the execution came from other people. Although he could not turn the charge into a boast, at least he could pretend not to have been involved in the deed. Yet some kind of involvement seems clear. When the real perpetrators of the crime were indicted by the *pankuš* and condemned to death, Telipinu granted them a pardon. His complicity is evident, yet he again tried to turn that suspicion into a boast, once more one of generosity, good will, and tolerance. Unwilling to kill even in order to execute the culprits legally, how could Telipinu have been suspected of any complicity in illegal murder?[31]

Telipinu was quite evasive concerning the third event, the killing of the queen and the prince. Perhaps he was too evasive; he did not even say that they were killed, just that 'they happened to die' (A ii 32). Now, if his wife and son had been killed by the opposite faction, he certainly would not have been so evasive.

---

[29] The phraseology of generosity is derived from Hattushili's Testament (i 30–36, iii 20–22 = Sommer 1938: 6–7, 12–13), and from Forrer 1926: no.10 (cf. von Schuler 1959: 444).

[30] The opposite interpretation by Hardy 1941: 210; still followed by Pugliese Carratelli 1958–59: 107–9 – a conspiracy against Telipinu, to the advantage of Huzziya – was based on an incomplete reading and is now excluded. Cavaignac 1930: 9–14 already clarified the relevant passage and identified the role of the executioners.

[31] The implicit argument of Telpinu was exactly like the explicit one used by Hattushili III in his letter to the Babylonian king *KBo* I 10, Rs. 14–23 (see especially his final statement: 'Now, people who are not used to executing a culprit, how could they murder a merchant?').

On the contrary, he would have taken advantage of it by protesting and making accusations in his turn. Or, if the deaths of the queen and the prince had been natural, how could we explain that this event was immediately followed by the delegation's protest? The blood that 'has become (too) widespread' was certainly not that of natural deaths. It is reasonable to hypothesise that Telipinu was not thought to be uninvolved in the deaths of Ishtapariya and Ammuna, the pair who were the key to a possible transmission of the throne. But their deaths probably took place in a way that was mysterious enough (perhaps through magical procedures),[32] so that it was impossible to make specific charges. Thus Telipinu did not have to formulate a defence on this matter.

Those are the points Telipinu used in his defence regarding episodes for which he was held responsible. Another line of defence was developed implicitly on a more general level, by making analogous references. Huzziya's murder at the order of his brother-in-law, Telipinu, was paralleled by the earlier murder of Murshili at the order of his brother-in-law, Hantili. The murders of queen Ishtapariya and her son were paralleled by the earlier murders of queen Harapshili and her sons. Telipinu's 'not knowing' of Huzziya's murder was paralleled by Hantili's 'not knowing' of Harapshili's murder. The use of an executioner (Tanuwa) in Huzziya's murder had parallels in the past: in more recent years, the case of the executioner Tahurwaili and Tarushhu, and earlier the case of Ilaliuma.

Why recall such episodes that were in the past, but certainly were not forgotten, and may even have caused endless feuds? Telipinu seems to have been interested in suggesting, while not openly stating so, that even if he had been a culprit, he had done nothing more than what had been done before him by many others. These other persons had not been charged, so why should he be charged? Telipinu also suggested that, if so many persons had acted in this manner, they had done so out of motives that transcended the personal. The cause should be looked for in the institutional organisation, not in individual responsibilities. It was therefore necessary to change the institutions, not to punish an individual. Finally, Telipinu suggested that, unlike others, he was good and generous: 'I pardon, I do not kill; I did not know, I was not there. I am the least culpable of all, so why do you get angry with me?' Telipinu conveyed the meaning of all this through references to similar cases, without stating anything explicitly. By inserting his own case in a long series, he understated his responsibility and overstated the relevance of general causes and possible remedies. In particular, he was able to divert the indignation of public opinion, which was certainly aroused by the *last* crime – that is, his own crime! – and to turn it against his predecessors, putting

---

[32] This hypothesis would explain the presence of the last paragraph of the Edict (50), where rules against the use of sorcery in the royal family are formulated.

himself on the side of the accusers, and crying more loudly than anyone else against ghosts.

5 LORDS AND SERVANTS

The social world of Telipinu's Edict was a strictly stratified one. It functioned correctly when everyone kept to his place. Society was viewed as divided into two parts: 'servants' and 'lords' (§7), or men of low and of high standing (§33).[33] The distinction between the two sets of people was twofold. At the behavioural level, servants were devoted to implementation, to physical and manual action, while lords were devoted to decision-making and to verbal expression. At the economic level, servants were devoid of property, which was owned by lords. This twofold distinction generated a fixed rule in the concrete case of crimes related to succession to the throne: the lords instigated the crimes (but this should be proven!), while the servants performed them, and they did so in order to take possession of the goods of the murdered lords.

Such an interpretation of the events is first stated in 'historical' terms, by explaining how the ideal situation of the early reigns had deteriorated over time:

> When afterwards the lords' servants became unfaithful, they began to devour their houses, they began to conjure against their lords, and they began to pour out their blood.   (A i 21–23, §7)

This statement explicitly links the execution of the bloody deeds to the appropriation of goods. It is set in Murshili's time, where it had no immediate actualisation, but it was useful to anticipate the interpretation of later occurrences. At the end of the historical section, when dealing with normative measures, Telipinu confirmed:

> Those who accomplish these crimes – be they a…, an *abubitu*, a chief of pages, a chief of the guard, a chief of wine – they wish to take possession of the royal houses. They say: 'This farm ('town': URU) will become mine', and he injures the farm's lord.   (A ii 61–65, §32)

We should bear in mind that the entire final section of the text (§§36–38) deals with problems of control and productivity of agricultural farms, of 'towns' or villages with storehouses (URU$^{DIDLI.HI.A}$ *ša* É$^{MEŠ \ NA_4}$KIŠIB), that were listed in

---

33 On the common binary view of social structures, cf. Ossowski 1966: 23–43. Obviously the concept of a 'servant' is relative; it expresses subordination, not a precise social position. Therefore it was the binary opposition that mattered in the Edict, even if among the lower level we find persons whose rank was not necessarily low.

detail.[34] There is an implicit appeal to the ruling class to keep effective administrative control over these farms, while charges and death threats are addressed to the peasants who 'drank the blood of the country' (iii 47').[35] Enemy raids and destruction and the disintegration of administrative control, seemingly caused the flight of peasants and the false recording of harvests (§§35, 39–40),[36] which was detrimental to the state's treasury and to the ruling class.

Not everything in the last section of the Edict is clear. Yet, while Telipinu's measures relating to the succession to the throne were fictitious, and even counterproductive, the measures relating to the protection of property were precise and effective:

> Now, if a prince transgresses, he has to pay for it with his own head. But do not touch his house and his son! It is not allowed to take away straw and wood from the princes!
>
> (A ii 59–61, §32)

In this way, economic incentives for political crimes would have been removed. It was forbidden for killers to take the victims' goods, and the victim's sons, who had to inherit their father's goods, were excluded from punishment.

The class distinction between servants and lords affected not only patrimony but also the establishing of personal responsibility. In political crimes the distinction made between executioners and instigators shifted most of the guilt onto the servants who carried out the orders, while the lords remained free. First, the aims were distinguished: the lords acted – if they acted, which is doubtful – for the 'noble' aim of kingship, while the servants acted for a low-ranking and disqualifying aim, namely the possession of material goods. Moreover, since the possession of goods would enable them somehow to rise in rank and in a certain sense reach the level of lords, their action implied an unnatural overturning of proper status relations, and this change had negative connotations. Conversely, the lords acted in a sort of competition among peers, a kind of trial by elimination, or a 'game' that could be played more or less correctly. This game, however, was exclusively for the ruling class.

---

[34] It is interesting to note here that the earliest (and most numerous) land grants, bearing seals nos 87, 88, 89 (only 'Tabarna', without personal names) perhaps dated back to Telipinu: cf. Riemschneider 1958: 327–8; also Otten 1971: 62–4. If all the land-grant documents belong to the period from Telipinu (or Hantili) to Arnuwanda, their connection with §§35–40 of the Edict would be relevant. This proposal becomes untenable if we accept the earlier dating for the land-grant documents with 'Tabarna' seal to the reign of Hattushili I, proposed by Balkan 1973: 72–6, on prosopographic basis (but the coincidence in personal names is not decisive when titles are different). Compare the similar proposal made independently by Bin Nun 1975: 156–7.

[35] Cf. also Sommer 1938: ii 75 – iii 5, with the new join *KUB* XL 65 by Kühne 1972: 257–60.

[36] Abuses in the recording of thefts were quite usual also in the 'Instructions', cf. e.g. von Schuler 1957: 50–1; Riemschneider 1965: 338; von Schuler 1959: 447.

The discrediting of servants was accomplished by treating executioners and instigators of crimes differently when it came to ascertaining their precise and unquestionable responsibilities. The executioner's responsibility was always physical and could therefore be recognised precisely. This was the more so because he had to declare openly the action he took, in order to take possession of the victim's property. By contrast, the instigator's responsibility, including Telipinu's, was only presumed. He could easily state that the executioner had acted on his own, beyond the instigator's control. Instigators 'do not know', so they are not responsible. Hantili did not know, he even went around asking, 'Who killed them?' (C ii 4). Telipinu was abroad – he had an 'alibi'– he was only informed of the deaths afterwards, and immediately took measures of justice.

The hierarchy of responsibilities was even threefold. It distinguished 'beneficiaries' (the future kings), 'instigators', and 'executioners'. In the case of queen Harapshili's murder there was only an executioner (the page Ilaliuma) and a beneficiary (Hantili), who denied having been the instigator, and therefore let the executioner be killed. But in two other cases there was a threefold distinction. In the events following Ammuna's death, the beneficiary was in fact Huzziya (the next king), the instigator was Zuru, 'chief of the guard', and the executioners were Tahurwaili (who killed Tittiya and his sons) and Tarushhu (who killed Hantili and his sons). In the subsequent events, Telipinu was the beneficiary, there were a number of instigators ('seven great men'), and Tanuwa was the executioner who killed Huzziya and his brothers. Telipinu, protected by the double line of instigators and executioners, could easily state he became a beneficiary by pure chance, and that he was innocent and of good faith.

The hierarchy of responsibilities was the basis for a very clear message, transmitted with a hint of complicity to members of the same class. Let us punish the executioners – said Telipinu to his peers – and let us save the instigators, let us save *ourselves* who are the instigators. This held true for the past, but since the past had gone, it would be useless to accuse the executioners. They should be punished, for sure, but not with a capital sentence. Telipinu had a different proposal for the future: what would be the advantage of using these executioners, who are covetous servants acting as cut-throats in order to take possession of our goods? Instead, let us act 'legally'! When a member of our class, our circle, commits a crime (in other words: if we want to eliminate someone, under pretext of a crime), instead of having him murdered, let's indict him. Let us punish him personally, but not touch his family (whose members generally are our relatives) and his property (which runs the risk of going to servants):

> When someone, among his brothers and sisters, commits evil, he has to pay with his royal head! Summon the tribunal and, if he is judged to be guilty, he has to pay with his head. But he shall not be murdered secretly, as Zuru, Tanuwa, Tahurwaili and

Tarushhu did. They shall not do anything against his house, his sons, and his wives. If a prince is guilty, he has to pay with his own head. His house and his sons are not to be touched. The reason for which princes are put to death will not affect their houses, their fields, their vineyards, their threshing floors, their servants, their oxen, and their sheep. (A ii 50–8, §31)

With respect to the sincere wish to obtain sentences and sanctions, we have to remember that the penalties announced by the assembly (*pankuš*) against the executioners of the last bloody deeds had been reduced, and almost nullified, through the direct intervention of Telipinu. He seems also to have been inclined to give more power to the tribunal (*tuliya*) at the expense of the assembly (*pankuš*). He gave more power to an organisation that was more restricted and probably more dependent on the king in the way it was appointed and functioned. This was at the expense of a larger organisation that could have escaped royal control and could have a will of its own. Is it only a matter of chance that after Telipinu we do not hear of the *pankuš* anymore? Perhaps Telipinu was looking for an organ more useful in hiding cases than in solving them.

6 THE EXTERNAL FRONT

In the positive model of the reigns of old, internal solidarity led to military successes over foreign enemies. This is described in the stereotyped sentences I quoted above, and is best exemplified in the prestigious actions of Murshili, the conqueror and destroyer of Aleppo and Babylon (§9). Military successes were not ends in themselves, but produced two effects. They enlarged a country that was originally 'small', and they supplied the members of the court with profitable political and economic possibilities in the conquered lands:

When he came back from an expedition, every son of his went to every (conquered) land… They governed the countries, and large towns were founded. (A i 8–9, 11–12)

The negative model, the reigns of the wicked regicides, was characterised by discord instead of unity and by failure instead of success in relations with enemies. About Ammuna, in particular, it is stated:

The country made war against him … but wherever his army went to battle, it did not come back victorious. (A ii 1–4, §21).

Moreover, military weakness led to the infiltration of enemies into the land of Hatti itself. Hurrians rode through the countryside, causing destruction and panic. This situation was the direct outcome of divine intervention (B ii 1–2

'Ammuna became king, but the gods claimed the blood of his father Zidanta'; A i 43 'the gods summoned the Hurrians'). The gods wanted to isolate the parricide and destroy his illegitimate kingship. At the human level, however, military failure was the unavoidable consequence of internal discord: a united country is strong, a divided country easily becomes prey to its enemies.

In this light, a passage describing the military activities of Telipinu acquires a precise meaning:

> When I, Telipinu, sat on my father's throne, I went to war against Hashuwa and destroyed Hashuwa. My army was in Zizzilippi and the battle took place in Zizzilippi. When I, the king, went to Lawazantiya, Lahha was hostile against me and made Lawazantiya revolt; but the gods gave it into my hands.   (A ii 16–22)

The divine favour manifested at the very beginning of Telipinu's reign was useful for emphasising his legitimacy or at least his ability to perform the role of king. Telipinu passed the military 'test', and his subjects were reassured about his kingship and the economic future of the country. The Hittite kingdom was 'small':[37] the Kashka people prevented access to the Black Sea, the new kingdom of Kizzuwatna separated it from the Mediterranean Sea, and the Hurrians cut access to Mesopotamia and Syria. But the old model showed that this was not an insurmountable inconvenience, provided that the king acted in the same way as the earlier paradigmatic kings. Two more references to Telipinu's present situation can be pointed out as linking the military passages of the Edict together. The first hints at appealing opportunities: military success in enemy countries could bring appointments to government posts in the annexed lands, as happened in the old paradigmatic reigns. Telipinu suggests: If we act in unity, we will again expand to the sea as in ancient times (whereas now Kizzuwatna is in between), we will acquire more towns to govern, and these appealing posts will be yours, members of the court. If, on the contrary, we continue our internal feuds, we have to fear more enemy raids, more destruction in our country, the flight of farmers, desertion of farms and towns, and problems in acquiring supplies.

The second remark was alarming and urged mobilisation. It invited courtiers to join forces in order to face dangers coming from the outside – a technique frequently used in support of a new regime. Internal conflicts were to be left aside, and a common effort had to be mustered against invaders, be they real or imaginary. In concrete terms, the possible invader seemed to be identified with

---

[37] I think that the definition by Telipinu of Labarna's kingdom as 'small' alludes to the dimensions of the kingdom controlled by Telipinu himself. The contradiction in the description of Labarna's kingdom, which is 'small' yet 'borders on the sea', has been noted by Kammenhuber 1958: 142–3, who explains the statement as a retrojection, not only from Hattushili's reign, but also from Telipinu's programme (§29). That suggestion is in line with the approach of my study.

the Hurrians, that is probably the recently constituted kingdom of Mitanni. Telipinu's military activities in Hashuwa and Lawazantiya were focused on the south-east of Anatolia, next to the Hurrian zone. The Hurrians were explicitly mentioned both in the good reigns (Hurrians were defeated by Murshili in connection with his Babylonian expedition, A i 30) and in the chaotic ones (Hurrian riders invaded the country, A i 43–46).[38] We have already noted that Telipinu was selective in the choice of events he quoted. Also during the paradigmatic reign of Hattushili Hurrian raids had taken place, but these could not to be mentioned, as they characterised the model of a bad reign. Since Telipinu was so selective, any hint at Hurrian raids must have expressed a very important message. References to Hurrian threats in the past would have been particularly meaningful to an audience that was confronted with such a threat in the present. Telipinu could exaggerate the Hurrian threat in order to mobilise forces, but he could not have invented it.

7 SOLIDARITY

By bringing together and summarising these observations, I think we obtain a substantially new picture of Telipinu's Edict in the juridical and political development of the Hittite state, a new evaluation of the historical introduction, and a new understanding of Telipinu's aims and actions.

Telipinu was accused. The arrival of a delegation of 'men of the gods' was the official manifestation of an atmosphere of hostility, or at least suspicion, about the way in which he had obtained the throne and had acted at the beginning of his reign. The condemnation issued by the assembly (*pankuš*) against the executioners of the last crime is another official feature that points in the same direction. Telipinu was under charge, he felt insecure, and decided to issue an edict in order to escape from this difficult situation. His personal involvement was twofold: on the one hand he was the person accused, while on the other hand he was the king, and had to judge and take measures. The twofold involvement was exploited in formulating the Edict, in which Telipinu as a king acted in order to save Telipinu as a person under accusation. He could not do so too explicitly, but the aims of the text are quite evident if we read it – as I have tried to do – at a 'deep' level, by deciphering allusions and cross-referencing passages. Telipinu obtained the desired effect. He transmitted a genuine message disguised under the formal one. We have to admire his ability to find the correct position for his

---

[38] It is legitimate to raise doubts about the historicity of Murshili I's defeat of the Hurrians. It is possible that Murshili's expedition through Yamhad, Hana and Babylonia was brought up to date by Telipinu with a mention of the Hurrians, who in his time were certainly the key polity for anyone who would try to repeat such an undertaking.

real message. It was not evident enough to be contested in moral or juridical terms, yet it was not so hidden as to remain unnoticed or ambiguous. The technique of disguise was effective.

The formal message 'on the surface' was simple, and can be summarised as follows: the kingdom of Hatti, at first characterised by inner concord and success against enemies, had undergone a negative evolution because of internal struggles, which had caused an institutional crisis and enemy raids. The state's fortunes had reached a nadir. Now I, the king, decided to remedy the situation through the promulgation of rules that will end dissent, and through practical measures that will bring peace. Starting from today, and starting with myself, everything will change. My reform restores the ancient model.

The genuine, 'deep' message was different, and contained recommendations about the charges against Telipinu. He urged people to remember that many other kings (practically all of them) had done the same in the past, so why should they get angry with him now? Telipinu advocated forgetting the episode, provided that it be the last one, and from then on everyone would be vigilant against a repetition of similar crimes. It is hardly necessary to recall that Telipinu was the one who would physically benefit from an interruption in the sequence of regicides. Finally, Telipinu advocated concentrating on moralising and punitive measures against the evil executioners, who belonged to the class of servants, thus saving the ruling class, and especially the king. If these recommendations were followed, the ruling class would have at its disposal government posts and economic gain, and would no longer be preoccupied with defending its properties against threats coming from below (servants) or from outside (enemies).

The substance of Telipinu's edict was a well articulated self-defence, a request for solidarity that sometimes became a denunciation of complicity, addressed to the entire ruling class. The entreaty to be united, to maintain concord and solidarity, which Telipinu proposed at first in terms of a historical model and then in terms of a direct appeal and of new norms, was not a generic appeal. It was a solicitation to be united to him, to be in concord and solidarity with him, against internal and external threats. The need for solidarity was the starting point of the entire edict, because it was its author's primary concern. Therefore, the insistence that solidarity had existed in the Hittite state and court during the early reigns was not an objective historical datum, one that was evident because it had actually existed. On the contrary, it was a rhetorical, persuasive device, a function of the aims of the author of the message. The paradigmatic solidarity of the Old Kingdom was a projection into the past of the denunciation of complicity and of the quest for solidarity that Telipinu addressed to the nobles in his court.[39]

---

[39]   Solidarity had already been recommended for the same purpose and in the same perspective by

The institutional history of the Hittite state given by Telipinu (concord → disintegration → renewed concord) was nothing but an application of the general pattern (good → evil → good) that characterises all edicts of 'reform'. The institutional history of the Hittite state should be rewritten on the basis of real data, forgetting Telipinu's pattern. I think that this 'real' historical reconstruction would be quite different in its details and general development. As to details, for instance, I do not think that Murshili's or Telipinu's accessions to the throne were very different – that is, better fitting the current criteria of legitimacy – from Hantili's, Zidanta's or Huzziya's. I do not think that military success was in direct correlation with internal concord. Lastly, I do not think that we can follow Telipinu in his distinction, implicitly adopted by most modern historians, between 'good' kings (the first three, and Telipinu himself) and 'bad' kings (those of the intermediate troubled period). As to general development, I do not think that the Old Hittite kingdom was a case of disintegration after original unity. On the contrary, it was the difficult and painful construction of a unitary state organisation starting from an extremely fragmented political situation. At the time of Hattushili we find clear traces of a situation of the 'Cappadocian' kind. Various city-states co-existed, sometimes fighting one against the other. Hattushili's Testament and Annals demonstrate clearly the roles of the cities Kushara and Hattusha, struggles against the cities Zalpa, Shanahuitta, Nenasha and many others, and their integration into the kingdom through marriages of the local chiefs with the king's daughters. Similar features can also be traced in the picture provided by Telipinu's Edict, even though it stresses unity! In this perspective of a painful, even violent, constitution of a union that (historically) was the end point, and not (mythically) the starting point, the court struggles are to be viewed as concentrating in the capital city the conflicts that had initially been spread over the entire territory. If this was (as I believe) the main trend in Old Hittite institutional history, we have to acknowledge that such a history has yet to be reconstructed.

Besides clarifying the real meaning of the concept of 'solidarity', the balanced juxtaposition of a 'superficial' and a 'deep' reading of the text also clarifies the meaning of the concept of 'reform'. The superficial reading is clearly reformist (enough with the recent past; from today on we shall do the opposite), but the deep reading is not. The substance of the measures did not bring about any real upset in the situation, as is clear in the procedure of access to the throne. Telipinu's appeals were made in a moralistic rather than a juridical tone. He insisted on a repetition of events and patterns. All these elements did not make a reform,

---

Hattushili (in reality, as said in n.19, by the young Murshili). We could not find a better expression of this than in the sentence: 'May your family be united like that of the wolf!' (Sommer 1938: ii 46) – where the wolf is a symbol of bullying, not of justice (cf. §37 of the Laws).

but a *fiction of reform*. As dreams serve to stay asleep, the issuing of an edict of reform could serve to continue political practice on its present terms. The emerging conflicts were solved by a form of words, but without introducing effective tools for change. A purely verbal reform has always been an effective and normal instrument of conservatism.

We do not know whether Telipinu's reign shaped itself according to the good old model – and it is hard to believe that it did – that the country became peaceful again and that there was internal concord, as well as success in war and expansion against enemies. According to available evidence, it was precisely during his reign that the Hittite court and country entered their most serious crisis. Meanwhile the states of Kizzuwatna and Mitanni consolidated power in the south and the south-east respectively. It is a very awkward historiographical mistake, but up till now a very common one, to take Telipinu's promises and statements of intent for the future and turn them into narratives of completed events. We cannot consider hopes and norms as historical episodes, nor see in them evidence that under Telipinu the Hittite kingdom recovered its unity and concord. The dream is not the awakening – it is rather the reverse.

3

*Shunashura, or: on reciprocity**

INTRODUCTION

The Hittites, who ruled Anatolia and large parts of northern Syria in the second half of the second millennium, have left us the largest number of political treaties from the ancient Near East. Those can be divided into two groups based on the status of the other treaty partner. There are parity treaties with equals and vassal treaties with subordinates, and the latter group is by far the largest. Treaties had to be renewed repeatedly as they were agreements between two individuals, the kings, rather than between two states. They also had to take into account changes in the political relations, and these shifts produced awkward diplomatic circumstances, when a previously equal ruler became subject. While the political reality was known to all, diplomacy did not permit a categorical statement of the fact. Such a situation is examined here. The south-east Anatolian state of Kizzuwatna had been equal to Hatti, but in the early fourteenth century it became a vassal to the Hittite king Tudhaliya II. That new reality was ascertained in a treaty, which was very careful in its language not to offend the king of Kizzuwatna. The discrepancies between political reality and diplomatic language are examined in this chapter.

The identity of the Hittite partner of the treaty as Tudhaliya II was determined by Wilhelm (1988). The Shunashura treaty and many other Hittite treaties mentioned in this chapter were recently translated into English by Beckman (1996).

> Eagle and snake made an alliance and swore to be friends; but the eagle stood at the top of the tree, and the snake at its base.
>
> (From the myth of Etana, Middle Assyrian version lines 9–12)

1 SYMMETRY AS THE FORMAL EXPRESSION OF RECIPROCITY

What immediately strikes one in the treaty between a king of the Hittites and Shunashura, king of the land of Kizzuwatna,[1] is its symmetrical structure. The

---

* Originally published as 'Storiografia politica hittita. I: Šunaššura, ovvero: della reciprocità', in *Oriens Antiquus* 12 (1973), 267–97.

[1] A list of manuscripts can be found in Laroche 1971: no.41. The Akkadian version, which is com-

prescriptive part of the treaty is made up of two mirror-like parts, repeating each other in an alternating sequence of clauses, once to the advantage of one partner and once to that of the other. Similarly, the historical introduction and the passage at the end of the treaty dealing with the problem of borders are built up through plays of parallelism and opposition, giving a strong sense of a mirror-like structure.[2] It is immediately evident that this literary structure – so pedantic in its technique of duplication – has been used in order to ensure and underscore the parity position of the two partners.

This formal structure is not found only in the Shunashura treaty. The historical period to which our treaty belongs is characterised by an approach to political relationships in terms of parity and reciprocity. This approach gives a privileged place to mirror-like forms in the acts that characterise political relationships (gift-exchange, marriage), and is found especially in the texts defining them (treaties, letters).[3] Texts or formulae with a mirror-like structure are as frequent and meaningful in the Near East of this period as they are rare in other periods. This is an obvious consequence of the far-flung international network that existed in this period. Political units that had traditionally been inward looking opened up to make contact with other units, both near and distant. Consequently they used diplomatic formulae that guaranteed everyone's prestige and rank.

More specifically, it seems that the parity treaty is linked especially to the state of Kizzuwatna – although this is probably due to the lack of available documentation. The treaty between Pilliya of Kizzuwatna and Idrimi of Alalah (Wiseman 1953: no.3) may exhibit the most rigorous mirror-like structure, which is used throughout the entire text. Moreover, a full set of treaties between Kizzuwatna and Hatti use the same pattern of mirror-like repetition. These are the treaties between Pilliya and Zidanta (*KUB* XXXVI 108 = Laroche 1971: no.25; see Otten

---

plete and is analysed here, has been transcribed and translated by Weidner 1923: no.7, 88–111, and partly by Goetze 1940: 36–42, 50–1. The fragment of the Hittite version has been transcribed and translated by Goetze 1924: 11–18; cf. also Petschow 1963: 242–3. The other fragment, *KUB* XXXVI 127 (Laroche 1971: no.131; cf. Petschow 1963: 244–5), belongs to another treaty, perhaps of another Shunashura, cf. Houwink ten Cate 1970: 5 n.17, 44 n.16, 60 n.20; against Kammenhuber 1965: 179 n.13; 1968: 37. On the name Shunashura, see Kammenhuber 1968: 87–93. A complete English translation of both the Akkadian and Hittite versions is found now in Beckman 1996: 13–22.

2   The other solution, which is equivalent in substance but much shorter, is to define the clause for one partner only and then to state that things are 'alike' (*QATAMMA*) for the other one; this was adopted in the Hittite version.

3   On this point, see Liverani 1990. The problems of symmetry have been the subject of much study, especially in structuralist studies of 'binary organisations' in kinship systems, exchange relations, etc. The present study is concerned particularly with the play between parity and imbalance, a much-debated problem, for which I limit myself to citing the contributions by Lévi-Strauss (1944; 1956).

1951), between Eheya and Tahurwaili (Otten 1971), between Ishputahshu and Telipinu (*KUB* XXX 42: iv 15–18 = Laroche 1971: 163–4; cf. *ibid.*, no.21), and between Paddatishu and an unknown Hittite king (*KUB* XXXIV 1 = Laroche 1971: no.26; cf. Meyer 1953; Beckman 1996: 11–3). Since these treaties are the direct forerunners of the Shunashura treaty, they were known and in the minds – if not the hands – of the scribes who produced this last treaty. Precise repetitions of phrases from earlier treaties in the Shunashura treaty do indeed occur, both in the introductory formula (as we shall see in detail below) and in the various clauses (cf. Otten 1951: 131–2; 1971: 66–7). So the Shunashura treaty fits into a well established pattern of relationships between Hatti and Kizzuwatna, a tradition that was revived from time to time with treaties whose symmetrical structure underlined the parity in rank of the two partners.

Although the king's name is lost and the exact date of the Shunashura treaty is uncertain (on older proposals for a lower dating, compare Weidner 1923: 88 n.6), the events recorded in its historical introduction point to a political situation that fits best in the first part of the reign of the Hittite king Shuppiluliuma. A scholarly consensus has grown up in favour of this dating.[4] The treaty certainly cannot be later, but an earlier date cannot be excluded.[5] The Shunashura treaty is to be dated to a time when a change in the political relationship took place, bringing about a corresponding change in the kind of statements employed to express that relationship. From the political point of view, we are at or close to the moment when the relations of parity between the two states were replaced by the submission of Kizzuwatna to Hatti. From the formal point of view, we are at the moment when the parity treaty is abandoned to be replaced by the vassal treaty.[6]

The correspondence between an actual evolution in political relationships and a formal evolution in their expression seems significant enough to be analysed

---

[4] Cf. Korošec 1931: 6 n.6, and Laroche 1971: 9. The dating is based on the historical events narrated in the introduction, so that its plausibility from the formal point of view is not a tautology but a useful confirmation. On the chronology of Shunashura (II) and of the Kizzuwatna dynasty in relation to the Hittite one (and to Mitanni and Alalah), see Goetze 1957b: 70–2; Kammenhuber 1968: 97–8; to be complemented by the synchronisms published by Otten 1971: 66–8. Note that the treaty is now thought to be from the time of Tudhaliya II (see Wilhelm 1988), who predated Shuppiluliuma by about half a century.

[5] Cf. Klengel 1968: 65 n.10. The peculiarities in the ductus and language of the Hittite fragments (see Kammenhuber 1965: 179 n.13) do not allow us to chose between Shuppiluliuma and his immediate predecessors.

[6] The establishment of the vassal treaty type by Shuppiluliuma's chancellery (cf. Liverani 1963: 45–6) has not yet been satisfactorily studied. The question is usually concealed in typological classifications that do not take diachronic changes into account, like those of Schachermeyr 1928 and Korošec 1931. More nuance has been introduced by von Schuler 1965b (cf. also 1964: 38–9), but he too avoided a diachronic view.

here. As is to be expected, the formal evolution comes slightly later than the political one. Statements that were proper to express a certain type of relationship were still in use when the relationship had undergone radical changes. The need in some way to express the changes that were taking place caused the old scheme to be marred by inconsistencies. We can use those inconsistencies as markers of the ongoing change. The inadequacy of a symmetrical pattern to express unbalanced relations is revealed by some unavoidable asymmetrical features.

The inadequacy and anachronism of a symmetrical pattern sometimes leads to the impression of 'sarcasm'. It is difficult to imagine that such 'sarcastic' effects are intended – or at least are meant to be noticed. Clearly the use of a traditional formula to express a new relationship aims at making the change less troublesome and less evident. It certainly is not meant to add derisory connotations to the actual detriment of becoming politically subordinate. Nevertheless, the contrast between formal parity and substantive imbalance is sufficiently evident to be noted by the addressee of the text. The authors in the Hittite palace chancellery willingly and consciously produced it. A few years later, when the political situation had been consolidated, the same Hittite chancellery had no difficulty in rearranging the whole pattern of the treaties *ex novo*. It retained only a few remains of formal parity, and those had little relevance – although they were not fully devoid of significance for political theory (cf. Liverani 1967a on reciprocal 'protection').

The fiction of symmetry – or the 'sarcastic' symmetry – therefore finds a precise historical setting in a dynamic moment, a moment of change between two static situations that are expressed through formulae that are neither fictional nor 'sarcastic'. From a tradition of parity in political relations expressed by parity treaties, we pass to a tradition of political subordination expressed by unilateral edicts with unilateral clauses. During these two static situations the political relations were so stereotypical and so obvious that the treaties defining them hardly transmit any information beyond their very existence.[7] Moreover, the information to be obtained from the formal pattern is as obvious and trivial as can be. But the Shunashura treaty needs to be read attentively in its entirety. The message it transmits is neither obvious nor predictable: it is a new message. Its structure is clearly different from the traditional usage, as is shown by the fact that it uses the mirror-like pattern to express unbalanced relations rather than the usual relations of parity. That in itself transmits a message, rich in information because unforeseen, and rich in connotations because identified by the way in which statements are made rather than by the statements themselves.[8]

---

[7]   On the well-known relationship between the predictability of a message and the amount of information it contains, it suffices to quote Pierce 1961.

[8]   These problems are not too different from those studied by Eco 1971 ('Semantica delle ideologie',

2 ANALYSIS OF THE JURIDICAL SECTION

2.1 THE SYMMETRICAL CLAUSES

As already stated, most of the text is built up through a rigorous symmetry of clauses. If the entire text were strictly symmetrical, or if there were no signs of alteration, the problem of our analysis could not even be posed. We would have a static correspondence of a sign and its usual meaning, of a form with the content which it is best fitted to express. It is not necessary, therefore, to insist here on the fully symmetrical clauses, which fill the text from i 49 to iii 33 and are summed up by a statement at the end, which is not mirror-like but nevertheless expresses perfect symmetry:

> The land of Kizzuwatna and the land of Hatti are truly united, they certainly maintain
> friendship.   (iii 31–35)

All the clauses preceding this summary, and intended to demonstrate its applicability, are characterised by a mirror-like repetition. This is most often of the simple type A = A'; the same clause is given twice, only inverting the positions of Hatti and Kizzuwatna. For example:

> If someone or some city rebels against the Sun and becomes his enemy, as soon as
> Shunashura hears about that, he will send (a messenger) to the Sun. (ii 16–18)

> If someone or some city rebels against Shunashura and becomes his enemy, as soon as
> the Sun hears about that, he will send (a messenger) to Shunashura. (ii 19–21)

Or:

> If a man of Hatti hears something concerning Shunashura from the mouth of an
> enemy, he will send (a messenger) to Shunashura. (iii 21–23)

> If a man of Kizzuwatna hears something concerning the Sun from the mouth of an
> enemy, he will send (a messenger) to the Sun. (iii 24–26)

And there are several other examples.[9] In some cases the mirror-like pattern is (so to speak) squared: inside each statement a further mirror-like feature is intro-

---

147–55 and 'I percorsi del senso', 48–50). They include the ideological character of assigning a fixed connotation to a given message (in our case the mirror-like form with the connotation of parity in rank), the propagandistic use of the normal connotation to hide other connotations, and the problems generated by the introduction of a new connotation.

9 The mirror-like clauses sometimes appear in pairs one after the other (ii 16–18 = 19–21; ii 22–23 = 24–25; iii 13–14 = 15–16; iii 17–18 = 19–20; etc.); sometimes two or three clauses are grouped

duced, by means of a correlation 'as...so...' (*kimē...qatamma...*). This type of mirror-like pattern is therefore A:A' = A':A. For instance:

> As the Sun protects his own person and country, so he will protect the country and person of Shunashura.   (i 50–52)

> As Shunashura protects his own person and country, so he will protect the country and person of the Sun.   (i 56–57)

Or:

> If any city in the country of the Sun begins hostilities – as it is the enemy of the Sun so it is also the enemy of Shunashura – they shall go together to battle.   (ii 26–28)

> If any city in the country of Shunashura begins hostilities – as it is the enemy of Shunashura so it is also the enemy of the Sun – they shall go together to battle.
>   (ii 34–36)[10]

It is evident that this 'squared symmetry', while adding almost nothing to the substance of the clauses, is very effective in underscoring the pattern of parity, and in bringing to the fore the parity in reciprocal treatment – and therefore in rank – between the partners.

In general, strict parity clauses are related to a wide range of topics: protection, acknowledgement of appointed heirs, treatment of rebels, intelligence, supply of troops, and extradition. These are the normal clauses in a parity treaty. I would even say that they are the normal clauses in *any* treaty: they lack a specificity that would apply only to that treaty and not to others. They are therefore stereotypical and abstract clauses; they do not prejudice in one sense or the other the substance of the relationship. If they are the only clauses in a treaty, they bring about a parity relation; but if they are accompanied by unbalanced clauses, they do not remove the imbalance.

Moreover, we get the clear impression of a prolixity and repetition, or at least of a concern to subdivide as much as possible topics that could be easily combined and summarised. The purpose is evident: it aims to get the maximum result, in terms of space and effect upon the audience, from clauses that in fact are less important. The devices of breaking topics up into fragments, of doubling them through a mirror-like presentation, even of quadruplicating them through

---

together (i 60–64 = ii 2–6, i 65–ii 1 = ii 7–15; ii 26–28 = 34–36, 29–30 = 37–38, 31–33 = 39–41; ii 42–45 = 52–55, 46–48 = 56–58, 49–51 = 59–62).

10 Additional examples of this type are: i 62–64 = ii 4–6; ii 42–45 = 52–55; ii 49–51 = 59–62; and iii 6–9 = 10–12.

the 'squared symmetry', provide emphasis. They do not transmit additional messages but underscore the already existing ones. They indicate: 'Pay attention, the message we are transmitting is important'. Obviously, the task of the author is to convince the audience of the importance of the message, but the very fact of using emphasis shows that the message is not really important in itself. Emphasis underscores here a feeble message, or a non-existent one. This is a typical procedure used in propaganda: it makes the audience concentrate on an 'empty' but pleasant message, and diverts its attention from a 'full' but unpleasant message, which runs parallel or lies underneath.

2.2 THE ALTERED SYMMETRICAL CLAUSES

Some clauses in the treaty keep the typical mirror-like structure, but include minor differences between what is valid for one partner and what is valid for the other. Such differences are of course anything but accidental; on the contrary, they turn out to be invaluable markers of the substance of the relationship. If it is necessary to introduce some change in a reciprocal clause, this means that complete reciprocity is, in reality, absolutely impossible. The changes relate to the personal involvement of the Hittite king and to his movements. In particular, they effectively keep him free from personal pledges. They effectively equate the king of Kizzuwatna with Hittite officials, and consequently set him below the Hittite king. The symmetry between Hatti and Kizzuwatna is kept, but not at the level of corresponding ranks. Instead, the highest rank of Kizzuwatna (the king) is equated to a lower rank in Hatti (the courtier).

The first example is already sufficiently clear. It states for Hatti:

> If a serious threat arises against the Sun, and the enemy enters his land in full force: provided that Shunashura's land is quiet, you Shunashura shall come to my aid with your *ḫurādu*-troops. But if there is some problem in your land, you can send your son at the head of the *ḫurādu*-troops, (but then) you have to come personally to my aid. (ii 63–69)

The statement regarding Kizzuwatna is parallel, except for the last sentence, which is changed to:

> But if there is some problem in the land of the Sun, I shall send a first-rank noblemen at the head of my *ḫurādu*-troops. (iii 4–5)

To sum up: if the Hittite king is busy, he can be replaced by a nobleman. It is easy to imagine that he is always busy and always replaced. But the king of Kizzuwatna has to go sooner or later personally in every case; he can be late but he is never excused. In practice, the troops of Kizzuwatna will be led by their king, the Hittite troops by a nobleman. In the general setting of the Hittite army, Shunashura is equated to any one of the (many) Hittite officers.

The second case is even more telling:

> If the Sun sends a messenger to Shunashura, Shunashura shall not plot evil against him, he shall not receive him with magical herbs'   (iii 27–29)

> If Shunashura sends a messenger to the presence of the Sun, or if Shunashura himself comes, the Sun shall not plot evil against him, he shall not receive him with magical herbs'   (iii 30–33)

The same observations apply to this case as to the earlier one: the Kizzuwatna king can go to Hatti – and as we shall see there are obligatory meetings – while the Hatti king will never go to Kizzuwatna. The Kizzuwatna king is equal in rank to a Hittite messenger. Note in particular the special nuance that someone is sent 'to the presence of' (*ana maḫar*) the Sun, while someone is sent simply 'to' (*ana*) Shunashura. The difference is clear: one goes 'to the presence of' a person of higher rank, while one goes 'to' a person equal in rank. Shunashura is therefore inferior to the Sun, and equal to Hittite noblemen serving as messengers.

But this case is even more significant because we can compare it to statements in the treaties concluded with the earlier Kizzuwatna kings Paddatishu (11–13) and Eheya (23'–24'). Those are identical to each other:

> If the Great King sends either his son or his servant to the presence of Paddatishu/ Eheya, Paddatishu/Eheya shall not plot evil against them; and if Paddatishu/Eheya sends either his son or his servant to the presence of the Great King, the Great King shall not plot evil against them.   (cf. Beckman 1996: 12)

The symmetry is perfect here, and has no special implications:[11] the two kings stay in contact while each one stays in his own palace and sends messengers to the other. The change between the earlier and the later treaties can be expressed schematically as follows:

---

[11] The entire Paddatishu treaty is fully made up of mirror-like clauses: 1–5 = 6–10, 11–12 = 12–13, 14–15 = 15–16, 17–18 = 18–20, 21–25 = 26–29, 30–33 = 34–37, 38–40 = 41–43. Only the last clause is formulated in a slightly different way, but I think without particular implications. What remains of the Eheya-Tahurwaili treaty is also perfectly mirror-like.

1. *Paddatishu/Eheya period*   **2. *Shunashura period***

| Hatti | Kizzuwatna | | Hatti | Kizzuwatna |

We clearly see the various elements: the king of Kizzuwatna is brought down from the upper to the lower level; he is put on the same level as Hittite officials (horizontal arrow) which is expressed by the preposition *ana* instead of the expression *ana maḫar* (oblique arrow) that indicates an unbalanced relation; Shunashura is forced to move (at the start of an arrow) while the Hittite king and Paddatishu/Eheya have the privilege to stay still; and finally, in general there is a persistence of the concept of reciprocity (one arrow pointing to the left and one pointing to the right) but not of equality in rank (one arrow pointing upwards vs. a horizontal one).

The comparison with the earlier texts is also illuminating on a strictly literary level. In the Shunashura treaty the very clause that was already present in the Paddatishu and Eheya treaties, as well as its terminology (*ana maḫar* X *šapāru, lemutta epēšu*), is deliberately changed to meet a substantially different situation. We see here in bold outlines how, at the level of literary technique, old patterns are adapted to new realities, and this is peculiar to the Shunashura treaty. If we bear in mind the old and 'neutral' use of the clause, how can we avoid the impression that it is being used 'sarcastically'?

2.3 THE ASYMMETRICAL CLAUSES

The less common asymmetrical clauses – i.e., those that are valid in one direction only – are characterised by greater actuality and specificity. Obviously the asymmetry is exclusively to the advantage of Hatti. However, the Hittite author of the treaty shows a constant concern for understating the imbalance, even for presenting unfavourable conditions as if they were favourable for Kizzuwatna. Three procedures are used: suggesting that the newly established condition is more favourable for Kizzuwatna than the earlier one; suggesting that every obligation brings about a reward (even if not its equivalent); and exempting Kizzuwatna explicitly from obligations that obviously should have been imposed. A good example is provided by the opening passage of the juridical section:

> The Hurrians called Shunashura a servant, but now my Sun made him a true king. Shunashura will come to the presence of the Sun, he will see the eyes of the Sun. When he will arrive in the presence of the Sun, the Great Ones of the Sun will rise from their chairs, no one shall remain seated facing him. Then, when (he wishes?), he will go back to the land of Kizzuwatna.   (i 38–44)

All three devices are employed here. The first contrasts the previous condition as 'servant' to the present one as 'real king'. The second views the visit to the Sun as a satisfactory reward for the trip, an honour not available to everyone, and rewards the displacement of Shunashura with the displacement of the Hittite Great Ones. As the displacement of the Kizzuwatna king occurs to pay homage to the king of Hatti who remains still, so the Great Ones rise to pay homage to Shunashura. The third device grants Shunashura the freedom to leave when he wants. He is not free not to go, but the author of the text considers it useless to underscore this fact. To sum up, the text views as a discharge ('deliverance') for Shunashura and as an expression of respect to him, what is really a restrictive clause. It is probably a newly devised clause, because the earlier kings of Kizzu-watna were certainly not forced to go to the presence of the Hittite king.[12]

The next passage runs along the same lines:

> Whenever the Sun shall call him: 'Come to my presence!' – if he does not wish to come, whichever of his sons the Sun shall designate, will come to the presence of the Sun. He will not have to pay tribute to the Sun.   (i 45–48)

Only the Hittite king has the right to summon the treaty-partner, not the oppo-site. Note also that the Hittite king designates the substitute, not Shunashura. Moreover, the exemption from tribute makes no sense at all in a parity treaty! This clause seems to be to Kizzuwatna's advantage, but it is the most heavily unbalanced clause. It implies that the payment of tribute would have been normal – were the Hatti king not so generous and well disposed. The exemption, which pretends to distinguish Kizzuwatna from true vassals, in fact differentiates it from truly autonomous states.[13] Such an 'exemption' has the same effect as the rhetori-cal trope of pretermission – it underscores what it pretends to conceal.

---

12 On this clause, Sommer 1932: 393–94 maintained that the intent of the Hittite king was to distinguish the visit of the Kizzuwatna king from the visits of the vassals with respect to ceremony. Therefore Shunashura would not be a vassal. This simple-minded opinion shows the efficacy of the cunning Hittite propaganda.

13 In this case too, Sommer 1932: 393 limited himself to a superficial reading and fell into the propa-ganda trap. Korošec 1931: 7 n.5 (against whom Sommer argues) had been more alert.

A final clear case is found toward the end of the treaty:

> Furthermore, when the Sun goes to battle against another country, such as the Hurri land or the Arzawa land, Shunashura shall give 100 teams of horses and 1000 soldiers, and shall go on the expedition together with the Sun. The travel provisions to be used until they reach the Sun, you – the Sun – shall provide. (iv 19–24)[14]

This case is not reciprocal; the Hittite king is not obliged to supply troops for Kizzuwatna's expeditions against third countries, for the simple reason that Kizzuwatna cannot lead an independent foreign policy. The clause is precise and imposes a heavy burden on Kizzuwatna because of the amount of supplies involved.[15] Yet it is presented in a favourable light through the concluding statement about provisions, a statement that would seem to introduce a sort of reciprocity: Shunashura provides the soldiers but the Hittite king provides the provisions. Also in this case we are close to sarcasm. On the material level the provisions clause may be to Kizzuwatna's advantage, but on the level of principle it underscores its subalternity. In fact the joint expedition ('together with the Sun') is not undertaken by two allied kings, each providing his own troops and his own provisions, but is undertaken by the Hittite king, who is using and supporting Kizzuwatna troops among others. He who pays, leads, one could say. Finally, if Hurrian towns are conquered, they will all be allotted to Shunashura, which is different from the equal division of the prisoners – each partner keeps the prisoners he takes. For geographical reasons it would have been impossible to do otherwise, but the Hittite king assumes the position of the authority that disposes. He gives to whomever he wants what actually belongs to himself, and by doing so affirms his rights at the very moment when he gives:

> My Sun shall give the territory of that town to Shunashura; my Sun shall enlarge his territory. (iii 42–43)

2.4 THE THIRD CHARACTER

Most of the asymmetrical clauses are asymmetrical because of the presence – more or less evident – of a third character, that is, the king of Hurri. As we shall see clearly in the historical introduction, the presence of a third character is the

---

14 Note that, among the differently formulated clauses, either spoken by the Hittite king in the first person, or referring to both kings in the third person (a variation that reflects well the difficult shift from parity treaty to edict), the clause about travel provisions is stated by the Kizzuwatna king as if he had decided it.

15 Sommer 1932: 393 mistakenly understood this clause as belonging to a general reciprocal obligation of supplying troops. In fact, only the supply of troops for defence is reciprocal, while here an offensive expedition is envisioned.

element that most effectively renders the treaty unbalanced. From a Hittite perspective, Hurri is located on the other side of Kizzuwatna. There should be no reason to have Hurri so heavily involved in the treaty unlike other countries located in a similar position or in a mirror-like position, that is, those located on the other side of Hatti from the perspective of Kizzuwatna. If the treaty were truly symmetrical, there would be no reason to mention Hurri. In contrast, the frequent mention of Hurri produces a situation of symmetry and opposition between Hatti and Hurri, with Kizzuwatna automatically set in an intermediate and qualitatively different position.

The two terms of the opposition are Hatti and Hurri; or better – since the problem refers to Kizzuwatna – the relations between Hatti and Kizzuwatna as compared to those between Hurri and Kizzuwatna. Indeed, a leitmotif that underlies the entire treaty is this:

> The Hurrians called Shunashura a servant, but my Sun has now made him truly a
> king.   (i 38–39)

This opposition follows two guidelines. The first depicts the former relations between Hurri and Kizzuwatna as bad, and the present ones between Hatti and Kizzuwatna as good. The bad relations are to be terminated: the tablet recording them needs to be destroyed (iv 25–28), and the exchange of messengers between Hurri and Kizzuwatna is to be interrupted (iv 28–31). If the Hurrian king tries to discredit the good relations between Hatti and Kizzuwatna, he should not be heeded (iii 55–58). The cutting of relations has to be definitive and complete:

> In the future, Kizzuwatna must never again turn toward Hurri.   (iii 47–48)

The second guideline in the opposition goes over the head of Kizzuwatna: the Hittite king pledges himself not to have friendly relations with the Hurrian king. Possible gifts from the Hurrian king, that is, friendly approaches with the intent to restore the past situation – namely the servitude of Kizzuwatna – are to be ignored (iii 49–54 and 59–62). This is presented as favourable to Kizzuwatna, since its apparent aim is to avoid that the 'true king' should become a 'servant' again. But it is very clear that the real advantage is for the Hittite king, who does not like to lose the newly acquired control over Kizzuwatna. Moreover, the Hatti king will not apply any pressure on Shunashura regarding the restitution of Hurrian prisoners in Kizzuwatna to their king (iv 5–10). This is another example of the ploy of graciously and explicitly granting something, thereby implying that it might not be granted and preparing conditions for the future. In both passages it is clear, however, that the diplomatic relations between Hurri and Hatti are above the orbit of Kizzuwatna, which is not in position to intervene.

In general, one could say that the Hurrian king acts as a negative model for the behaviour of the Hittite king. Hurrian behaviour is always negative: the king breaks the oath (i 25), commits serious crimes (i 33), forces the cities of Kizzuwatna to revolt (iii 36–38), tries to bribe by means of gifts (iii 49–54), and spreads biased reports (iii 55–58). The result of this behaviour is the subjection of Kizzuwatna (i 38, iv 27). The Hittite king reverses that situation, since he behaves according to the norms of justice, and replaces subjection with freedom. We have an algebraic inversion of two elements that are opposite in quality but equal in quantity: Hurri is Hatti preceded by a negative mark. Between these two elements there is, however, a possibility for symmetry and confrontation. By considering the value of its relations with Hurri as negative, Kizzuwatna has to bear in mind that its relations with Hatti, which are positive, are of the same quantity. The model of the 'bad lord' underscores that the new lord is 'good', but it does not deny – and even implies – that he too is a lord. The danger of subjection is carefully exorcised, because it is very present. By insisting on denying, something of it will remain.

2.5 THE BORDER

The final part of the treaty, in which the border between Hatti and Kizzuwatna is determined, calls for a similar analysis. The border is defined by way of a bipartition that sets the two partners on an equal level. Bipartition is obtained by means of different procedures: opposing those sites belonging to the Hittite king to those of Shunashura (mostly alternating, but without consistency); underscoring the parallel operations of 'measuring' (*madādu*) and 'dividing' (*zâzu*); and prohibiting the crossing of the border when this is made concrete by a river. The three procedures are co-ordinated and linked, so as to provide the effect of a highly abstract patterning. For example:

> (Starting) from the sea: Lamiya belongs to the Sun, Pitura belongs to Shunashura. They shall measure and divide the boundary between them.   (iv 40–42)

> Sherigga belongs to the Sun, Luwana belongs to Shunashura; the border is the Shamri river. The great king shall not cross the Shamri river to the side of Adana, and Shunashura shall not cross the Shamri river to the side of Hatti.   (iv 58–61)

The carefulness is evident and underscores that the division is done in equal amounts – like an inheritance shared by two brothers whom the father wants to set on a level of absolute parity.[16]

---

[16] *Zâzu* is the technical term for inheritance partitions, cf. *CAD* Z, 77.

The text runs so smoothly that we almost do not realise that this equal and brotherly partition concerns a territory whose *previous* ownership is not revealed. How is this border to be set in a historical perspective? The text does not state this point, since the (Hittite) author has no interest in doing so. But something can be grasped through an attentive reading. First, there are some clauses about the right to 'fortify'[17] (or not) certain sites:

> The Sun may not fortify Lamiya. (iv 42)
> The Sun may not fortify Anura. (iv 45)
> The Sun may fortify Shaliya. (iv 48)
> The Sun may fortify Anamushta. (iv 51)

The Hittite king is allowed to fortify some localities; Shunashura is not even mentioned. Therefore the Hittites can provide the border with a new military set-up; Kizzuwatna does not have this right.

Moreover, the first part of the description of the border (iv 40–52) is quite different from the second part (iv 52–66). The former seems to be the definition of a new boundary, in contrast to the confirmation of an old one. Different elements favour this interpretation: fortification clauses are present in the first part but not in the second one; also the actions of 'measuring' and 'dividing' are present in the first part only; the grammatical tenses qualify the first part as related to current operations and the second part to operations already completed (see Goetze 1940: 49 n.192).

The border between Hatti and Kizzuwatna, as defined in the Shunashura treaty, is therefore built up of two parts: a part already valid before the treaty, and a new one. A (partial) displacement of the border took place, and is now defined by the treaty. If we bear in mind the substantial imbalance of the treaty, it is easy to imagine in which direction there was a displacement. The Hittites acquired a part of the Kizzuwatna territory, and established a new border and the right to fortify it. Historically, a dynamic event occurred, a change that was the result and the marker of subordination. Yet the formal presentation is one of parity, with the evident aim of concealing – or at least not underscoring – the change. Also in this case symmetry is used in a 'sarcastic' way: the equal sharing is underscored, but any statement that the shared territory previously belonged to one partner only is avoided.

---

17 Akkadian *banû* 'to build'. A clause about '(re)building/ fortifying' border cities was already present in the Zidanta-Pilliya treaty, *KUB* XXXVI 108: 6–10 (Otten 1951: 129), but in a fragmentary and unclear context.

2.6 THE HEADING OF THE TREATY

Now that we have become more alert through the analysis already accomplished, we can consider the preamble of the treaty itself, in order to detect even there an interesting play between tradition and innovation, symmetry and subordination. As I have pointed out, phraseology links the Shunashura treaty strictly to the earlier Kizzuwatna treaties, that are parity treaties also in their substance. The Shunashura treaty takes the characteristic introductory formula from them: *inūma...nīš ilāni izkurū u riksam annītam ina birišunu irkusū*, 'when...they pronounced the oath of the gods, they stipulated this treaty between them'. But our treaty presents a highly significant change from the older ones. In the older treaties, where symmetry was accepted with no problem, the heading was as follows:

> When X and Y pronounced the oath of the gods, they stipulated this treaty between
> them.   (cf. Wiseman 1953: no.3: 2–5; *KUB* XXX 42: iv 15–19)

In the Shunashura treaty the heading is instead:

> Thus speaks X: when together with Y they pronounced the oath of the gods, they
> stipulated this treaty between them.[18]

So the oath and the treaty are reciprocal, but they are stated by one side only: the 'contaminated' formula marks the passage from treaty to edict (*umma...* 'Thus speaks X').[19] In substance there is a change from an inter-state to an intra-state kind of document. The Hittite king proclaims a pact between himself and another king, just as he could proclaim a pact between two of his own subjects. In the older type the gods were the guarantors of the pact while Hatti and Kizzuwatna were only contracting parties on the same level. Now Hatti itself

---

[18] Based on the two texts just quoted, I think we can reconstruct the heading of the Shunashura treaty (*KBo* I 5: 1–4) as follows:

⌜*um-ma Ta-ba-ar*⌝-[*na* X LUGAL GAL LUGAL KUR URU *Ḫa-at-ti*]
⌜*e*⌝-*nu-ma* x (erasure) *it-ti* ᵐ[*Šu-na-aš-šu-ra* LUGAL KUR URU *Ki-iz-zu-wa-at-ni*
i-na bi-ri-šu-nu ni-⌜*iš*⌝ [DINGIR.MEŠ *iz-ku-ru ù*
ri-ik-ša-am an-ni-⌜*e*⌝-[*im*] ⌜*i-na bi-ri-šu-nu ir-ku-šu*⌝

The erasure after *e-nu-ma* (see Weidner 1923: 88 n.b), that is exactly at the point where the new formulation diverges from the traditional one, could be significant. It could point to the moment when the inertia of tradition was overwhelmed by the will to innovate.

[19] Schachermeyr 1928: 182 considered true treaties (*Verträge*) only to be those stipulated with independent states (his only example beside the Ramesses II treaty is, in fact, the Shunashura treaty, p. 180), while vassal treaties are properly edicts (*Erlässe*). On the difference between edicts and treaties, see also von Schuler 1959: 440–1; 1964: 34–53.

becomes the guarantor, in addition to being one of the contracting parties, so it places itself on a higher level. Indeed, somewhat later – in the 'new' type of treaty, which is also unbalanced in form – the gods were to disappear from the headings, although not from the entire texts. The treaty then acquired the form of a true edict – a series of provisions the leader of the Hittite state addresses to a servant or a category of servants of his.

3 ANALYSIS OF THE HISTORICAL SECTION

3.1 A STRUCTURE WITH FOUR CHARACTERS

Before the properly juridical clauses, the Shunashura treaty – as is usual for Hittite treaties – places a long historical introduction to explain how and why the parties came to conclude a treaty, and that specific treaty in particular. We expect the introduction to deal with the relations between the two contracting states – in our case Hatti and Kizzuwatna – and in a parity treaty we expect such relations to be presented on an equal level. We therefore expect a structure with two characters, since symmetry naturally requires a paired number of items. On the contrary we see from line 8 on a third character entering the scene as a protagonist: Ishuwa. The loss of symmetry is only apparent, and soon the play on opposition and harmony is fully re-established. This is done by establishing a precise correspondence – by reversal, as we shall see – between the events in Ishuwa and those in Kizzuwatna, and by giving an increased role to a fourth character, Hurri, first mentioned in line 7, and subsequently given a primary role.

In such a play with four characters, the roles are immediately evident: there is an opposition between Hatti and Hurri, and one between Kizzuwatna and Ishuwa. The binary symmetry still exists, but not between the two states concluding a treaty that has parity in form but not in substance. Hatti puts itself at the level of someone else, yet not of the present partner Kizzuwatna, but of Hurri. Also Kizzuwatna is put at the level of someone else, yet not of Hatti, but of Ishuwa. The four characters are arranged into pairs, not only for the sake of horizontal symmetry, but also for the sake of vertical asymmetry. There is an analogy in the behaviour of the characters in the pair Hatti-Hurri and in the pair Ishuwa-Kizzuwatna, but there is a difference between the two pairs. As in chess, the white and black kings have the same 'moves', one against the other, and those 'moves' differ from those reserved for the white and black bishops. Symmetry in parties (white vs. black) and asymmetry in rank (king vs. bishop) together build up a closed system, in which it is impossible to misunderstand as equality in rank what is simply an opposition in colour. At the very moment when it concludes a treaty with Hatti, Kizzuwatna cannot presume equality in rank, because the role of the 'black king' is clearly occupied by Hurri.

Let us look at the 'moves' that are made. Hatti and Hurri do not move because their position is unassailable and not subject to change. In contrast, Ishuwa and Kizzuwatna do move: they enter and leave one of the greater and stable entities, or better, they 'detach themselves' from one (*paṭāru*: i 7, 27, 32), or 'address themselves' to the other (*saḫāru*: i 7, 28, 32; in i 14–18 simple *alāku* 'to go' is used in both directions). Hatti and Hurri generate movement: they 'give back' (or not) to each other (*târu* D: i 12, 20) the smaller entities that moved; they accomplish punitive expeditions (*ana tāḫāzi alāku*: i 9; *šapāru* said of troops and chariots: i 21), by moving not their entire body but only their tentacles, and so forcing the smaller entities to flee (*naparšudu*: i 11), or they carry them away as booty (*ḫabātu*: i 22). Moreover, Hatti and Hurri talk to each other but never *to* the lower entities. When they do talk to each other, they talk *about* the lower entities (i 12–13, 25–29). Finally, Hatti and Hurri know each other, and they know the lower entity that is active, while the lower entities do not know each other. The stories of Ishuwa and Kizzuwatna run parallel, but are unconnected. The links are in their connections with Hatti and Hurri. The game is between Hatti and Hurri, and it is divided into two sets, one about Ishuwa, the other about Kizzuwatna.

In practice, the historical introduction views the relations between Hatti and Kizzuwatna as part of the game between Hatti and Hurri. We can sum up the 'message' clearly by saying that Hatti explains to Kizzuwatna its position as a secondary and passive element in a game between Hatti and Hurri. This unpleasant message is concealed in a set of peer-ranking oppositions and clever connotations (which I shall analyse below), so that the addressee, Kizzuwatna, can receive it as a guarantee of its parity with Hatti.

3.2 KIZZUWATNA AND ISHUWA

The parallelism mostly dealt with in the historical introduction is the one between Kizzuwatna and Ishuwa. Their displacements are parallel in relation to the fixed points – and major powers – of Hatti and Hurri. The displacements are of a chiastic nature, that is, equal but opposed – and since there are three 'acts', each character moves twice in different directions and occupies three positions, the first and third being the same, and coinciding with the second position of the other character.

The three 'acts' are introduced by the same clauses for each character. The first is introduced by *pānānum* 'in the past' or 'once' and characterises the original and optimal situation:

Once, in the time of my grandfather, Kizzuwatna belonged to the land of Hatti.

(i 5–6)

> Once, at the time of my grandfather, these towns (= Ishuwa) had come to the land of Hurri and settled there.   (i 14–15)

The second act is introduced by *arkānum* 'later on' and points out a change in the optimal situation. Therefore, it means '(but) later on'.

> Later on Kizzuwatna detached itself from the land of Hatti and turned to the land of Hurri.   (i 6–7)

> Later on they returned to the land of Hatti as refugees.   (i 16–17)

The third act is introduced by *inanna*, and points out a restoration of the optimal situation, by now a definitive one. Therefore, it means 'now (at last)'.

> But now the oxen have recognised their stable, and have come into my country.
>   (i 17–19)

> But now the people of Kizzuwatna are Hatti oxen, they have recognised their stable: they have detached themselves from the man of Hurri and turned to the Sun.
>   (i 30–32)

It is easy to observe that the positions and moves of Kizzuwatna and Ishuwa are always equal and opposed, so that the intersection of the three 'acts' (*pānānum, arkānum,* and *inanna*) with the two positions (Hatti, Hurri) generates the following pattern:

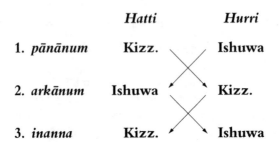

If we see the changes as displacements of the border between Hatti and Hurri, and not as physical displacements by Kizzuwatna and Ishuwa across the border (as the text reads), we get the following pattern:

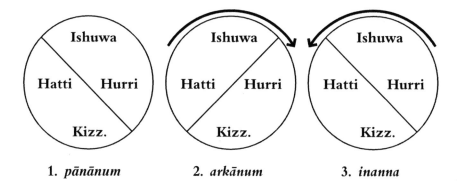

1. *pānānum*   **2.** *arkānum*   **3.** *inanna*

However we read these schemes, two points become unavoidably clear. First, Kizzuwatna is made equal to Ishuwa in rank (because of its position inside the system) and in history (because of its displacements inside the system). It is made equal – or at least comparable – to a country that in no way could be considered a honourable term of comparison for Kizzuwatna in terms of its size, historical role, or position in the political and cultural world of the time. Ishuwa never had any pretension to taking the title of 'Great King', which had been assumed by the predecessors of Shunashura (cf. Goetze 1940: 73; Gelb 1956: 246–7). It always remained isolated in the Upper Euphrates valley, outside political events, trade exchanges, and cultural relations. Today we would know almost nothing about it (cf. Klengel 1968), were it not for this treaty and the Shattiwaza treaty (Beckman 1996: 38–50), which provide some information, but always incidentally in contexts related to other countries.

The second point is that Kizzuwatna, in the historical pattern provided by the Hittite chancellery, is always a part of some larger political system, being subject to a great king, and thus – in the idiomatic language of our text – cattle belonging to some stable and owner. Later the text goes on to try – rather boldly, or at least surprisingly – to depict the final displacement from the Hurrian to the Hittite sphere as a process of liberation:

Kizzuwatna rejoices exceedingly in its liberation (*ina piṭriš*).   (i 34–35)

Now (*inanna*) my Sun restored the land of Kizzuwatna to freedom (*ana andurāri*). (i 36–37)[20]

---

[20] Note that the verb *paṭāru* (whose semantic field goes from 'to separate' to 'to ransom') is used neutrally to indicate the separation both from Hatti and from Hurri. In line 34 it becomes a joyous

The move is also viewed as a restoration of the legitimate royal rank, as opposed to the earlier move from the Hittite to the Hurrian sphere, which was viewed as a subjugation:

> The Hurrians called Shunashura a servant, but now (*inanna*) my Sun has made him a
> king in a legitimate way (*kittam*).   (i 38–39)

There is a conscious effort, on the one hand, to provide a reading of events that is the most favourable to Kizzuwatna, and on the other hand, to imply and to conceal within the internal logic of the text, the true interpretation, which Kizzuwatna would not like.

3.3 TRADITION AS A CRITERION FOR JUSTICE

The interrelations of the three acts are not left to chance, but are set up in such a way as to convince the audience that the present situation – the one the treaty has to ratify – is the right and definitive one, and that it should become definitive because it is right. It is *the* situation. The treaty makes use of the normal procedure of retrojecting into the past the situation that is to be proved right, in order to embed it in the original and therefore perfect condition of the world (on the archetypal character of the past, see Eliade 1949; van der Leeuw 1949). The vague *pānānum*, which introduces the first act, is indicative of this procedure. By being vague it presents the past as an optimal condition, not as a historically defined time. Also the qualification *ana pāni abi abiya* 'at the time of my grandfather' is only apparently more specific. It does not refer to the grandfather in the proper sense, but generically to the ancestor (*CAD* A/1, 70) the elder who when alive guaranteed tradition and justice (hence the role of elders as judges; cf. Klengel 1960; 1965a; McKenzie 1959), and after death continued to embody it.

So the original situation is the correct one, and originally Kizzuwatna 'belonged to Hatti' (*ša Ḫatti ibašši*). It is therefore correct that now and forever Kizzuwatna will belong to Hatti. In an analogous way, Ishuwa originally belonged to Hurri, and therefore Hatti does not claim it. In contrast, the intermediate phase was the time of alteration: Kizzuwatna and Ishuwa detached themselves from their natural lords, and approached another lord. So they produced an alteration in the correct state of affairs. Clearly the function of the intermediate phase is to underscore the opposite and correct state. It functions like a pair of parentheses that encloses the negative quality, while outside it and in clear view is the positive quality that precedes and follows it. This is what emerges from the interior logic of the text and from the author's intent.

---

fact ('detachment' as 'liberation' from a bond), and is used as a synonym of *andurāru* in the nearby
line 37, which means 'freedom' (relief, liberation from bonds).

But, if we are aware of the biased character of this historiographic pattern and of the mythical character of the 'original' condition, we should restrict ourselves to the real and well documented events. We should realise that the displacement leading to the final state constitutes the real alteration and the real 'injustice'. Kizzuwatna, a former vassal of Hurri, has been absorbed by Hatti. The Hurrians protest and do so correctly in legal terms – in political terms the strong party is the correct one, of course. The perspective that we could label as Hurrian can be summarised as follows: the original positive state is Kizzuwatna's vassalage to Hurri and the alteration is its subjection to Hatti. In order to rebalance the pattern and let justice triumph, Hurri should change the situation again and restore its control over Kizzuwatna. On the other side, in order to keep the pattern in balance, Hatti needs only a simple 'historiographic' device. It needs to introduce a former 'original' situation that corresponds to the present one and so automatically transforms the phase of Kizzuwatna's vassalage to Hurri into a negative and ephemeral interlude that has now been eliminated (cf. Liverani 1973a: 184–8).

It is clear that the 'artificial' phase, whose purpose it is to arrange the other phases into a coherent pattern, is the first one, not the second. By considering the first phase as mythical, I do not need to ask the purely historical question of whether or not the events belonging to the first phase really happened. If we would investigate that question, the mythical character of the first phase would probably turn out to be even more evident. Only after our treaty does Kizzuwatna lose its political independence. Before its subjection to Hurri – or perhaps its alliance with Hurri – Kizzuwatna was an autonomous kingdom. We have to go back two to three centuries to the Old Hittite kingdom to find the region of Kizzuwatna as a subject of the Hittites. But in that period Kizzuwatna did not yet exist as a kingdom with that name, its political life as a state had not yet begun. In any case, the historiographic pattern adopted by our treaty is to be considered as incorrect, because it omits as irrelevant an entire phase of autonomy, the period when the Kizzuwatna kings used the title of 'Great King'.

But, as already stated, it is not necessary to enter into a properly historical kind of analysis, because by its very wording the statement 'in the past Kizzuwatna belonged to Hatti' has a mythical character in itself. The author of the text supplies no historical details because he does not want his statement to be historically embedded. If it were, he would run the risk of pushing even further back the period of 'origins', which functions as a model of justice because it precedes every accident or alteration. An absolute statement, on the contrary, cannot be falsified because it refers to an archetypal and not to a historical time.

This historiographical procedure is quite common. Some years later, for instance, the Hittite chancellery had to establish relations with Ugarit. This was a difficult case since Ugarit had been a long-time vassal of Egypt, and there had been no previous political link with Hatti. The Hittite chancellery solved this problem easily by inventing previous relations, or at least by giving a political value to relations that were not political in nature. 'In the past your fathers were friends and not enemies of the Hatti king, so now you also, Niqmepa, should be a friend of my friend and an enemy of my enemy' (Nougayrol 1956: 35–6: 7–13). Here too the lack of a precise historical setting underscores the mythical character of the time-honoured relationships that function as a prototype. The astonishing brevity of this historical introduction, underscores that previous relations really were absent.

The best example of the archetypal value of origins is supplied by the treaty between Hattushili III and Ramesses II, whose introduction states that the friendly relations established by treaty are the optimal and original type of relations between Hatti and Egypt. Later on a negative interlude took place, namely the war in Muwatalli's time, but now the positive situation is restored forever (see especially the Egyptian version: ARE III, §374).

The force of this pattern of three acts, of which the first is endowed with an archetypal value, is also evident in its deprecatory use in the Talmi-Sharruma treaty (Weidner 1923: no. 6: Vs 11–14 and Rs 11–12). In the story of the relations between Hatti and Aleppo it is to be acknowledged that 'once' (*ina pāni*, corresponding to *pānānum*) Aleppo was a 'great kingdom'. Later on, 'after Hattushili', (*arki Ḫattušili*, corresponding to *arkānum*) the Hittites brought the great kingdom of Aleppo to an end. Therefore it is to be feared that in the future (*ina arki ūmi*) Aleppo could 'grow up' again at the expense of Hatti. The new king of Aleppo, a cousin of the Hittite king, is urged not to try anything like that, in the name of family unity. So, in one way or another, the Hittite chancellery was always able to use the archetypal model of relationships in the most convenient way.

3.4 RECIPROCITY AS A CRITERION FOR JUSTICE

While the idea of tradition as the model for correct behaviour is only implicit – although clear – in the Shunashura treaty, the text openly states another idea that is supplementary yet not in opposition to the other: what is reciprocal is correct since it is valid in both directions (cf. Perelman and Olbrechts-Tyteca 1958: 297–305). The Ishuwa story is explicitly narrated as a model for the Kizzuwatna case. To seem more convincing, the idea that reciprocity is just is stated by the Hurrian king, that is, the person who could now make a claim on Kizzuwatna:

> My Sun sent as follows to the Hurrian: 'If some country would detach itself from you and address Hatti, how (would you consider) this?' And the Hurrian sent to the Sun as follows: 'Exactly the same'.   (i 26–29)

A sarcastic and triumphant tone is clear when the Hittite side repeats about Kizzuwatna the very phrase used by the Hurrian about Ishuwa. The idea once expressed by the Hurrian is now turned back against him:

(The Hurri king says about Ishuwa:) Now the oxen have recognised their stable, and they have come into my country. (i 17–19)

(The Hatti king says:) Now the Kizzuwatna lands are Hittite oxen, they have recognised their stables; they have detached themselves from the Hurrian and have turned to the Sun. (i 30–31)

The Hurrian cannot complain, because in the past he rejected a similar claim by the Hittite king and created the model now accepted and used by the Hatti king.

This logical and very simple procedure is applied in other texts of the time (cf. Zaccagnini 1973: 103–4). The most explicit case, and the one most similar to the Kizzuwatna-Ishuwa case, is found in a letter relating diplomatic contacts between Murshili II of Hatti and Horemhab of Egypt (*KUB* XIX 15, cf. Stefanini 1962; 1964). The Pharaoh did not even bother to answer, and so implicitly rejected the Hittite request for the extradition of the rebel Tette (the king of Nuhashe), who had gone over to the Egyptian side. When later on the Pharaoh requested the extradition of his vassal Zirtaya, who had gone over to the Hittite side, the Hittite king refused, recalling Egypt's behaviour in the case of Tette. Here the balance is perfect, and there is no problem.

In the Shunashura treaty, by contrast, the situation is more complex, and a connotative analysis can contribute additional elements to an evaluation. If the norm of reciprocity were accepted 'in good faith', we would expect the actions in both directions to be presented with the same words, and to be evaluated morally in the same way. But this is not how it is: the Hittite author uses every occasion to imply that the two cases, considered as equal, are not really equal, and that the Hittite king, with superior magnanimity, allows them to be equal just for the sake of peace.

The original situation, which functions as a model, is presented as follows. In the case of Kizzuwatna, it is a static situation and therefore truly archetypal (as already pointed out above): 'Once the land of Kizzuwatna belonged to Hatti'. On the contrary, in the case of Ishuwa, it is a secondary situation, not static but the result of a displacement: 'Once, these towns went into the Hurri land and settled there'. The Hurrian king makes this statement so that no doubt can arise. The Hurrian king himself recognises the secondary character of Ishuwa's belonging to Hurri. The Hittite king – very kindly! – agrees to consider this event as representing the original situation, while he could raise objections and deny that such an event is an adequate basis for Hurrian rights to Ishuwa.

The first displacement, the one leading to the intermediate and troubled state, is also presented with a different wording. Kizzuwatna 'detached itself from Hatti and turned to Hurri'. The wording has no particular connotation, but this 'detachment' from the original seat is an action that cannot be evaluated as positive. On the contrary, the Ishuwa communities 'went to Hatti as refugees (*ana munnabtūti*)'. Their action is entirely excusable: it is clear that their displacement is really a 'coming back', as opposed to a 'going (out)' which slightly earlier had created the pseudo-original situation. It is also an 'escape' from an intolerable situation. The Hurrian interpretation of the event as a disturbance is mixed with the Hittite interpretation of it as a restoration. From the Hittite point of view it is postulated that Ishuwa originally belonged to Hatti, in an earlier phase that the Hurrians try to conceal.

Finally, the second displacement, the one leading to the restored state, is once again differently worded. For Kizzuwatna the same expression is used as for the first displacement ('they detached themselves from the Hurrian and turned to the Sun'), with the evident aim of making it algebraically a zero-sum situation. So the final status is indeed the restoration of the original one. For Ishuwa the text clearly mentions a rebellion: 'When the Ishuwa land, subject of the Sun, began hostilities (*nukurta iṣṣabtū*) against the Sun'. Such an action is objectively offensive.

So the Hittite attitude is presented as being generous and full of equity. Hatti agrees to consider as original Ishuwa's belonging to Hurri, something that was not really true. It agrees to put the 'detachment' of Kizzuwatna and the 'coming back' of Ishuwa on the same level. It even agrees to put the 'deliverance' of Kizzuwatna and the 'hostility' of Ishuwa on the same level. The play on connotations leads the audience to think that the Hurri king has no reason to complain.

3.5 FORCED ANALOGY

While the play on connotations used by the Hittite chancellery aims to create an imbalance, even to suggest that a reciprocal interpretation is a major concession by the Hittite side, there is no doubt that a historical analysis of the events would produce completely different results. The analogy between the events in Ishuwa and in Kizzuwatna, which intended to prove the legality of the Hittite annexation of Kizzuwatna, is a forced one. It is the result of a manipulation of historical events.

The difference in importance between the two kingdoms has already been pointed out: an 'exchange' of Ishuwa for Kizzuwatna is not at all equitable, and Hatti gets all the advantage. To consider Ishuwa as equal to Kizzuwatna in terms of exchange is itself a real mockery to Hurri. But the reality is even worse. An attentive reading of the text shows that the 'exchange' (or the analogy) is not between the kingdoms of Kizzuwatna and Ishuwa in their entirety, but between the entire Kizzuwatna kingdom and some refugees from Ishuwa. The story of Kizzuwatna – as told by our text – is linear. The kingdom, with its entire territory, originally belonged to Hatti, then it left Hatti to join Hurri, and finally it left Hurri to join Hatti again. The entire territory 'moved', not in a physical sense but in its political relations. These changes in political allegiance had great significance in the international setting: they moved the border between the Hittite and Hurrian spheres of influence from the Amanus to the Taurus mountains, from Syria and the Euphrates to well within Anatolia. Either Hatti or Hurri got access to the sea in Cilicia. The changes determined whether or not Hatti had access to any sea and to Syria. In sum, the control of Kizzuwatna determined the political destinies of the contenders.

The story of Ishuwa – always as told by our text – is different, and only a very inattentive reader can be fooled by the analogy with Kizzuwatna and understand that Ishuwa similarly (but in reverse directions) moved twice between Hatti and Hurri. In fact, the status of Ishuwa is as a 'servant of the Sun'; this stable position is never called into question. During a rebellion by Ishuwa and a Hittite punitive expedition, it happened that some groups of its inhabitants escaped into Hurrian territory. The number of these groups is never recorded, and it is obviously in the Hittite interest to suggest that it was larger than in reality. At first they are called 'Ishuwians' (an almost complete, yet reasonable, restoration: URU [*I-šu-wa-i-*]*ú*), then some 'towns' (URU.DIDLI. ḪI.A), evidently in the sense of 'communities' (since they physically move), that is, inhabitants of settlements close to the border who are able to cross it.[21] The territory of Ishuwa remains in place together with most of its population, and in fact soon afterwards the Hurrians plunder the land and take prisoners. All that had crossed the border were a few groups of refugees.

The Hurrian king answered the Hittite request for extradition with a refusal, and told the story of these communities – not the story of the entire Ishuwa land! – from his perspective as follows: these groups had already taken refuge in Hurri in the past (the archetypal model), and then they went back to Hatti 'as refugees' (therefore temporarily). Now they have chosen their stable and have decided forever; the Hittite king cannot demand their extradition.

This trivial story about Ishuwa refugees is repeated by Hatti as a valid analogy and a precedent that will establish the correctness of the annexation of Kizzuwatna. The analogy is purely formal and not substantive at all. It refers to the manner of displacement, not to the number and quality of the displaced items.

---

[21] On moving communities that cross the border, see also the Paddatishu treaty (*KUB* XXXIV 1: 17–20 in Meyer 1953: 116–7). The phenomenon fits well in the hilly and pastoral areas at the borders between Ḫatti, Kizzuwatna, and Ishuwa.

An 'exchange' is made between a group of Ishuwa mountaineers and the important kingdom of Kizzuwatna. The Hurrians must have been astonished when
they heard that the irrelevant and forgotten story of Ishuwa refugees was now
revived to counter their protests against the annexation of Kizzuwatna.

3.6 BIASED HISTORIOGRAPHY

Our analysis can stop here, because the picture is clear enough. The historical
introduction to the Shunashura treaty makes use of a symmetrical pattern – built
up of analogies and binary oppositions – with the clear aim of reassuring Kizzuwatna about the parity of the relationship. But the symmetry is altered, or at least
questioned, by biases of two kinds: (1) a forced analogy is established between
two events not comparable in reality, and (2) the symmetry between Hatti and
Kizzuwatna is submerged by the one between Hatti and Hurri. The latter point is
so disruptive that in the historical introduction – as against the juridical section –
almost nothing is left of the symmetry Hatti-Kizzuwatna. The historical introduction is much clearer than the juridical section in indicating that the age of
independence for Kizzuwatna is finished forever, and that its position is that of a
Hittite vassal. The persuasive effect of the many parity clauses is greatly reduced
when they are read after the message of the historical introduction. Only a literal
reading of the treaty would produce an image of Kizzuwatna as equal. Only too
often the equality of treatment is underscored, while the real imbalance in rank is
never stated explicitly. But it is implied between the lines. It seems as if the
Hittite king did not consider it suitable to tell the Kizzuwatna king what the
situation really was, leaving him instead to understand it for himself.[22]

Obviously, the audience was larger than the king alone. It included the court,
which had been accustomed to cultivate certain ambitions, to preserve certain
ranks, and to pursue certain policies. It included the entire population, which was
also interested to some extent in the political destiny of the kingdom. This
audience had to be informed and convinced, with due caution, that the autonomy
of their country was over.

The discourse is by its very nature biased – since it aims at specific conclusions – but it is composed from historical events. The oft-repeated appreciation

---

22   The discussion between Schachermeyr 1928: 180–6; Korošec 1931: 6–7 and *passim*, and Sommer
     1932: 344–5, 392–3, about whether the Shunashura treaty is one of 'parity' or of 'vassalage', reveals
     the limits of an overly rigid and elementary juridical classification that does not take into account
     the differences in time or the complex semantic purposes of the texts. The flexible position of
     Korošec is more acceptable than the strict one of Sommer ('Das der Vertrag…seinem Inhalt und
     seiner Formulierung nach as Ganzheit paritätisch gedacht ist, davon kann man wirklich nicht
     zweifeln').

of Hittite historiography as unbiased, concrete, and impartial,[23] is senseless when applied to the historical introductions in the international treaties – and I think it has no sense at all.[24] These introductions are indeed historical in the full sense. Far from being randomly put together, the 'events' are arranged with great attention to a specific purpose; they aim at a precise meaning. The 'events' are selected and presented in a way that is most useful for proving the author's assertions.[25] The selection is so biased as to conceal true events and to fabricate others. The presentation is characterised by the attribution of precise moral judgements to the events. They are evaluated as positive or negative depending on who the actor was. Selection and moral judgement produce meaningful pictures and express a strong intent to impart a meaning. It would be incautious to use the historical introductions – what they literally state – to reconstruct the history of relations between two countries. On the other hand it is correct – and moreover much more interesting – to use them to reconstruct the ideological groups who presented different interpretations and the play in reciprocal confutation.

In the case studied here, the stories of Kizzuwatna, and even more so of Ishuwa, are completely overshadowed by the intent of the Hittite author to construct a pattern. They are phantom stories, unrecognisable and misleading if used as 'true stories'. What emerges correctly, however, are the opposed evaluations, interpretations, and reactions that arose when the treaty was written down. There is the public opinion of Kizzuwatna, with memories of grandeur and with

---

23 This appreciation is repeated, more or less consciously, both in general treatments of Hittite culture and in more specific studies on Hittite historiography. Two studies by Furlani (1939a; 1939b) need to be mentioned here; their ingenuity is now evident, yet some points are still valuable. Güterbock 1938: 96–7 revealed his dependence on historiographic models, dominant in Germany at the time, that aimed at objectivity and non-engagement. He searched for a historical tradition for its own sake, 'die nicht der offiziellen Geschichtsschreibung dient', excluded the entire political historiography, and only accepted fairy tale stories of the Old Kingdom like the 'Siege of Urshu'. This still seems to have been the methodological background of Kammenhuber (1958).

   The debate then was whether Hittite historiography could be considered 'true' historiography or not, whether 'true' historiography begins with the Hittites or with Israel, whether or not 'true' historiography could be found in the rest of the ancient Near East, and whether the Hittite talent for history writing should be connected to their Indo-European origins (Kammenhuber 1958: 152, contested the details but not the basic approach). Such questions should be abandoned today, or rephrased in different terms.

24 See the treatments by Archi 1969 and Klengel 1969: both authors make clear that Hittite history writing aims at propagandistic demonstration rather than a 'search for truth'.

25 On the characteristics of persuasive discourse, see Perelman and Olbrechts-Tyteca 1958: 154–60, 169–174, and *passim*. The rhetorical techniques studied in this book could be largely exemplified in the Shunashura treaty (compare, for example, the pages on model and anti-model, on analogy, etc.).

difficulties in accepting a diminution in rank. There is the 'victorious' interpretation by Hatti, and its interest in understating and showing that the situation is settled. There is the Hurrian interpretation, made up of recriminations and protests. The opinion in Kizzuwatna is borne in mind by the Hittite author, who makes use of positive tones and understates the relevance of change. But the Hurrian claims are also borne in mind by the Hittites, who were always concerned with contradicting them at the juridical level, as they were active in combating them at the military level.

We are therefore dealing with a biased historiography endowed with a practical function, as a channel for precise messages addressed to precise and different audiences. This is a political historiography in its fullest sense: not one *dealing with* historico-political events, but one *making* politics, using the raw material of events in order to construct the right and wrong behaviour of polities confronting each other.

4 LEVELS OF DISCOURSE AND AUDIENCES OF THE MESSAGE

As a result of my analysis I have pointed out, both in the historical and the juridical sections of the Shunashura treaty, a correspondence between the symmetrical pattern of the text and its political aim of presenting relationships as based on parity. More specifically, I have pointed out the correspondence between changes in the formal symmetry and in political parity. A certain delay in the formal structure recording changes that had already been accomplished in their political substance results from the attempt by the (Hittite) authors of the treaty to make the change in relations less burdensome and evident, because it was certainly painful for Kizzuwatna.

Behind the declining symmetry between Hatti and Kizzuwatna another symmetry emerges of the treaty: one between Hatti and Hurri, which is quite real yet not pertinent to a treaty between Hatti and Kizzuwatna. The two levels of the symmetrical pattern – the more intentional symmetry Hatti-Kizzuwatna (especially clear in the juridical section) and the more concealed symmetry Hatti-Hurri (especially clear in the historical introduction) – can also be understood as components of a general patterning of the entire text on two levels.

One level of the discourse deals with the relationship between Hatti and Kizzuwatna: this is a completely conscious level, underscored by emphatic procedures. It fits best the case that is officially at issue. This is the level of discourse we expect to find in a treaty between Hatti and Kizzuwatna, and indeed in the earlier treaties, when the correspondence of political situation and treaty form was full and unquestionable, this was the only level of discourse.

But there is also a second level, dealing with the relationship between Hatti and Hurri: this is an unconscious level – or if it was conscious, it is cunningly presented as unconscious. We discover it by reading the concealed intent rather than the explicit words. This is the level that fits the concrete political situation. Through this treaty the Hittite king formalised a change in the political situation that was to the detriment of Hurri. Consequently, in drawing up the treaty the Hittite chancellery was attentive to – or preoccupied with – the Hurrian position. This preoccupation penetrates the treaty deeply and becomes an unavowed yet evident feature of it.

In this way Hurri too was an addressee of the message contained in the treaty text. Some clauses in the juridical section, and especially the entire historical introduction, have little meaning as a message from Hatti to Kizzuwatna, but are a clear message from Hatti to Hurri. In parallel with the two levels of discourse we perceive two addressees of the message, for whose benefit the discourse is differentiated on two levels. The official, natural, and explicit addressee is Kizzuwatna, to whom the upper, conscious level of discourse is addressed. Hurri is the secondary addressee, not pertinent but in fact more important, to whom the concealed level of discourse is addressed. It seems as if Hatti made use of the opportunity offered by the Kizzuwatna treaty to send a message to Hurri – speaking out loud to an irrelevant addressee in order to make another distant person, who was not officially listening, receive a warning. Kizzuwatna was used in order to establish communications between Hatti and Hurri, which at that time were officially broken. We do not know how in practice Hurri could have received the message of which it was the ultimate addressee. There are various possibilities, such as through a pro-Hurrian party at Shunashura's court. In any case, the semiological complexity of the text studied here corresponds to that of a cunning political action – built up of worries and justifications, reticence and ambiguity – which our analysis has been able to reconstruct, at least in part.

PART THREE
Syria

4

*Leaving by chariot for the desert**

INTRODUCTION

In the early fifteenth century a local ruler of the city of Alalah, today in southern Turkey some 50 km west of Aleppo in Syria, left a statue of himself with an inscription recounting his career. He started out in Aleppo, was chased from the city with his family, crossed the desert and fled to Emar on the Euphrates. There he decided to join bands of warriors called *ḫabiru*. Seven years later he conquered the city of Alalah, and was eventually recognised by the ruler of the region, Barattarna, king of Mitanni.

The story provides a justification for Idrimi's rule over a city with which he had no previous connections (see chapter 7), and was manufactured in order to make the king look especially qualified for the task. It includes a literary motif of the hero taking off by himself into hostile territory where he can prove his worth. The chapter here identifies that motif, akin to what is found in fairy tales, and traces it through other literatures from the ancient Near East. It analyses the motif using V. Propp's methods for the analysis of fairy tales. The Egyptian tale of the 'Doomed Prince' provides the clearest parallel to the Idrimi story. In it the only son of an unnamed Egyptian king, whose death through a crocodile, snake, or dog was prophesied at birth, is kept in a safe house by his father. But one day he takes off by himself on his chariot to Nahrin in Syria where he is chosen to marry a local princess because he alone is able to pass a test. Afterwards his wife urges him to protect himself against his fate, and he probably ends up escaping it, although the end of the text is not preserved. That text is clearly a fairy tale, but several other Near Eastern texts of various genres contain parts of the motif. Such texts then have to be analysed as what they truly are, fictional stories, rather than as historical accounts.

Idrimi's inscription has been translated numerous times. The most recent English translation is by Longman (1997).

★   ★   ★   ★

---

* Originally published as 'Partire sul carro, per il deserto', in *Annali dell'Istituto Universitario Orientale di Napoli* 22 (1972) 403–415.

In two earlier publications I have pointed out details and structural features that force us to consider the autobiographical inscription on the statue of Idrimi as an expression of the literary genre of the fairy tale, or better as an example of a historiographical text that makes use of patterns and narrative modes similar to those of the fairy tale. On both occasions, however, the focal point of my analysis was different – the number seven (Liverani 1967b) and Ugaritic epics (Liverani 1970) – so that some points of comparison and some analytical approaches were not taken into account. I think it useful to present them here.[1]

1 IDRIMI AND THE DOOMED PRINCE

The Egyptian tale of the 'Doomed Prince' (Lichtheim 1973–80: II, 200–3) provides the best comparison, in the genre of fairy tales, for epics like the Ugaritic one of Keret (Coogan 1978: 58–74), and historical texts like that of Idrimi (see already Liverani 1970: 868). Their styles differ since the three texts had different purposes, but the narrative development is basically the same. The texts cover a timespan of only a couple of centuries (Idrimi c. 1480, Keret c. 1360, Doomed Prince 13th century), and the contemporaneous use of the same pattern in three literary genres that have different sociocultural functions warns us against possible evolutionary mirages. The study of these texts that I propose is not a matter of looking for the 'origin' of a pattern and then for its secondary or derivative uses. Instead it is a matter of studying three different but parallel applications of the same pattern, which was clearly suitable for expressing widespread political and social tensions.

We cannot compare the story of Idrimi and the fairy tale of the Doomed Prince in their general pattern alone. At least one passage points out that both stories use a precise literary *topos*. Here are lines 13–15 of the Idrimi story:

> I took my chariot, my horse, my groom; I crossed the desert and entered into the midst of the Suteans.

And here is the corresponding passage in the tale of the Doomed Prince:

---

[1] After Liverani 1970, esp. 861, I worked with the assumption that the story of Idrimi uses the fairy tale pattern (as defined by Propp 1966) in its essential features. We could formalise the story according to Propp's symbols, and would get something like XW↑R↓LVRmPSN∗. I would not go further than that, because the most detailed part in Propp's analysis can be applied only to the corpus from which it is derived, and also because the result often seems only to reintroduce a factual content rather than deepening the formal analysis (as was noted by Lévi-Strauss, in Propp 1966: 185).

Then a chariot was harnessed for him, equipped with all sorts of weapons, and a servant was given to him as an attendant. He was ferried over to the eastern shore and was told: 'Go wherever you wish', and his greyhound was with him. He went northward across the desert, following his heart and living on the best of all the desert game.
(Lichtheim 1973–80: II, 200–1; on the fairy tale features of this texts see Pieper 1935: 41–4).

Apart from the fact that the Egyptian text is more detailed, while the passage in Idrimi is only an epigraph using a limited space, the resemblance between the two passages is evident. The hero enters the desert with his chariot, horses, and groom, leaves his original community – and in particular his paternal family – and starts his adventure. The *topos* is so similar that we cannot explain it as accidental, and should entertain the possibility that the authors of the two texts both used it consciously.

2 OTHER OCCURRENCES OF THE *TOPOS*

In its basic outline the *topos* consists of introducing the hero alone, and with minimal equipment (chariot, horses, groom), venturing into the desert. Both Idrimi and the Doomed Prince set this *topos* in the same and precise narrative sequence, as we shall see better in a moment. In other texts this motif is used with a different – or vaguer – specific function, although the general purpose always is to emphasise the hero's valour by pointing out his loneliness. I will give some examples, all dating to c. 1500 to 1200 BC.

In some instances the motif is included in a battle narrative, and the desert setting is absent. But in every case the hero is alone, either because he was abandoned by the rest of the army or because he himself left the army, and he finds himself in a hostile environment, surrounded by enemies. A passage from the Memphis stela of Amenophis II uses the motif as follows:

His majesty proceeded by chariot to Hashabu, alone, without having a companion. He returned thence in a short moment, and he brought back 16 living *maryannu* on the two sides of his chariot...   (*Urk* IV 1304; J. A. Wilson in Pritchard 1969: 246)

Other passages in the same inscription emphasise the king's being alone while he carries out his enterprises, and his usual association with chariots and horses. The motif becomes more complex in the poem on the Battle of Qadesh, starting with the following passage:

> The great horse that bore his majesty was Victory-in-Thebes of the great stable of Usermare-sotpenre, beloved of Amun. Then his majesty drove at a gallop and charged the forces of the foe from Hatti, being alone by himself, none other with him.
>
> (Lichtheim 1973–80: II, 64)

The poem continues to emphasise over and over again the loneliness of the king who is abandoned by his army – an emphasis that is not devoid of polemic aims (Posener 1963: 64). In his loneliness, the king does not fail to mention the contributions provided by his assistants, that is the charioteer Menna and the two horses, whose names are recorded and whose help will be duly rewarded.[2]

Otherwise, the *topos* can also be used in relation to hunting, as shown by two examples, one Egyptian and one Babylonian. On the 'Sphinx stela' of Tuthmosis IV we read:

> He took his leisure amusing himself on the desert plateau at Memphis, at its northern and southern ends, shooting arrows at a copper target, hunting lions and gazelles, and driving on his chariot, with his horses faster than wind, and only one person in his escort, no one else knowing. (*Urk* IV 1541, 8–15; *ARE* II 813)[3]

And in the Babylonian 'Dialogue of Pessimism', one of the ideas put forth by the protagonist for a possible accomplishment is this:

> Quickly, fetch me the chariot and hitch it up; I will drive into the steppe.
>
> (Lambert 1960: 144–5: l. 18)

From what follows it is clear that he wanted to go hunting. But note that in both passages something more than a simple hunt is at issue. In the case of the young pharaoh the hunt allows him to prove his valour. But above all this is the occasion when in a dream he receives the promise that he will become king. The dream comes when he falls asleep near the Sphinx while having a rest in the desert after the effort of a hunt (on the political implications, see Donadoni 1959: 179–80). In the case of the protagonist of the Babylonian dialogue, hunting is a way to do 'something' meaningful, a possibility that is eventually dismissed, as are all of the other suggestions the main character makes. But perhaps – bearing in mind the heroic character of our *topos* – the purpose of leaving by a chariot for the desert is

---

2   In Egypt, this *topos* is naturally connected with the well known iconographic motif of Pharaoh alone on a chariot subduing his enemies.

3   On the literary pattern of this and similar texts see Hermann 1938, where our motif is not analysed, however. For hunting too, the *topos* is frequently depicted in pharaonic iconography of the time.

not only a question of 'going hunting', as the servant will trivialise it, but rather a matter of 'starting on an adventure' (Buccellati 1972: 91).

In my last example, that of the Amarna boundary stelae of Akhenaten, the *topos* is used in the context of 'foundation of a city':

> The king appeared mounted on the great chariot of fine gold, like Aten when he dawns in lightland and fills the Two Lands with his love. Setting out on the good road to Akhet-Aten on the first time of finding it, which his majesty had done so as to found it... Having proceeded southward, his majesty halted upon his great chariot before his father Aten at the southeastern mountain of Akhet-Aten...
>
> (*Urk* IV 1982–83; Lichtheim 1973–80: II, 49–50)

Here we again find all the basic features: the hero is alone, on a chariot, and ventures into the desert (the 'mountain'), in order to initiate a decisive action.

3 THE POSITION OF THE MOTIF WITHIN THE NARRATIVE SEQUENCE

In these passages, and in other available examples, the motif is modified in order to adapt it to different situations and aims. In the stories of Idrimi and of the Doomed Prince, however, the motif is clearly used with a specific meaning, and at a fixed point in the narrative sequence. After the stories provide the setting, centred on the heroes' troubled predicament, they relate the sudden decision to act. In both texts the hero's decision puts an end to a period of inactivity. In Idrimi's story, his family's loss of a kingdom is followed by an inglorious refuge with the maternal relatives, which the hero alone can put to an end:

> My brothers, who were older than I, stayed with me, but none of them had the plans I had. I (said to) myself: 'Someone wants to own his father's house, (while) someone wants just to be a slave of the people of Emar'. (So) I took my horse, etc.
>
> (Idrimi 7–12; cf. A. L. Oppenheim in Pritchard 1969: 557).[4]

In the Doomed Prince, the young hero puts an end to the paralysis brought upon his parents by a bad omen:

> Now when many days had passed and the boy was fully grown in all his body, he sent to his father saying: 'To what purpose is my sitting here? I am committed to Fate. Let me go, that I may act according to my heart, until the god does what is in his heart.' Then a chariot was harnessed for him, etc.
>
> (Lichtheim 1973–80: II, 200–1).

---

4   On the interpretation of this passage, whose details are disputed although the general sense is clear, see Buccellati 1962: 96.

It is evident that the opposition between the earlier inactivity and the hero's decision to act is effective in emphasising his valour, by setting him apart from his family members (parents, brothers) who are antiheroes because of their inability to act.[5] In the development of the story, the decision to act has a discriminating function: it differentiates the hero (who leaves) from nonheroes (who remain), and the main character's behaviour before (kept within the family) and after (responsible for his own destiny) his decision.

The position of the motif within the development of the story is thus fixed as a function of its meaning. In the pattern of a fairy tale not only is the same motif found – or better, the same pair of motifs: decision to act + departure from home – they also appear at exactly the same point, after the troubled setting has been laid out. This is because these motifs have the same narrative function in the stories. In Propp's analysis (1966: 44–5), the motifs correspond to the elements 'Beginning of reaction' (symbol W) and 'Departure' (symbol ↑). Their presence, their close association (W↑), their position in the sequence, their relationships with the background and with the further developments leading to the final solution – in particular its connection with helpers and magic tools, as we shall see presently – are the best established elements of the entire analysis of the fairy tale pattern. The story of Idrimi, and still more the tale of the Doomed Prince, are consequently part of a large corpus of narratives that share the same pattern of development. This allows us to ascertain, by way of comparison, what is already clear from the analysis of the texts themselves, namely the meaning of the narrative details in the overall story, and their relation to the aim of its composition.

4 THE BASIC FEATURES

Besides the functional placing of the motif in the narrative sequence, its constituent parts also help to determine its meaning. A comparison of the tales of Idrimi and of the Doomed Prince – and to some extent the other similar texts of the same period – shows two specific elements as characteristic of the motif: the direction 'into the desert' and the presence of assistants (chariot, horses, groom).

By cutting the hero's links with his family, his departure transfers him to a different human and natural environment. He leaves the town, the well known, frequented, interior and secure space, and faces the desert, the unknown, lonely,

---

5   The 'chorus-like' function of relatives, officers, courtiers, etc. in their relation to the hero is evident in many more texts. For Egyptian examples, see Hermann 1938: 14–18. In Hermann's data the chorus is usually in agreement with the hero, rarely in opposition (p. 18). I think, however, that this is due to the specific Egyptian context, where pharaonic ideology leaves little space for opposition. In the more open Syrian and Anatolian worlds opposition is more frequent and quite effective.

exterior, uncertain, and quite frightening space.[6] In the Near Eastern setting the 'desert'[7] is the equivalent of the 'forest' into which the hero ventures in European fairy tales (cf. Propp 1949: 90–2), an equivalence dictated by the obvious climatic and ecological differences between the two regions. The isolation, frightening nature, and difficulty of travel characterise the departure not only as a transfer necessary for the development of the story, but also as a 'trial' (Propp). Consequently the arrival, after crossing the desert or forest, in another inhabited space, one different from the town of departure but comparable to it in that humans live there, already constitutes a success. It allows one to hope that the later and more demanding tests will also be overcome.

The second element, the helpers or the tools – the distinction is not always easy to make or meaningful – at the disposal of the hero, at first seems to contradict the hero's isolation, an isolation that is crucial to the story. But it is well known also in fairy tales that the hero is always given helpers or tools of a magical nature; or he is otherwise able to obtain them. Without them he could never overcome the tests (cf. Propp 1949: 75–81; 1966: 88 and *passim*). In the cases of Idrimi and the Doomed Prince, as in others mentioned above, chariots, horses, and grooms constitute a unit that is the equivalent of the magical helpers or tools in fairy tales. Both in fairy tales and in the ancient Near Eastern texts such equipment has a dual function.

Their first, and more trivial, function is that the equipment serves as a means of transport: helpers and magical tools help the hero in his displacement through space (Propp 1966: 85), and this is the reason why they appear in connection with his decision to leave. In this sense, chariots and horses are the equivalent of other means of transportation found in fairy tales, which are often technologically more modest because of the protagonist's lower social status, such as shoes – even iron shoes – walking-sticks, or magical boots (Propp 1949: 75–81).[8] It is not surprising

---

6   On the opposition between inner space (known, stable, ordered, reassuring) and outer space (unknown, unstable, chaotic, frightening), see Vernant 1971: I, 124–70; Barthes 1972: 141–5; Ščeglov 1969: 129–31; etc. More generally, the opposition between a central, inner, cosmic space, and a peripheral, external, chaotic space, has been especially emphasised by M. Eliade (esp. 1965) and by other scholars who have treated the qualitative differences of space in so-called 'mythical thinking'.

7   On the desert in the ancient Near East and its symbolic implications, especially as a transitional space where a trial is to be overcome, and as a metaphor for the netherworld, see Haldar 1950; Talmon 1966.

8   In other Egyptian tales the hero as a commoner leaves with sandals and a walking-stick. For example, in the tale of the Two Brothers 'he took his staff and his sandals, as well as his clothes and his weapons, and he started to journey to the Valley of the Pine' (Lichtheim 1973–80: II, 208), and in the tale of Truth and Falsehood 'he went off to avenge his father. He took ten loaves of bread, a staff, a pair of sandals, a waterskin, and a sword' (*ibid.*, 212).

to find horses as the most prestigious means of transportation, and as such they feature quite often in fairy tales (Propp 1949: 271–89; 1966: 88; cf. already Aarne and Thompson 1928: 86–8; Thompson 1936: VI, 282–6; 1946). The prestige of the horse, a symbol of social status, and its privileged connection to the hero, have a psychological and social basis that is very strong and concrete in the Near East of the fifteenth to thirteenth centuries BC. Exactly in this period the first nobilities of 'knights' emerged. The same motif was to become stereotypical in the fairy tale, to be revived from time to time when 'knights' were popular.

The social prestige attached to the ownership of a horse introduces us to the second function of the assistant or tool: it is indispensable if he is to overcome the trials and achieve success. In the fairy tales the trials are such that the hero cannot overcome them without magical help. In fact, they are never surmounted by his rivals who have no magical assistance. The hero would not be a hero, he would not stand out among the common and indistinct mass of nonheroes, if he did not have magical support. The same holds true for Idrimi and comparable characters in the ancient Near East: the conquest of the throne, the victory in battle or the like, are goals that would be unattainable without this minimal basis. The effect of the magical support is at once technical and social, since it expresses itself both at the material level and that of prestige. Idrimi might have been able to get from Emar to Ammiya on foot, but if he had arrived on foot he would never have been recognised by the refugees there as 'the son of their lord'.

5 ACCESSORY FEATURES

The comparison between the story of Idrimi and the pattern of the fairy tale has demonstrated a close similarity in the position and function of the motif of 'departure' in the narrative sequence. There is also a close similarity in the main features of such a departure: the hero is alone, he has helpers or means of transportation, and he sets out into the desert or forest. This comparison can help us understand the meaning of other secondary features as well.

A common narrative feature is the astonishing speed of the trip. Idrimi leaves Emar and spends the night in the desert; the next morning he arrives at Ammiya. So he covers the distance from the Euphrates to the Mediterranean coast – 300 km – in a single day, a feat which is clearly impossible. From the narrative point of view, it is easy to understand that the inscription ignores meaningless details and emphasises only significant stages. Yet the way the trip is narrated does not seem to abridge the process of its recording, but rather the great length of the journey. Someone unaware of the geographical position of Ammiya who reads: 'On the next day I arose and went to the land of Canaan', can get the impression that the entire trip was concluded on the second day. Now, this tremendous shortening of the hero's journey is typical of fairy tales (Propp 1949: 76), especially in the case of the specific trip of the hero that occurs at this particular point in the narrative sequence. Sometimes the speed of travel is explained by the use of magical helpers or tools, such as the winged horse, the 'seven league' boots, and the like. Speed in displacement can be a stylistic and psychological device – in the framework of a narrative technique largely unconcerned with conditions of space – but even so, it is not insignificant for the development of the story. It is an important aspect of the ease with which the hero surmounts difficulties that would be much more serious for other people. The speed is therefore a constituent detail in the protagonist's heroic nature, and as such it has a definite function to the narrative itself.

A second relevant point is that Idrimi runs into the Suteans. This event corresponds to the fairy tale hero's frequent accidental encounter with a group of brothers, mostly hunters or brigands (Propp 1949: 188–92). That such an encounter is recorded in the Idrimi inscription could seem meaningless, and indeed it has no relevance in the development of the plot.[9] But its psychological implications are meaningful. In the desert or forest, the hero typically encounters 'irregular' populations that are different from the usual urban ones. He encounters people who produce the same psychological effect as the natural landscape – desert or forest – that hosts them: a feeling of insecurity and fear generated by the unknown and possibly hostile environment. But, although the hero runs into this difficult situation, he is able to overcome it, and even to find in it the help he needs in order to continue.[10]

Finally, the almost irrelevant detail, 'I spent the night in my covered chariot' may have its equivalent in the fairy tale when the hero, once he has entered the forest, spends the night in a hut, in some cases the dwelling of a witch, or the like (Propp 1949: 93–103). I do not believe that this goes beyond a common psychological point, which in the Idrimi story seems to be its only motivation, while in the fairy tale it may be complicated by other factors. The psychological point consists simply in emphasizing the worries caused by entering a hostile, or simply unknown, environment, that intensify when night comes. At that moment, the availability of an enclosed space – chariot or hut – for overnight shelter generates a relief by providing a defence against the hostile forces of the unknown space outside (see n.6 above).

---

9 There is, however, a further reference in ll. 84–86 where Idrimi gives permanent abodes to the Suteans. The motif of the hero rewarding his helpers or punishing his enemies once he achieves final success is also normal in fairy tales.

10 The fact that Idrimi spends the night with the Suteans implies that they hosted him, instead of robbing him, as city-dwellers would probably have expected them to do.

6 THE FAIRY TALE PATTERN AND HISTORICAL TRUTH

I have compared Idrimi's story to the fairy tale simply in order to point out the specific function of details in the psychological setting and in the mechanics of the narrative plot. It seems to me that all the details basically converge in the same direction, the one already pointed out for the central motif: the nature of the departure and the eventual journey is a kind of 'trial', permitting the protagonist to qualify as a 'hero'. The trial consists of detaching the hero from his family, where he had no possibility for acting autonomously, and of inserting him into a new world – one unknown and potentially hostile – a world that he is easily able to master, thus enabling him to qualify as a hero.

In this sense we cannot deny that the hero's adventures possess features of 'initiation', an aspect that Propp emphasised strongly for the fairy tale.[11] In Propp's opinion, initiation and fairy tale are linked by a diachronic subordination. The adventures of the hero are interpreted as an echo or a residue – no longer functional and no longer understood – of ancient initiation rituals. I see the relationships as synchronous, as going back to a more general psychological core, the different manifestations of which (dependent on different social and cultural environments) are on the one hand initiatory procedures, with their strong institutionalising of symbolic behaviour, and on the other hand stories or fairy tales in which the same motifs are present at a vaguer level of consciousness.[12]

At this point, I am concerned that a too facile opposition between history and literary motif, or between history and fairy tale pattern, might lead to misunderstandings.[13] By pointing out the use – conscious or not – of stereotyped motifs and narrative patterns by the author of the Idrimi story, I do not mean to deny the historical reliability of the narrative. I have no problem in accepting that Idrimi really did leave with horses and groom, that he really did spend the night in his chariot, that he really did encounter Suteans, and so on. In short, I believe that the story of Idrimi is a 'true' story, that what was recorded in the inscription took place more or less as described. Two points must, however, be considered more carefully.

---

11 Propp's thesis (1949) is that fairy tales derive from ancient initiation rites, as well as from the event of death (and rebirth) – the latter being an overstressed form of initiation, adumbrated by initiation itself.

12 Although synchronised, the relationship does not loose its historical concreteness. In any case it refers to the influence of various sociocultural structures that shape a fact whose remote roots remain generally human.

13 My study (1970) was partly misunderstood by Archi 1971: 187–8 with n.8. I never meant that a literary *topos* is necessarily false. On these problems cf. Liverani 1973a.

The first point is related to the qualification 'more or less' that I have added in order to account for some ahistorical details, such as the motif of the 'seven years'. Although the storyteller wants to provide us with a 'true' story, he has a concept of 'historical truth' that is in general slightly different from ours. In fact, since we ourselves have different concepts of historical truth, depending on the literary genre and the function of the text we discuss, I should refer to a specific type of document of ours – the historical document – that has been considered arbitrarily to be equivalent to Idrimi's story. The storyteller clearly makes use of narrative patterns that he considers to be appropriate for his genre of composition. The line between historical exactness and literary motif is not clear-cut, because it is not considered very important and meaningful. What does it matter if a period of time was seven years, or six, or nine? Such a piece of accuracy has no relevance whatsoever in a society – like the Syrian society of the Late Bronze period – that does not keep records of the lengths of reigns, that has no dating formulae or any other system to distinguish the single years of the past, and that 'dates' its juridical documents only insofar as it says that they are valid 'from now on' and 'forever'.[14] The storyteller cannot know, and is not interested in knowing, how long a period was. He just states that it lasted 'seven years', in order to emphasise that 'in the seventh year' the situation was reversed. And his audience knows that 'seven' has no numerical significance, but has a specific narrative function related to the reversal of a given situation or the end of a given phase (cf. Liverani 1967b).

We are left in doubt about the accuracy of other details because we cannot check them. For example, Idrimi states that he is the youngest among his brothers ('my brothers, who were older than I…'). Was it true? We cannot dispute it, but this is not enough. It is possible, for instance, that Idrimi had both older and younger brothers, which would be a quite trivial state of affairs. To the storyteller the 'truth' of such a remark has no more relevance than the years of exile being seven or eight, and the length of the trip being one day or one week. But from the narrative point of view the identification of Idrimi as the 'youngest son' is quite effective. The brothers remain inactive although they are older, have been able to act for a longer time, and are more advanced in the family hierarchy of rights and responsibilities. Idrimi acts although he is the youngest and the weakest, the one we least expect to solve problems that the older ones do not dare to face.[15] Therefore the storyteller deliberately emphasises the more advanced age of the brothers, while he remains silent about the presence of younger brothers.

---

[14] Such temporal references are usual in juridical documents of the Late Bronze period in Syria, at Alalah (Wiseman 1953: nos.15, 17, etc.), Ugarit (Nougayrol 1955: *passim*), and Karkemish (Nougayrol 1956: *passim*).

[15] Cf. also the opposition between chorus and hero (n.5 above).

He emphasises and conceals certain things according to the function of a specific remark in the framework of the entire narrative. This is the reason why the heroes of fairy tales, like the protagonists of some 'historical' autobiographies, are *as a rule* the youngest in a long line of brothers, a fact that is statistically improbable but semantically most effective.[16]

This brings us to the second and most relevant point to be considered. The adoption of an overall fairy tale pattern, as well as of some fairy tale details, has a meaning. The pattern was chosen – consciously or not, by the king or the storyteller – in order to express a specific meaning. The problem then is not to understand whether a detail is exact or not, but to understand why such a detail was used – be it true or false. The problem is not so much checking whether the events took place in a certain way, but rather appreciating how and why they were told according to a particular narrative pattern. Idrimi tells the story of his life along the lines of a fairy tale, because he has a definite interest in doing so: he has to face the opinion of a public that was troubled by the irregular way he ascended the throne. In fact most protagonists of 'fairy tale' stories in the ancient Near East are usurpers: Idrimi, Sargon of Akkad, Hattushili III, David, Darius, and so on. They all rose to power in an irregular way from a modest background. It was appropriate and necessary to recount their story as a fairy tale accomplishment, in which the hero's bravery, assisted by magic or divine help, and notwithstanding an unfavourable starting point, succeeded in surmounting every obstacle and in achieving success. The story of Idrimi is therefore a 'true' story, even if its narrative pattern preceded it. *That* pattern was used to narrate *that* story with a precise purpose. Idrimi needed to demonstrate to public opinion that his accession to the throne was the result of his heroic capabilities and of supernatural assistance.

---

16 I have quoted contemporary examples (Liverani 1970: 863), but the motif is quite widespread in the ancient Near East: suffice it to recall the boast by Esarhaddon *ša aḫḫīya rabûti aḫšunu ṣiḫru anāku* 'of my elder brothers, I was their younger brother' (cf., *CAD* Ṣ, 182), or the story of David, the youngest among the 'seven' sons of Jesse (1 Sam. 16: 10–11). The motif of the younger brother has been studied for the ancient Near East by Redford 1970: 88–9. On the opposition of elder and younger brothers, and the prevalence of the younger, in fairy tales compare Thompson 1946: *passim* (Olrik's rule no.6); 1936: 5–6 (motif L 10), 8 (motif L 101); also motifs L 111, on p. 9: 'Exile returns and succeeds' (cf. Idrimi 30–39) and R 155.1 on p. 210: 'Youngest brother rescues his elder brothers' (cf. Idrimi 39–42).

5

*Rib-Adda, righteous sufferer**

INTRODUCTION

Rib-Adda was king of the harbor city of Byblos, on the coast of present-day Lebanon, in the early fourteenth century when Egypt controlled the Syro-Palestinian area through a system of vassals. The king of Byblos was a prolific correspondent with the court of Egypt, under kings Amenophis III and IV, and between 59 and 63 letters from him are preserved in the Amarna archive (EA 68–71, 73–95, 102–9, 112–4, 116–9, 121–7, 129–34, 136–8, 362; EA 101, 110, 111, and 120 are probably also his). In those he portrays himself as the victim of the kings of Amurru who pressure states in the region to abandon their allegiance to Egypt. As loyal vassal to Pharaoh he sees himself under constant threat and implores the king to help him. Ultimately, he was indeed overthrown, not by outsiders but by his own brother, and he died in exile.

The Amarna correspondence presents a rich source of information on how Egypt administered this area through a hands-off policy. Local dynasts, called mayors (*ḫazānu*) by the Egyptians while acknowledged as kings by their own subjects, had to provide annual payments whose collection was Egypt's main concern. The Syro-Palestinian area was divided into three provinces, Kinahni (= Canaan), Ube, and Amurru, each of which had one centre of Egyptian administration, where a governor (*rābiṣu*) resided. The local kings competed with one another over territory and in their struggles hoped to gain Pharaoh's support by presenting themselves as loyal vassals and the others as Egypt's enemies. It is in this context that Rib-Adda's letters have to be read. The kings of Amurru are the primary targets of his accusations and he claims that they rely on marauding bands of outcasts, the *ḫabiru*, in their aggression. This chapter cautions against a literal reading of Rib-Adda's letters, and interprets their style and contents as a reflection of the author's self-portrayal as a righteous sufferer.

Everything that is known about Rib-Adda derives from the Amarna letters (referred to as EA with the numbers typically assigned in the discipline). These have been recently retranslated into English by Moran (1992). Liverani's own complete translations into Italian were published in 1998–99.

★   ★   ★   ★

* Originally published as 'Rib-Adda, giusto sofferente', *Altorientalische Forschungen* 1 (1974), 175–201; the manuscript was completed in December 1971.

The current reinterpretation of the Amarna correspondence aims at understanding the overall historical situation underlying the individual letters, rather than at an uncritical historical use of the 'items of information' contained in them. The process focuses primarily on pointing out stereotyped procedures, patterns, and expressions, both administrative and literary in character (see already Liverani 1967a; 1971a). Recurring stereotypes are especially revealing of the concepts and worries that prompted the writing of the letters. Moreover, the very fact that they occur frequently warns us against using individual and specific statements as independent evidence. In letters, especially diplomatic letters, such statements can easily be biased, because the author takes up a subjective stance in order to convince the addressee.

It would be particularly interesting to define the existential position of the authors, and the patterns with which they interpreted reality. How did they feel themselves as part of the world that surrounded them? How did they conceive their relations with other people, and with the gods? How did they evaluate the connections between behaviour and success? How did they characterise the present in the perspectives of the past and of the future? The Amarna letters seem to supply useful and adequate material to study how these questions apply to concrete historical events. It is possible to establish a basis for evaluating what parts in individual letters pertain to concrete events, and what parts are interpretative patterns applied to reality – whether consciously or unconsciously – by the authors of the letters.

By so doing, we tackle the world of 'wisdom' (in its broader meaning), which is poorly documented in second millennium Syria.[1] Yet this is not a difficulty. It may even be an additional reason for our interest, namely to recover some elements of the lost Syrian 'wisdom' of the Bronze Age. We would recover those elements not from remains of learned or literary reflection, but from documents composed of practical needs that are spontaneous and germane to the historical moment. We can at once anticipate that the interpretative pattern that results from a detailed analysis of the letters will show close connections with a well known motif in Near Eastern wisdom, one commonly called the 'righteous sufferer'.[2] The analysis that follows is based on the procedure of deconstructing single letters and then reassembling them according to the 'righteous sufferer'

---

[1]   The situation is such that when Albright (1955) tried to point out parallels between the wisdom of the Old Testament and that of the Bronze Age 'Canaanite' world, he could not find more than a few proverbs (cf. now Cazelles 1963), and some stylistic parallels.

[2]   At one time the parallel between texts like the biblical Book of Job and the late second millennium Babylonian composition *Ludlul bēl nēmeqi* was rather weak in historical terms. Today the gap is being filled through the publication of new texts and by the identification of wisdom elements in texts of different genres. So I believe that I am justified in estimating that the 'righteous sufferer' motif was a widespread cultural model in the ancient Near East.

pattern. The aim of this is assuredly not to deny the necessity of reading a single letter as a unit (a necessity on which I insisted in an early study, Liverani 1971a, and on which I still insist). Quite the contrary, this is done in order to provide a unitary reading, using a pattern of reference of which each letter is a materialisation. Deconstruction is therefore a transitional and instrumental procedure, with a more conscious and organic recomposition in mind. In a sense it seems possible to consider the letters as stanzas of a long wisdom poem, each stanza repeating (with only accidental, even merely stylistic, variations) the same concepts, always in the framework of the same pattern.

I have selected the correspondence of Rib-Adda, not because it has a peculiar character when compared to other groups of letters, but simply because it is by far the most extensive corpus of Amarna letters, and it supplies a documentary basis that is less likely to be influenced by happenstance. Rib-Adda's letters show more precisely, and with greater clarity, what we indistinctly perceive in the correspondence of other Syro-Palestinian kings, such as Abdi-Heba or Abi-Milki. Moreover, I have preferred to limit my analysis to a single group of letters only, which can be viewed as homogeneous in literary terms. In principle this allows one to isolate a personalised characterisation, which is especially useful in the patter of the 'righteous sufferer', since it presents a highly personalised analysis of the surrounding reality.

1 THE PRESENT

1.1 THE RIGHTEOUS SUBJECT

It is necessary to start from the subject, the writer of the letters, since their general focus is extremely egocentric. With some simplification we can say that the world is made up of just two elements: the subject and the others. The subject is at the centre; the others are all around him. The others' movements are always considered in relation to him: either they press (in a hostile way) toward the centre where the subject is located, or they flee (also in a hostile way) to an 'outside' space, where they tend to disappear. Any judgement on others is given in function of the subject and is based on their relations to the subject. Matters are quite simple: the others are enemies. The moral characterisation of the two is one of basic contrast: the subject is just, the others are unjust.

On the whole, Rib-Adda's correspondence is highly autobiographical, but more in the sense of establishing a pattern than of narrating a chronicle. From the many hints Rib-Adda gives regarding himself or, less frequently, his city (which is exactly the same) we get an extremely stereotyped and elementary 'self-portrait': Rib-Adda is 'just', Rib-Adda is 'alone'.

First, Rib-Adda is characterised by 'justice'. The Akkadian term used is *kittu*, which can hardly be translated simply as 'justice', because its implications are more complex.[3] *Kittu* (from the verb *kânu*, 'to be stable') is the fact that one persists in one's own place in the world, and remains loyal to one's own existential mission and to the one who established this mission, in other words god. Therefore it is justice in a cosmic sense; it measures how well one's own conduct fits the established rules. In practice, in the political language of the time, *kittu* is the 'loyalty' of a vassal to his overlord, and the loyalty to the (sworn) agreement between them (cf. Liverani 1971b). A typical expression of the Amarna letters, and exclusive to it, *arad kitti*, means the 'faithful servant', he who remains steadfast in the place appointed to him by his lord (the god) in the political system (the cosmos).

Rib-Adda and his city behave according to *kittu* 'righteousness/faithfulness', in the frame of the political system established by Pharaoh. Rib-Adda states: 'Byblos is a faithful city, from of old. My lord is the Sun of lands. And look: I am the stool under the feet of my lord, I am his faithful servant' (EA 106: 4–7); 'I am a faithful servant of the King, the Sun. As to my mouth: the words I spoke to the King are loyalty. Let the King, my lord, listen to the words of his faithful servant' (EA 107: 8–13; also 34–6); 'Consider that I am your faithful servant… My loyalty is very great… Let the King listen to the words of his faithful servant, and grant life to his servant and to Byblos, his maid-servant' (EA 116: 14–5, 29, 44–7). Some of the statements that qualify Rib-Adda as a faithful servant are stereotypical and recurrent. 'Let the King, my lord, listen to the words of his faithful servant' (EA 85: 16–17; EA 103: 5–7, 23–4; EA 116: 44–5; etc.), 'Consider your faithful servant' (EA 114: 54; EA 116: 14–5; EA 124: 11; EA 132: 8–9 referred to Byblos), or 'Let the King know that Byblos, the city loyal to the King, is safe' (EA 68: 9–11; EA 74: 5–7). He also simply states 'I am a faithful servant' (EA 108: 22; EA 109: 42; EA 116: 57; EA 134: 25–26, referring to Byblos; etc.), or 'If my lord loves his faithful servant' (EA 123: 23–24). This faithfulness dates from time immemorial (see below, p. 113; EA 74: 5–12; EA 88: 42–45; EA 118: 39–41; etc.), and Rib-Adda intends it to continue forever in the future, until his death. 'I will never forsake the word of my lord' (EA 88: 28–29); 'As long as I will be alive, I will protect the King's city for him, but if I die who will do that?' (EA 119: 15–18; EA 130: 49–52); 'I live in order to serve the King my lord' (EA 112: 23–24); 'My

---

3   Semantic studies that analyse this term are lacking (as for many words in the Akkadian lexicon). References are to be found in the articles *kânu(m), kīnu(m)* and *kittu(m)* in *AHw*, 438–40, 481, 494–5, and in *CAD* K, 159–71, 389–93, 468–72. What is stated in the present article is limited to the Syrian milieu of the second millennium, where the semantic field of *kittu* was presumably influenced by Northwest Semitic *ṣdq*, on which see Pedersen 1926: 336–2; Fahlgren 1932; Rosenthal 1950–51.

purpose is to serve the King my lord' (EA 119: 43–44; EA 118: 39–40; cf. EA 89: 15–16); 'Let my lord know that I would die for him' (EA 137: 52; cf. EA 138: 27). Rib-Adda's faithfulness distinguishes him from his colleagues, and distinguishes Byblos from the other cities in the region (cf. below pp. 111–12).

Sometimes loyalty is stressed because of a particular circumstance, for instance, when charges of falsehood reached the palace. 'Let my lord know that there is no evil in the words of his servant. I did not tell any false word to the King my lord… People who told false words to the King my lord, they are false!' (EA 94: 5–8, 14–5); 'My lord knows that I did not write false words to my lord' (EA 362: 51–3); 'Let the King know that I am a faithful servant to him: let the King not listen to the slanders against his faithful servant… No one reported my faithfulness to the King my lord. Let the King know, know my faithfulness… Now, this judgement is a judgement about my righteousness' (EA 119: 24–27, 36–39, 44–45). But more often faithfulness is proclaimed in absolute terms, in function of a general problem: Rib-Adda needs to obtain from Pharaoh the means and assistance necessary to assure the 'protection' of the city, which is after all the very substance of loyalty (cf. Liverani 1971a: 259–60). Basically Rib-Adda asserts, 'I am a faithful servant and I protect the city, but you must send me troops and food' – that is to say, 'I want to be faithful, but you have to give me the concrete possibility'. If 'justice/faithfulness' is the persistence of the subject in his correct location in the framework of the cosmic (here: political) order, following the dispositions of the god (here: of Pharaoh), a state of security and gratification should follow. Yet it is not so, and this painful observation is at the core of the drama that Rib-Adda lives: 'You see: we are faithful servants of the King, from the beginning. Moreover, you see: I am a faithful servant; yet I am doing badly' (EA 116: 55–58). In fact (as we shall see more fully later on) this 'loyalty' of Rib-Adda is an exceptional behaviour – or better, it is perceived as exceptional by the subject – that differentiates him from and contrasts with the entire surrounding world. The behaviour is morally correct, but statistically anomalous. The result is the 'isolation' of Rib-Adda, and the 'hostility' of all the others towards him.

Rib-Adda feels this isolation strongly. The question, 'what can I do in my isolation?' recurs frequently (EA 74: 63–64; EA 81: 50–51; EA 90: 22–23; EA 91: 25–26; EA 134: 15–16).[4] At its most basic level, the question reveals the dismay of being alone in a world that is totally different and completely hostile. 'What can I do, I who reside in the midst of the *ḫabiru*?' (EA 130: 36–38).[5] Rib-Adda needs help, but cannot find anyone willing to give it: 'The men of Maspat are hostile to

---

[4] The expression *ina ìdini-ia/ši* is exclusively used in the Amarna letters (cf. *CAD* E, s.v. *ēdēnu* 2a).

[5] On *ḫabiru* as meaning 'enemy', cf. below p. 102. Notice that the expression *ša aṣbati ina libbi ḫabiri* in EA 130 takes the place of the more usual *ina ìdini-ia*, pointing to a correspondence between the feeling of being 'isolated' and that of being 'surrounded'.

me, and behold, there is no one to help me out of their clutches' (EA 69: 21–24); 'I am afraid that there is no one to rescue me from their clutches' (EA 74: 43–45). Rib-Adda has to accomplish a task that is too great for his forces alone: 'Know that hostility against me is strong, all my cities have been taken, Byblos is left to me in its isolation' (EA 90: 5–9; cf. EA 91: 19–22); 'In my isolation I protect...' (EA 122: 19–21, etc.). His isolation is stressed by the surrounding hostility: it is therefore necessary to analyse it in the context of the conduct of the others, the 'enemies'.

1.2 THE ENEMY

A hostile world puts pressure on the subject from all directions. In every letter Rib-Adda denounces hostility; we can even say he wrote them in order to denounce hostility. The denunciation is mostly formulated in general terms. 'Hostility against me is very strong' is a recurring statement, with minor variants (EA 90: 6; EA 106: 8–9; EA 116: 7–8; EA 117: 89–90; EA 118: 21–22; EA 121: 18–19, etc.). The instigator of such hostility is not even mentioned. Rib-Adda simply declares that the hostile pressure has become unbearable. In other cases the instigator of hostility is designated by the term *ḫabiru*, a term that should to be understood as having a vague meaning in this context: 'Hostility of the *ḫabirus* against me is very strong' (EA 68: 12–14; EA 74: 13–14; EA 75: 10–11, etc.). *Ḫabiru* here means generically the 'enemy' (cf. already Campbell 1960: 13–15), that is, the perpetrator of hostility against Rib-Adda. Originally the term had a precise technical meaning ('exile', 'outlaw'; cf. Liverani 1965b, with earlier bibliography), but here it is used in an emotional sense, as is usual for political terms, encompassing the sphere of 'hostile', 'enemy', also 'rascal', and the like. In linguistic terms I could say that a rendering 'refugee' belongs to the denotative level, while renderings like 'enemy', or 'rascal', belong to the connotative level. Rib-Adda gives a negative moral judgement of the *ḫabirus*' behaviour and the way they behave as enemies.

Sometimes the enemy has a more concrete, individual personality. An immediate rival becomes the embodiment of the generic hostile force that presses from every direction. Abdi-Ashirta is the prototype of this character.[6] He is always detested, he is labelled 'the *ḫabiru*' (that is, 'the rascal'), or 'the dog'.[7] In

---

6   For the use of 'prototypes' or fixed 'characters' in the pattern, cf. EA 280: 30–35: 'Lab'aya, who used to take our cities, is dead; but now Abdi-Heba is a second Lab'aya, and he takes our cities'.

7   In the Amarna corpus, the label 'dog' often refers to Abdi-Ashirta. Rib-Adda labels him so in a deprecatory sense ('Who does he think he is, Abdi-Ashirta, the servant and dog?...': EA 71: 16–18, etc.; see Coats 1970). Abdi-Ashirta labels himself a 'dog', obviously in a positive sense ('I am the servant of the king and the (guard) dog of his house': EA 60: 6–7; cf. EA 61: 3–4, and perhaps Aziru in EA 159: 17). His usage may not be without an ironic and polemic nuance against that of Rib-Adda. See already Baikie 1926: 353.

the stereotyped denunciation of hostility, his name is a free variant of the term *ḫabiru*: 'The hostility of Abdi-Ashirta against me is strong' (EA 76: 8–9; EA 78: 8–9; EA 81: 7; etc.). The connection lies in the fact that Abdi-Ashirta is at the head of the *ḫabirus*, that he instigates and co-ordinates them in their hostile actions against Byblos (see Artzi 1964; Liverani 1965a). 'All the *ḫabirus* are set against me, instigated by Abdi-Ashirta' (EA 79: 10–12); 'Since Bit-Arha was taken at Abdi-Ashirta's instigation, they have been trying to do the same to Byblos and Batruna, and all the lands go over to the *ḫabirus*' (EA 79: 21–25). Abdi-Ashirta's identification in the role of 'the enemy' is so strong that Rib-Adda sometimes hints at him without even naming him, so evidently is he the instigator of every hostile action. 'Behold, three times he stood against me this year, and for two years I have been short of grain' (EA 85: 9–10, Abdi-Ashirta is not mentioned until line 64); 'People knew that there were no troops with him (= the messenger coming back from Egypt), and Batruna went to him (= Abdi-Ashirta)' (EA 87: 18–20, Abdi-Ashirta is never mentioned in this letter).

After Abdi-Ashirta's death, his sons, in particular the one called Aziru, inherit his kingdom, his policy, and his hostility toward Rib-Adda (as well as Rib-Adda's toward them). Consequently, they play the role of 'enemies' in Rib-Adda's existential pattern. 'I am doing very badly, hostility is very strong, the sons of Abdi-Ashirta entered Amurru and the entire land (belongs) to them' (EA 103: 7–11); 'The sons of Abdi-Ashirta took all the cities and initiated hostility against me' (EA 133: 6–8); 'The King's enemy (=Aziru) is hostile to me, and his *ḫazānus* decide on their own. So I am doing very badly' (EA 114: 47–50); 'Aziru took all my cities' (EA 124: 7–8); 'Let the king my lord know that Aziru is hostile to me' (EA 114: 6–7). Another individual enemy, who does not belong to the Amurru group, is also mentioned, namely Yapah-Adda, king of an unknown city: 'Yapah-Adda behaves badly, badly against me' (EA 116: 40–42); 'What did I do to Yapah-Adda, who behaves badly, badly against me?' (EA 113: 11–13). Other hostile characters are vaguely present: Zimrida king of Sidon, the usurper of the throne at Tyre, the people of the city Arwad, an Egyptian official who is not sufficiently attentive, and so on.

In the case of Yapah-Adda the question seems to be one of personal quarrel, with judicial implications (cf. EA 117–119). But in the other cases the generic hostility is seldom concretely formulated. Once a ransom is considered too high ('Aziru is hostile to me: he took twelve people of mine and established 50 shekels of silver as a ransom between us', EA 114: 7–9; for the normal price of 30 shekels per person, see EA 292: 49–50). Once it is a question of slander ('Let the King not listen to the slander against his faithful servant', EA 119: 26–27; cf. EA 94: 14–15). But almost always the hostile action is that of 'taking cities' at Rib-Adda's expense, first by Abdi-Ashirta, then by Aziru, and always by the *ḫabirus*. 'Let the King, my lord, know that Abdi-Ashirta's hostility against me is strong: he took all my cities. Behold: two cities are left, and he tries to take these too' (EA 78: 7–13; cf. EA 76: 7–10; EA 79: 20–29; EA 81: 6–11, etc.); 'Know that hostility against me is strong. All my cities have been taken, Byblos is left in her isolation' (EA 90: 5–9); 'The sons of Abdi-Ashirta took all my cities, they started hostility against me' (EA 133: 6–8). These examples could be easily multiplied. Such actions are without doubt politically serious. Indeed, a picture of serious political and military difficulties for the kingdom of Byblos has been derived from them – the city being hemmed in progressively, as if in a vice. It is legitimate, however, to ask whether this reconstruction is acceptable. From his first letter to his last, for a period of some ten to twelve years,[8] Rib-Adda always complains about the loss of cities, 'taken' by the enemies or 'gone over' to them by themselves. This is always the case for all but two cities, whose names vary while they are always two in number. They are the 'last' two remaining, Shigata and Ambi (EA 74–76), Byblos and Batruna (EA 79–81), or Sumura and Irqata (EA 103). Clearly this is a stylistic device rather than a precise figure. One could argue that there was a progressive worsening of the situation, with Byblos at first excluded from the computation ('Byblos and two cities are left' in EA 74: 22) and then included. But we must bear in mind that the chronological ordering of Rib-Adda's letters has been arranged since Knudtzon (1902; see Campbell 1964: 77–83) precisely on the basis of this kind of 'information'. The letters have been placed in a sequence on the assumption that there was a progressive crisis in the king's control over his kingdom. If we are dealing here not with 'facts' about abandonment, but with a 'feeling' of being abandoned, everything is different. The changes are then not unidirectional and progressive, but cyclical, and the situation is therefore basically static. Some loss is always taking place, only the last bulwarks ever remain, and they too are always on the point of collapse (see below, pp. 115-16). It is also clear that the cities are not taken by military action; they are simply transferring their political and tributary affiliations toward Amurru rather than to Byblos, probably in an alternating and unstable process that changes with the balance of power. Rib-Adda himself says to Pharaoh: 'Don't you know that the Amurru people go with whoever is strong(er)?' (EA 73: 14–16). Therefore the phenomenon is a recurrent one, and its importance is questionable. The cities alternately ally themselves with one or the other of the contending parties. It is generally believed that Rib-Adda at first progressively lost all his cities to Abdi-Ashirta. Then he would have retrieved all of them after the chief of Amurru died, and finally he would have lost them again under the pressure of Aziru. This reconstruction is an unacceptable transposition of the cyclical view of events, which is

---

8   For the length of the Amarna correspondence I adopt the estimate of Campbell 1964: 83–9. For
     longer estimates of around twenty years, see the studies by Riedel and de Koning quoted there.
     For a minimal estimate of about five years, see Kitchen 1962: 41–5.

typical of Rib-Adda's milieu,[9] onto a historical level. A precise example is provided by the 'information' on the murders of the kings of Irqata and Ammiya. Rib-Adda accuses Abdi-Ashirta (EA 73: 26–29; EA 74: 25–29; EA 75: 25–26, 32–34), while Ili-rapih accuses Aziru (EA 139: 14–15; EA 140: 10–14). It is possible that these episodes took place even before Abdi-Ashirta's time – the two kings were killed in local peasant revolts, and it is only Rib-Adda's opinion that this was at the instigation of the kings of Amurru – being eventually recalled when it was expedient, as admonitory anecdotes.

Rib-Adda's psychosis of feeling besieged has a concrete historical basis, but it is certainly exaggerated by him. He tries to substantiate his problems by mixing personal and political facts, trivial and serious episodes, as if they were all on the same level. He even quotes episodes that do not concern him personally, as in the case of the city of Sumura. 'As to Sumura, hostility against it is very strong, and it is strong also against me' (EA 106: 8–9); 'I am doing very badly, the hostility of the sons of Abdi-Ashirta is strong: they entered Amurru, all the lands (belong) to them, (only) Sumura and Irqata are left to the Great-One' (EA 103: 7–13); 'There is hostility against me and against Sumura, and now its *rābiṣu* is dead' (EA 106: 21–23), etc. In complaining about the attacks against Sumura, and in listing it among the cities that are left, Rib-Adda tries to identify himself with that city. However – as was the case with Irqata – it was not and had never been part of his territory, being the seat of the Egyptian governor (*rābiṣu*). Pharaoh himself noticed the oddity and asked Rib-Adda: 'Why did Rib-Adda write a letter to the Palace, and why is he worrying more than his colleagues about Sumura?' (EA 106: 13–16; cf. Liverani 1971a: 265). A typical symptom of Rib-Adda's psychosis is that he considered attacks that were not his concern at all to be directed against himself. The all-encompassing character of the surrounding world's hostility against the subject underscores that the situation is psychological rather than historical. 'You know that everything is hostile. Why do you abandon me to the enemy? Behold, because of this I am afraid' (EA 102: 25–28); 'All my cities are my enemies, with the sons of Abdi-Ashirta. Therefore they are strong' (EA 109: 58–60); 'In Amurru, they are all allied, I am (the only) enemy' (EA 114: 14–15); 'All my cities went over to the *habirus*, and all of them are hostile to me' (EA 116: 37–40); 'Aziru is hostile to me, and all the *hazānus* are in agreement with him' (EA 126: 9–11); 'All the lands are hostile to me' (EA 130: 43). Rib-Adda no longer knows from which direction the attacks are coming. The enemies are everywhere, both inside and outside his territory. 'From whom should I protect

---

[9]   The recognition that the events of Aziru's time are a repetition of those from the time of Abdi-Ashirta's is explicit in EA 105: 25–26: 'Everything which belonged to Abdi-Ashirta, they gave to his sons'. So the vicissitudes started again.

myself? From my enemy or from my peasants?' (EA 112: 10–12; cf. EA 117: 89–90). Sometimes he identifies the surrounding hostile forces clearly: 'The cities of Ambi, Shigata, Ullaza and Arwad are my enemies... These cities on ships, and the sons of Abdi-Ashirta on land, are standing against me, and I cannot leave' (EA 104: 40–51); 'I cannot send my ships there (i.e., to Ugarit) because Aziru is hostile to me and all the *ḫazānu*s are in agreement with him' (EA 126: 7–11). Are these real attacks? Or are they just the expression of a siege psychosis? Just think how frequently Rib-Adda depicts his dire situation by using the metaphor of a bird in a cage: 'As a bird caught in a trap, so am I inside Byblos' (references in Knudtzon 1915: 1417 s.v. *ḫuḫāru*).

1.3 THE DISTANT GOD

A third protagonist of the present situation, after the subject and the enemy, is the god whom the subject addresses in order to obtain help and justice. The distant god in this case is Pharaoh. He fits the role well. Not only is he in fact endowed with all the qualities of divinity according to the traditional Egyptian ideology of sacred kingship, but he is, above all, the unchallenged arbiter in the present political situation of the Syro-Palestinian area. Both the 'righteous' Rib-Adda and the 'hostile' Abdi-Ashirta are the servants of Pharaoh, who could therefore – by a simple decision, if he wanted to – settle the dispute forever, redress the evil, and put an end to disorder and enmity. If omnipotence is a distinctive feature of God-Pharaoh in the future perspective (as we shall see later on), in the tragic and concrete present he is characterised by remoteness and absence.

First, Pharaoh is physically remote. Rib-Adda never had, and never will have, direct contact with him. He knows that Pharaoh exists because messengers and soldiers sometimes arrive from his distant Palace. He knows that Pharaoh personally came to Syria once (EA 85: 69–71; EA 116: 61–63; cf. below §2.1). But now he no longer does so, and the hope for a direct encounter is only projected into the future, as a secretly languishing hope: 'It would be nice for me to stay with you, whereas what can I do in my isolation? Behold, so I hope day and night' (EA 74: 62–65). In the present situation any contact with the distant god is entrusted to messengers. The quite different and unbalanced rhythm of the correspondence in the two directions clearly reveals the different attitudes of the two correspondents. On one side, Rib-Adda's eagerness for contact produced an unbelievably intensive, even irritating, epistolary activity. On the other side, Pharaoh's indifference gave rise to infrequent answers, or even complete silence (cf. Liverani 1971a: 155–7).

It is indeed immediately clear that Pharaoh is not only physically distant, he is completely absent from the affairs of this world. He 'does not listen' to requests for help. He 'does not care' about the serious events that take place so frequently.

Rib-Adda comments on Pharaoh's indifference with apprehension, even despair. In many passages the king of Byblos complains that his letters remained unanswered, or that his requests were not fulfilled – which is practically the same (see Liverani 1971a: 255 for references).

The absence of answers – which was in fact a common practice of the Egyptian chancellery – is explained by Rib-Adda as an attitude of 'indifference' by Pharaoh, consistently expressed by the Akkadian verb *qâlu* 'to keep silent'. Rib-Adda complains about this indifference. He uses an exclamatory form, denoting astonishment: 'The King my lord is indifferent!' (EA 88: 8–9; EA 126: 57; cf. EA 84: 16); 'The King my lord is indifferent to his servant!' (EA 88: 12); '(The King) is indifferent to his land!' (EA 84: 10); 'But you are indifferent!' (EA 76: 37; EA 109: 13; EA 121: 53); 'You are indifferent to your cities, that the *ḫabiru*s take . them' (EA 90: 23–25), or an interrogative form, denoting incomprehension: 'Why are you indifferent to your land?' (EA 74: 48); 'Why are you resting and indifferent, while that dog of a *ḫabiru* takes your cities?' (EA 91: 3–5); 'Why are you indifferent?' (EA 91: 7–8), or also a deprecatory form, denoting worry: 'Let the King my lord not be indifferent to his city!' (EA 68: 30–32; EA 137: 59–60); 'Let the King my lord not be indifferent to the deed of that dog!' (EA 137: 25–26).

Some passages are more complex. Pharaoh's indifference can be linked on the one hand with the dramatic present condition, and on the other hand – should no change in attitude take place – with even more dramatic future perspectives. 'If the King remains indifferent to his city, not one of all the cities of Kinahni (will remain) to him' (EA 137: 75–77); 'Formerly they took the cities of your *ḫazānu*, and you remained indifferent. Now they drive your *rābiṣu* out and take his city for themselves. Behold, they take Ullaza! If you remain indifferent until they take Sumura and kill its *rābiṣu*, (at that point) what will the auxiliary troops who stay in Sumura be able to do?' (EA 104: 24–37; cf. Moran 1960: 7 n.3); 'Let my lord not be disinterested about Sumura, otherwise she will go over to the *ḫabiru*s!' (EA 68: 14–18); 'Let the King not be indifferent to this deed, (namely) that a *rābiṣu* was killed! If you are indifferent now, Pihura will not stand in Kumidi, and all your *ḫazānu*s will be killed' (EA 132: 43–50).

As time goes by, indifference becomes a real 'abandonment' of the faithful servant and of his city into enemy hands. A clear opposition exists between the actions of 'protecting' (*naṣāru*) and of 'deserting' (*ezēbu*).[10] As the faithful servant 'protects' the post entrusted to him, and does not 'desert' it, so Pharaoh should in his turn protect the faithful servant, yet in fact he abandons him. 'Former kings protected Byblos: do not desert her!' (EA 129: 46–48); 'Behold, the King deserted

---

10 Both terms are often used by Rib-Adda (cf. Knudtzon 1915: 1407–8 s.v. *ezēbu*, and 1483–4 s.v. *naṣāru*), and both are endowed with political implications. Compare especially the opposition of 'to guard the city' (*āla naṣāru*) and 'to abandon the city' (*āla ezēbu*).

his faithful city, (leaving it) off of his hands' (EA 74: 8–10); 'You know that everything is hostile to me: why do you abandon me to the enemy? Therefore I am afraid' (EA 102: 25–28). More examples could be quoted.

This painful astonishment at Pharaoh's actual indifference, joined to the hope for a future change in attitude, characterises Rib-Adda from the beginning to the end of his political 'career'. Perhaps it is no accident that the last sentence of his last letter, written when everything had been lost and Rib-Adda had to project his hope for a change of fortune into the lifetime of his sons, still contains – once more in the form of astonishment and incomprehension – the usual question: 'When I die, my sons, servants of the King, will be alive, and will write to the King: "Give us back our city!" Why is the King my lord so indifferent to me?' (EA 138: 136–137).

1.4 THE ABANDONMENT BY PEOPLE

The dramatic isolation perceived by Rib-Adda is an existential, and therefore permanent, condition, which is with him from the beginning until the end. Yet this condition is not static, it is dynamic. The isolation is the product of an ongoing process, namely the process of abandonment. The subject feels alone, because he sees himself to be continuously abandoned by people who should remain with him and support him, and who in the normal (by now past) situation were indeed with him and supported him. To feel abandoned, even if the feeling is based on specific historical events, is fundamentally a situation outside history. The process is not becoming increasingly serious, with more and more abandonment: it is always at the maximum level of seriousness. The desertions that take place are always – so to speak – the ultimate possible ones. After them the protagonist would be fully and definitively left alone.

Already at the beginning of his correspondence Rib-Adda feels alone: 'All the cities located on the highlands or on the seashore went over to the *ḫabiru*s. Byblos and two (more) cities are left' (EA 74: 19–22).[11] This early letter already makes use of the previously mentioned *topos* of the last two remaining cities: the identity of the two can change, but they are always the last two. This is relevant for showing the connection between the process of abandonment and the feeling of isolation.

The process of abandonment can have different features, according to its actors: either single peasants (*ḫupšu*) or entire 'cities' and 'lands'. Peasants 'flee' or 'desert' (the Akkadian term *paṭāru* indicates an illegal flight, connected with the servile status of the population toward the king). They shift not only in their

---

11 Note the expression of totality by means of a pair of opposite terms; on this device, see Boccaccio 1953.

mental attitude, but also physically. 'My peasants try to desert' (EA 114: 21–22); 'Hostility against me is strong, there are no provisions for the peasants, so they desert to the sons of Abdi-Ashirta, to Sidon and Beirut' (EA 118: 21–28); 'There is no grain left to eat, and the peasants desert to cities where there is grain to eat' (EA 125: 25–30); 'The men who are in the city desert, all of them' (EA 134: 16–18). This desertion by peasants is clearly caused by economic factors (famine, debts). It means, however, a transfer of allegiance to the enemies, making their victory easier: 'If the peasants desert, the *ḫabiru*s will take the city' (EA 118: 37–39, cf. Moran 1950: 169). They become hostile by the very fact of moving, going over to the other side: '(Abdi-Ashirta) has tried to take Byblos and to cut my gardens down, so that my men have gone away/become hostile' (EA 91: 13–14);[12] 'If there are no provisions of the King for me, my peasants will go away/become hostile' (EA 130: 39–42).[13]

In the case of 'cities' or 'lands' the expression used is *nēpušu ana* X, which has more nuances in its meaning: 'to go over to someone's side' (Campbell 1960: 15; *CAD* E, 235 'EA only'; on the sociohistorical implications see Mendenhall 1962; Waterhouse 1965: 192–9). This 'someone' is always the enemy: either Abdi-Ashirta in person or the *ḫabiru*s in general. There are many examples. 'If there are no archers, all the lands will go over to the *ḫabiru*s' (EA 79: 18–20 and 25–26; cf. also 39–44); 'Does the King my lord consider good what Abdi-Ashirta, the dog, is doing, that all the lands go over to him?… Behold: now Sumura, the stable of my lord and his storehouse, went over to him' (EA 84: 6–13; cf. EA 76: 33–37); 'If the King my lord will not listen to the words of his servant, Byblos will go over to him (= Abdi-Ashirta), and all the King's lands up to Egypt will go over to the *ḫabiru*s' (EA 88: 29–34); 'All my cities went over to the *ḫabiru*s, and everybody is strongly hostile against me' (EA 116: 37–40; cf. EA 85: 69–75; EA 87: 18–20; EA 104: 51–52; EA 117: 92–94).

This kind of abandonment is seldom the result of a particular, violent, episode: '(Abdi-Ashirta) told the Batruna people: "kill your lords!", and they went over to the *ḫabiru*s, like Ammiya' (EA 81: 11–13). This is an open revolt. But more often the shift takes place in an unperceived, indefinite way. It is more a fact of will than of action, more a question of attitude than of conduct. The cities 'go over to the *ḫabiru*s', while, of course, they remain perfectly fixed in their place, simply by cutting off their relations with Rib-Adda and by carrying on relations with the enemy. Therefore, the act is not irreversible, and Rib-Adda's fears can

---

12　The verb used is *nakāru*, which includes the aspect of 'being different' and that of 'being an enemy': cf. *AHw*, 718–20; *CAD* N, 159–71.

13　The verb used is *šanānu* Dt; cf. Rainey 1970: 81 ('to become hostile'); *CAD* Š/1, 366–70; and compare the parallelism between *nkr* and *tn* in Ugaritic (Gordon 1965, n.2705).

hardly be set in a diachronic order and used to reconstruct a progressive lessening of his power. They should rather be viewed *in toto* as a permanent sign of weakness in his rule.

'Cities' and 'lands' naturally act under the authority of their chiefs, the *ḫazānu*s, 'mayors' or 'city-rulers', and the *rabûti*, 'great ones'. In practice those are the people who come to an agreement (*šalāmu*)[14] with the enemy and who abandon Rib-Adda. 'Moreover, all the city-rulers are in agreement with Abdi-Ashirta' (EA 90: 27–28); 'You know that the great ones and the city-rulers are in agreement with the sons of Abdi-Ashirta' (EA 102: 21–23); 'Aziru is hostile to me, and all the *ḫazānu*s are in agreement with him' (EA 126: 9–11); 'All my cities are hostile to me, with the sons of Abdi-Ashirta, therefore they are strong. And the *ḫazānu*s do not remain by me' (EA 109: 58–61). The result of this general 'agreement' among the others is that Rib-Adda remains totally alone: 'In Amurru everyone is in agreement, I am (the only) enemy' (EA 114: 14–16).

The feeling of being abandoned, of remaining alone, practically coincides with the feeling of being 'outside' the community – which is in fact the 'enemy' community, yet now encompasses everyone else. The subject feels excluded from something in which everyone else takes part. He is disqualified, placed on the margin. Why, then, should he not pass over to the 'other' side, why should he not adjust his own behaviour to that of the community? Rib-Adda is led to the point where he asks and threatens: 'Give me an answer, otherwise I will come to an agreement with Abdi-Ashirta, as Yapah-Adda and Zimrida (have done), so that I will survive' (EA 83: 23–27). But when his city spurs him on to this accommodation, he finds the answer: 'The city told me: "Desert him (= Pharaoh) and let's go over to Aziru", but I answered: "how could I go over to him and desert the King my lord?!"' (EA 138: 44–47; see below on EA 136: 8–15). It is the bond of loyalty that prevents him from joining the others: the others deserted 'righteousness' (*kittu*) – that is loyalty toward god – and for this reason they are 'enemies'. They do not suffer materially, because they are not isolated. They all behave in the same way and are 'integrated'. But the price they pay is renunciation of *kittu* 'justice/loyalty'. Rib-Adda chooses *kittu*, and remains alone. 'I am not like Yapah-Adda, I am not like Zimrida: all (these) colleagues deserted' (EA 106: 18–20); 'Behold, I am a servant of the King. There is no (other) *ḫazānu* of the King like me for the King: I would die for my lord' (EA 138: 25–27); 'Byblos is not like the other cities, Byblos is a city faithful to the King my lord from the beginning' (EA

---

14   *CAD* A/1, 388 (on EA 102: 21–23) and A/2, 108 (on EA 114: 14–16) translates *šalāmu* simply by 'to be at peace'. I prefer 'to agree with', which is more specific. Compare *šalmu* as 'pact' in EA 136: 13 (Moran 1963: 174); and see in general Eisenbeis 1969: 25–6.

88: 42–45). The awareness of not being like the others is moralistic, it is that of a man who believes himself to be the only one who acts correctly – according to *kittu* – in a world where everyone else 'deserts'.

In his last letters, written from Beirut after he was expelled from his own town, Rib-Adda's feeling of 'abandonment' naturally has grown. It has become much more concrete, and turned into a basic element of his meditations on his political fate. Ruin came because the withdrawal by the distant god combined with the desertion by his neighbours (even those closest to him). When the first signs of abandonment by his closest circle appeared, Rib-Adda did not pay attention to them. 'The people of Byblos and my house and my wife told me: "Let's go behind the son of Abdi-Ashirta, and let's make an agreement (with him)", but I did not pay attention' (EA 136: 8–15). But when finally his brother betrayed him, which was a kind of abandonment, the situation came rapidly to a conclusion. '(When) I went back home, my house shut in front of me' (EA 136: 33–35); 'My brother, who is younger than me, led Byblos to revolt, in order to give the town to the sons of Abdi-Ashirta… (My brother) committed the sin of driving me out of the town' (EA 137: 16–19 and 24–25; cf. also 57–58).[15] When abandonment becomes total, isolation becomes complete, and the political 'death' of the subject ensues.

1.5 THE FORTUNATE COLLEAGUES

We can guess that Rib-Adda's condition was not different from that of the other Syro-Palestinian kings of his time. All of them were caught between Egyptian control and their own desire for autonomy, between the expansionist pressures of their neighbours and the difficult economic circumstances of their countries. In fact, other – albeit much smaller – groups of Amarna letters could be analysed similarly. Rib-Adda's feelings are generated by a specific historical situation. Yet, in presenting his own analysis, he does not intend to frame his existential feelings within a historical context. His analysis starts from a sharp distinction and opposition between himself and the surrounding world. Certainly, according to him, the others' situation is completely different from his own.

We can check this opposition point by point:

(1) Rib-Adda and Byblos are loyal – the other kings and cities are not. 'Look, Byblos is not like the other cities, Byblos is a city loyal to the King my lord, from the beginning' (EA 88: 42–45); 'Behold: I am not like Yapah-Adda, I am not like Zimrida: all (these) colleagues deserted' (EA 106: 18–20); 'Behold, I am a servant

---

15 Rib-Adda vividly relates the desertion by his city in a passage (EA 138: 36–75) that is in literary terms perhaps the most notable of his entire correspondence.

of the King, there is no (other) *ḫazānu* of the King like me for the King: I would die for my lord' (EA 138: 25–27; cf. EA 109: 41–44); 'Who will love you, if I die?' (EA 114: 68).

(2) The distant god abandons Rib-Adda to his fate – but he takes care of the others' needs. 'Let the King my lord listen to the words of his faithful servant, and let him send grain on ships, and let him keep his servant and his city alive, and let him give 400 men and 30 teams of horses, as have been given to Zimrida, in order to protect the city for you' (EA 85: 16–22); 'Moreover, why did the King give something to keep alive the *ḫazānus* my colleagues, while he did not give anything to me?' (EA 126: 14–17; cf. Moran 1960: 8; *CAD* B, 52; *CAD* I, 6).

(3) Finally, Rib-Adda is abandoned by his cities, and comes close to disaster – whereas, quite to the contrary, the others easily keep control over their respective kingdoms. '(You asked me) why I cannot send a man to the Palace, as my colleagues do. Their cities belong to them, and they have peace' (EA 113: 28–32); 'You wrote: "Why are you writing more than all the (other) *ḫazānus*?" Why should they write? Their cities (belong) to them, my cities have been taken by Aziru' (EA 124: 35–40; cf. Moran in Campbell 1964: 85; Liverani 1967a: 8 n.1); 'Moreover, why is the King comparing me to the (other) *ḫazānus*? These *ḫazānus*: their cities (belong) to them and their chiefs are submitted to them, while as for me: my cities (belong) to Aziru, and he desires (to take) me too' (EA 125: 31–38; cf. Liverani 1971a: 264 n.61).

Sometimes the comparison with his more fortunate colleagues extends to ridiculous and banal features: 'The messenger of the King of Akko is more honoured than mine, because a horse has been given to him' (EA 88: 45–48). But on the whole the comparison is serious and it is an important feature in the overall picture. In fact, these more fortunate colleagues, who receive a privileged treatment by Pharaoh and who do not have to face the pressures to which Rib-Adda is continuously submitted, are clearly – as a category, if not necessarily as single persons – the same colleagues who 'deserted' *kittu*, and adopted an easy, common conduct. The inexplicable condition of the 'righteous sufferer', abandoned by god, is underscored by the contrasting condition of the 'unrighteous fortunate' colleagues. No doubt the decisive point is the conduct of god, who is the arbiter of human fate. Why does god assist those who betray him, and does he leave to die those who love him? The question is formulated explicitly, not by Rib-Adda but by one of his colleagues, each one convinced that he suffers a drama analogous to Rib-Adda's. Abdi-Heba asks – addressing himself more than Pharaoh – what Rib-Adda was never able to formulate so clearly: 'Why do you like the *ḫabirus* and hate the *ḫazānus*?' (EA 286: 18–20), in other words, why do you like the rascals and dislike your loyal servants? This is the pivotal point, around which the whole theme of the 'righteous sufferer' revolves.

2 THE PAST

2.1 THE GOLDEN AGE

Rib-Adda's present tragic situation was not always thus. At one time things were different, and Rib-Adda often makes reference to the past by way of contrast, in order to be more persuasive.[16] If we collect all the passages in his letters that use the term *pānānu(m)* 'formerly', 'once', and all the allusions to the 'time of the fathers' (*ina ūmē abbūti*, or the like), we obtain a homogeneous picture, not without insistent repetitions. The picture is of a kind of golden age, a paradisiacal state now lost. Of course, in the past Rib-Adda was already a loyal servant of the King. 'In the past the Mitanni king was the enemy of your fathers, but your fathers never separated from my fathers' (EA 109: 5–8); 'Behold, my purpose is to serve the King, as was my fathers' custom' (EA 118: 39–41; cf. Moran 1960: 5 n.1); 'Safe is Byblos, the faithful servant of the King since his father's days… Let the King look at the tablets in his father's house, whether the man who resides in Byblos is a faithful servant' (EA 74: 6–8 and 10–12). The loyalty of Byblos and of Rib-Adda is a permanent fact, it exists 'from of old' (*ištu dārīti*). 'We are faithful servants of the King, from of old' (EA 116: 55–56); 'Byblos is not like the other cities, Byblos is a faithful servant of the King, from of old' (EA 88: 42–45; cf. EA 106: 4); 'Let the King my lord know that Byblos, your servant from of old, is safe' (EA 75: 7–9).

In the past also, reasons for trouble and worries were not lacking, but these were easily surmounted thanks to a different attitude on the part of Pharaoh. At that time, he was not a distant god, but a good father concerned with the needs and difficulties of his servant. 'In the past, hostility against my fathers was strong, but a King's garrison was with them, and the King's provisions were with them. Now hostility against me is strong, and there are neither King's provisions nor King's garrisons for me' (EA 130: 21–30); 'Let (the King) send garrison troops to protect his faithful servant and his city, and also Nubian soldiers with them (i.e. the troops), as was your fathers' custom' (EA 117: 78–82; more passages quoted below, p. 114); 'In the past Abdi-Ashirta stood against me, and I wrote to your father: "Send royal troops, and we will take all the lands". Was not Abdi-Ashirta caught, with all his possessions?' (EA 132: 10–18); 'I wrote to your father, and he

---

16 In Rib-Adda's cultural environment there is a strong idea that something is correct when it has always been the same. Traditional behaviour is correct, and change is for the worse when compared to an archetypal optimal condition. Also in practice in legal cases tradition is a norm for decision. For instance, in Nougayrol 1956: 64 the Hittite king Murshili allots cities to their traditional (*ša laberti*) owners (a similar case *ibid.*, 78: *ultu dārīti*), and *ibid.*, 219 tradition (*ultu dārīti*) and the testimony of elders (*abbē āli*) are quoted in a dispute about taxation.

listened to my words, and he sent troops. Was not Abdi-Ashirta caught?' (EA 108: 28–33; cf. Moran 1960: 16). To sum up: in the past Pharaoh protected Byblos, while now he abandons her. 'In my fathers' (time), previous Kings protected Byblos: may you not abandon her!' (EA 129: 46–48). Rib-Adda himself, protected by the King, was stronger and better able to defend himself: 'My lord, when in the past Abdi-Ashirta came against me, I was strong, while now…' (EA 127: 30–33).

Pharaoh's concern for his lands, so different from the present indifference, even materialised in his appearance in person. 'Did not your father come out, did he not inspect the lands and his *ḫazānus*?' (EA 116: 61–63). After the king's presence came to an end, the situation deteriorated. 'Since your father came back from Sidon, since that day the lands go over to the *ḫabirus*' (EA 85: 69–73). That presence assured a quite different prestige to Egyptian authority and to Egyptian military forces, both of which are now in crisis: 'Once the *rābiṣu* of Sumura used to decide among us, but now no *ḫazānu* listens (to him)' (EA 118: 50–54); 'In the past, just at seeing an Egyptian, the kings of Kinahni fled before him, while now…' (EA 109: 44–46; cf. Moran 1950: 170).

The practical consequences of the change in Pharaoh's attitude are serious. In the past his care manifested itself in the sending of garrison troops and provisions, where now his indifference manifests itself in the refusal of troops and provisions. 'Once there were King's provisions for me…now there are neither King's provisions nor King's garrisons' (EA 112: 50–51 and 54–56); 'My fathers (had) King's guards with them and King's provisions for them, while now I have no provisions and no guards of the King for me' (EA 121: 11–17; cf. EA 130: 21–30, quoted above); 'Formerly, in my fathers' days, there were King's guards with them and everything of the King for them, while now I have no King's provisions and no King's guards with me' (EA 122: 11–19); 'In the past, silver and everything was given by the Palace to my fathers for their survival, and my lord gave soldiers for them, while now…' (EA 126: 18–23). This happy situation was linked to two places, Sumura and Yarimuta, the strongholds of pharaonic control, and the bases from which Egyptian interventions came on both the political-military and the economic level. 'Once Sumura and his men were a fortress, and gave garrison troops' (EA 81: 48–50); 'Once my peasants were provided from Yarimuta' (EA 114: 54–57); 'In the past (there were) King's guards with me, and the King gave grain from Yarimuta for their sustenance, while now…' (EA 125: 14–19); 'May it seem good to the King my lord to give grain, the product of Yarimuta. What once was given to Sumura, let he now give to Byblos' (EA 85: 33–37); 'Suggest to your lord to give the product of Yarimuta to his servant, as in the past it was given to Sumura' (EA 86: 31–35). In Rib-Adda's memory these two places acquire a paradisiacal quality. They are totally different from the present condition: now Sumura is lost and Yarimuta has become a place of enslavement.

Rib-Adda clearly projects the model of the correct situation into the past – a vague past, sometimes that of his fathers', sometimes that of his own first regnal years. He was always the 'righteous/faithful' servant, and this is the only feature of the proper picture that still survives in the abnormal present. But then Pharaoh rewarded faithfulness with care: he was present, he was helpful when necessary, and he supplied the tools needed to ensure the protection of the place. Now he still pretends that this service is being supplied, but he does not in fact provide anything any more. The unhistorical character of the past as a model and an archetype is made evident by at least one detail. The first years of Rib-Adda's reign and the initial fighting against Abdi-Ashirta were described as abnormal and disastrous at the time when they occurred. But when they were past – namely at the time of the fights against Aziru – the period became idealised as a happy and effective one. Rib-Adda does not supply a historical analysis of the situation, but fits the vicissitudes of his own life into a preconceived frame.

3 THE FUTURE

3.1 THE EVE OF THE END

The situation is so serious that it cannot be sustained much longer. Since Rib-Adda is the only faithful survivor in a collapsing world, his end would mean the uncontrolled rampaging of the enemy forces, and lead to the total loss of pharaonic authority all over Asia. Therefore Rib-Adda resists not only on his own behalf, but also, and especially, on behalf of Pharaoh. In a letter written when he had already been expelled from his city and was trying to recover control over it, he clearly expressed how the case of Byblos was an example for the fate of the entire Egyptian empire. 'If the King remains indifferent to his city, not one of all the cities of Kinahni will remain to him. (Therefore) let the King not be indifferent to this fact' (EA 137: 75–77). But even before that, he consistently underscored this point. 'If the King is unable to rescue me from the hands of his enemy, all the lands will go over to Abdi-Ashirta' (EA 79: 39–44); 'If the King my lord will not listen to the words of his servant, Byblos will go over to him (= Abdi-Ashirta), and all the King's lands up to Egypt will go over to the *habirus*' (EA 88: 29–34).

The most insistent reproach relates to the urgency of sending troops. Troops must be sent immediately, otherwise it may be too late. 'If within this year the archers do not come out, all the lands will go over to the *habirus*' (EA 77: 26–30; cf. EA 79: 18–20; EA 117: 56–58); 'If within two months the archers do not come out, Abdi-Ashirta will come and take the two cities' (EA 81: 45–47; cf. EA 81: 29–30); 'If troops do not come out within this year, they (i.e., the enemies) will take Byblos' cities' (EA 129: 40–42); 'All the guards who are left are feeling bad, and only a few people are left in the city. If you do not send archers, no city will remain to you. But if archers will be (present), all the lands will go over to the King' (EA 103: 47–57). From this last passage it is clear how decisive the 'coming' of the troops is supposed to be (see also below). This act could produce a complete restoration of order, and, if it does not happen, the final collapse will follow. All depends on Pharaoh's decision. Since no decision seems to be forthcoming, ruin would unavoidably follow. So Rib-Adda starts to think about his personal safety. 'If within two months there are no archers, I will abandon the city, and desert, and (so) I will save my life' (EA 82: 41–45); 'If there are no troops within this year, send ships to take me away alive with my gods, to my lord' (EA 129: 49–51); 'If you do not say so, I will abandon the city and desert, together with the men who love me' (EA 83: 45–51).

These invocations are often repeated, in terms of an ultimatum, from the beginning to the end of Rib-Adda's correspondence. When considered in isolation every entreaty seems to imply a historical diagnosis, that is, the situation has reached such a point that a resolution (in whatever direction) will come soon. Yet the very fact that the invocations are repeated proves that they are not based on a historical diagnosis but only on a general existential feeling. Throughout the course of his reign, Rib-Adda continually feels – or at least says – that he is on the brink of the end, whatever the actual situation may be. His feeling is outside historical time. It is fixed once and forever, and does not evolve. Indeed, it is a basic feature of the emotional pattern in Rib-Adda's correspondence, not of the historical state of affairs.[17] Even if the difficulties of Rib-Adda's position in Byblos cannot be denied – although the end will come from an unexpected direction – it is to be excluded that a general collapse of the Egyptian empire, which is the pivotal point in Rib-Adda's thesis, could have been imminent.[18]

3.2 MESSIANIC EXPECTATIONS

Even if a situation has arisen – or better, has always existed – where Rib-Adda is on the brink of final disaster, nothing is prejudiced. The situation is so only because (and as long as) Pharaoh is uninterested. A simple intervention by him would solve all problems. Rib-Adda's ultimatum-like appeals point the way

---

[17] I think, therefore, that it is dangerous to use the expressions 'within one year' and 'within two months' in order to make precise calculations of the length of trips or of the time required to organise an expedition, as has been sometimes done (e.g., Campbell 1964: 67).

[18] I have already analysed (Liverani 1967a) how the misunderstanding of the emotional nature of the Amarna letters often leads scholars to accept as historically founded a thesis (namely, the collapse of Egyptian control in Asia during the Amarna age) that is based only on the way the Syro-Palestinian kings carried on their relations with Pharaoh. On the continuity of Egyptian control and of military engagement there, see Klengel 1965b; Schulman 1964.

toward salvation: the arrival of Egyptian troops. Requests like 'Send archers in great number, and you will drive the King's enemies out of his land, and all the lands will go over to the King' (EA 76: 38–43) are a fixed point in almost all of Rib-Adda's letters. The arrival of troops is imagined in two different forms, and with two levels of efficacy, according to the type, number, and function of the soldiers. In some cases it is a question of small groups of armed men, mostly defined as 'garrison troops' (*amalūti maṣṣarti*), whose function it is 'to protect' (*naṣāru*, whence the noun *maṣṣartu* 'garrison' is derived) the city against enemy pressures and assaults. Their presence is mostly symbolic and its value lies in expressing pharaonic support. A single man by himself can obtain this result – one Egyptian official who takes responsibility for protecting the city. 'Let the King my lord send his *rābiṣu* to protect the city of my lord' (EA 84: 26–28); 'Let the King send his *rābiṣu* and take care of the place' (EA 94: 71–72). Some economic measures, such as the shipment of grain, are also viewed in this way (discussed above). In all these cases, the measures are partial, they ensure a delay in the collapse, but do not solve the heart of the problem.

The 'coming out' of the Egyptian army, in its fullest sense, is different. In this case the verb *aṣû* 'to come out' is mostly used, while for garrisons, officials, and provisions, the verb *uššuru* 'to send' is mostly used.[19] This 'coming out' has a clear messianic connotation. It is considered so effective that it could completely eliminate the causes of trouble, and therefore ensure a restoration of the peaceful state, which is, after all, the normal one, or at least the desired one. It is often stated in explicit terms that the sending of garrisons (or provisions) is only a temporary solution, while one waits for the definitive arrival of the full army. 'Send me Egyptian and Nubian soldiers…until the archers come out' (EA 70: 17–19, 22); 'Let the King my lord listen to the words of his servant, and let him send garrison troops to protect the city of the King, until the archers come out' (EA 79: 13–17); 'Let my lord send garrison troops to these two cities, until the archers come out' (EA 79: 29–32); 'Send as soon as possible auxiliary troops to Sumura, to protect it until the arrival of the archers of the King, the Sun' (EA 103: 25–29); 'Let my lord give 100 soldiers and 100 Nubians and 30 chariots, and I will protect the land of my lord, until a large army comes out, and my lord takes Amurru for himself, so that the lands will be pacified' (EA 127: 35–42). The decisive 'coming out' is preceded by – or equated with, being its obvious consequence – an act of 'thinking' (*idû*),[20] or of 'decisive measures' (*malāku*) by the king regarding his

---

[19] Studies of the expression *aṣû ša ṣābē piṭāti* were published by Pintore (1972; 1973). The translation of *ṣābē piṭāti* as 'archers' is conventional. In fact, they are a complete army corps; cf. Albright 1966: 7; Bernhardt 1971: 139.

[20] *Idû ana* in the sense of 'to think about', 'to be concerned with' is attested only in the Amarna letters, cf. *AHw*, 188 s.v. *edû(m)* B7; *CAD* I/J, 28 (b').

land. 'Send a garrison to protect your city and your servant, until the King thinks about his land and sends archers to pacify his lands' (EA 112: 33–38); 'Let the King send auxiliary troops to Sumura, until the King decides measures for his land' (EA 104: 14–17); 'May it seem good to the King my lord to give grain … and we shall survive until you decide measures for your city' (EA 85: 33–39; cf. EA 86: 31–37).The liberating 'coming out' of the army is not only awaited by Rib-Adda but by the entire country, or at least by those who possess goodwill toward Pharaoh. Therefore the 'coming out' will not meet any opposition – after all, who could resist? – and it will automatically restore order. 'Let the King my lord know that Amurru is longing night and day for the coming out of the archers. The day the archers reach Amurru, all (of Amurru) will go over to the King my lord' (EA 70: 24–30); 'Do you not know that Amurru is waiting night and day for the archers?… Tell the King: come as soon as possible!' (EA 82: 47–52). Even after his expulsion from Byblos, Rib-Adda continues to be sure of the automatic effects of a 'coming out' of the Egyptian troops. 'At the coming out of the troops, they will know it, and on the very day of their arrival, the city will go back to the King my lord' (EA 137: 49–51; cf. Moran 1950: 170).

Of course, the apex of messianic expectations is a possible 'coming out' of Pharaoh in person. If he would repeat the visit to Sidon, he would restore order everywhere. 'Let the King listen to the words of his servant and send chariots and archers as soon as possible, to protect the city of the King my lord and the city of his servant, until the King my lord arrives' (EA 88: 23–27); 'Let the King my lord come out to inspect his lands and take everything! Look, on the day you come out, all the lands will go over to the King my lord. Who could stand against the troops of the King?' (EA 362: 60–65). But the possibility is so remote that Rib-Adda seldom hints at it.

3.3 PARADISE REGAINED

The ease of the remedy – it would be sufficient for Pharaoh to 'think' about his land and let the archers 'come out' – is effective in concealing the dramatic nature of present condition. It is easily understood that, when Rib-Adda formulates his vision of the future, which is basically pessimistic, he can also imagine paradisiacal features of justice and peace as an ultimate outcome. It is nothing but the restoration of the original conditions. The paradisiacal features are centred around two recurrent terms: 'to be at peace' (*pašāḫu*) and 'to live' (*balāṭu*) (see *CAD* B, 46–63; Hirsch 1968–69).

The wish for peace is obvious, and contrasts with the troubled and painful present. Peace will be restored throughout the country by the arrival of the troops. 'Let the King send his troops, and let him pacify his land under the *ḫazānus*. (If) the cities will belong to them, they will be at peace' (EA 118: 42–45);

'Let the King listen to the words of his servant, and let him send the archers to protect the land of the King for the King; let him pacify the *ḥazānu*s of the King with grain' (EA 121: 45–51); 'Let my lord give 100 soldiers and 100 Nubians and 30 chariots, and I will protect the land of my lord, until a big army comes out and my lord takes Amurru, and the land will be at peace' (EA 127: 35–42);[21] 'Send troops and pacify the land!' (EA 132; 58–59); 'Think of your land, and pacify your land' (EA 74: 58–59); 'Send a garrison to protect your city and your servant, until the King thinks about his lands and sends archers to pacify his lands' (EA 112: 33–38, with the full pattern).

The paradigmatic character of this longing for peace, and its value in the political ideology of the time, are clarified by the converse use of the same terms in Abdi-Ashirta's propaganda pieces. These have been preserved as quotations in the letters of Rib-Adda, so the coincidence of terminology cannot be accidental. Rib-Adda expects that peace will result from the arrival of the Egyptian troops and from the guarantee that the *ḥazānu*s will control their lands. On the contrary, in Abdi-Ashirta's program, peace for all lands is the result to be achieved by driving out the *ḥazānu*s, and *notwithstanding* the possible arrival of the Egyptian troops and of Pharaoh himself (cf. Liverani 1965a: 275–6, where the utopian character of Abdi-Ashirta's program was already underscored). The two programs of Abdi-Ashirta and Rib-Adda are neatly contrasted; both aim at the same condition of 'peace' by way of completely opposite measures.

In case a general pacification of all lands turns out to be unattainable, Rib-Adda hopes to reach at least his own personal 'peace'. He wishes to escape physically from his present troubles and find shelter with Pharaoh, where the condition of peace is naturally permanent, always present, and not just projected into the future or into the past, as it is in the human condition of Rib-Adda. The hope for personal rescue is expressed as the last possibility. 'It would be pleasant for me to stay with you: I would be at peace!' (EA 116: 48–50); 'May it seem good to the King my lord to send a man here, and I will come to the King my lord. It would be pleasant for me (to stay) with you, (while) what could I do in my isolation? Behold: this I hope day and night' (EA 74: 59–65; cf. EA 114: 44–46).

Rib-Adda's basic expectation is 'life'. Life is now uncertain, and the realisation of his hope is projected into the future – when Pharaoh will 'think' about his land and send help. 'Day and night I am waiting for the archers of the King my lord; may the King my lord take measures for his servant. If the King does not adopt a different attitude, I will die. May the King my lord let his servant live' (EA 136: 37–43; the interpretation in *CAD* B, 70 is wrong); 'Let the King

---

[21] The full pattern is present here: preliminary sending (*uššuru*) of troops to protect (*naṣāru*) the city, until the definitive coming out *(aṣû)* which brings back peace *(pašāḫu)* in the entire territory.

listen to the words of his servant and give life to his servant and let his servant live' (EA 74: 53–55); 'If the King will protect his servant, I will live. But if the King will not protect me, who will protect me? If the King sends as soon as possible Egyptian and Nubian soldiers and horses led by this man of mine, I will live to serve the King my lord' (EA 112: 14–24); 'Let the King listen to the words of his faithful servant and give life to his servant and to Byblos his maid-servant' (EA 116: 44–47). Quite often the expectation of 'life' is linked to the material shipment of food. 'Let the King my lord listen to the words of his faithful servant and send grain on ships and let his servant and his city live' (EA 85: 16–19);[22] 'Moreover, may it seem good to the King my lord that grain be given, the product of Yarimuta. What once was given to Sumura, may it be given now to Byblos, and we shall live' (EA 85: 33–38; cf. EA 86: 31–37). As is the case with 'peace', if 'life' is not restored to the land in general, it could at least be granted to Rib-Adda alone, provided he could escape from the present situation. 'If within two months there are no archers, I will abandon the city and desert, and I will save my life' (EA 82: 41–45; cf. EA 83: 45–51); 'Send me an answer, otherwise I will make an agreement with Abdi-Ashirta, like Yapah-Adda and Zimrida, and I will live' (EA 83: 23–27; cf. Moran 1960: 12 n.1). In his insistence on 'life', Rib-Adda consciously hints at the image of Pharaoh granting life.[23] He even refers to specific statements of Pharaoh in this sense. 'You are the King, the Sun, my lord – Rib-Adda writes – and you let your faithful servant live' (EA 80: 31–34);[24] 'You let (people) live – you let (people) die' (EA 169: 7–8; EA 238: 31–33).

Rib-Adda lives in a state of eschatological uncertainty: he is either on the brink of complete disaster, or on the brink of rescue. 'If you do not send archers, no city will remain to you – if archers do arrive, all the lands will go over to the King' (EA 103: 51–57). The decisive element is Pharaoh's attitude: if he will only decide to 'think' of his land, he will rescue it; if he remains 'indifferent', he will ruin it. Rib-Adda cannot but wait, stubborn in holding on to his 'faithfulness' and stubborn in reminding Pharaoh of the gravity of the situation.

---

[22] In cases like this one, *CAD* B, 61 (7. *bulluṭu*) adopts the translation 'to provide with food' and Moran 1960: 5 (on EA 74: 53–55) 'to provide means of sustenance'.

[23] *CAD* B, 55 correctly devotes a special section (2d: 'due to royal charisma') to some of these passages (like EA 112: 23). But when one uses special renderings such as 'be safe', 'take courage', 'acquire new courage', 'gather fresh strength', 'feel safe', the sense of the technical term gets lost.

[24] Outside Rib-Adda's correspondence see also passages like EA 147: 5–9 'My lord is my Sun ... who keeps alive by his good breath'; EA 149: 21–23 'What is the life of a man, if no breath comes out of the mouth of the King his lord?' On these passages (and their Egyptian models), cf. Williams 1969: 93–4.

4 HISTORY AND WISDOM

The coherence of the various features, which I have separated here for purposes of analysis, is evident from the numerous cross-references and from the frequent use of one and the same passage in different contexts. Such coherence is not reconstructed *a posteriori*, it is already present in Rib-Adda's epistolary construction. When we read the letters in the light of my scheme – reading them (as stated at the beginning) as single documents, each endowed with a precise motivation, but as part of a larger unit – it becomes evident that in every letter the various elements are explicitly linked in a functional way. The memory of the past is opposed to the dramatic condition of the present in the perspective of a future resolution. The contrast between the subject's loyalty and the hostility of his surroundings makes evident the contradictory attitude of the indifferent god, and the consequent perspective of an imminent disaster. The protagonist's isolation is linked to his just behaviour, the alliance of the others derives from their common treachery. The possibility of remaining loyal, and at the same time recovering earlier prosperity, is conditional upon a different attitude by the god. It would be possible to assemble a complete network from the various elements isolated in my analysis. Rib-Adda's existential condition would emerge clearly – in its coherence and completeness – in every single letter.[25]

The coherence of the picture and its existential character are particularly emphasised in the final stages of the political events in Rib-Adda's life. His end is sad, and seems to substantiate and justify the fears felt by the king of Byblos throughout his reign. It seems to give a historical reality to his role as 'righteous sufferer'. Yet this is not the case. The final blow to his career comes from an unexpected direction, namely his brother, who probably acts for personal and banal reasons – ambition, envy – which are not mentioned in Rib-Adda's laments. Most importantly, as soon as the usurper is installed on the throne of Byblos, he too begins to write letters to Pharaoh, the distant god (EA 139–140). He too requests help against the enemy (Aziru, as usual), who presses on all sides and makes it difficult for him to remain loyal. The wisdom model of the 'righteous sufferer' is fixed. It is the focus of concern and worry, whatever happens, and whoever the protagonist may be. What really happens is immediately forced into the pattern if at all possible; otherwise it is ignored.

---

[25] I hope not to be misunderstood here. In underlining the existential character of the picture, I do not mean to deny its historical basis. Rib-Adda's situation is truly difficult and he really suffers from the expansionist pressures of Amurru. In the end he loses his throne, and perhaps he is truly affected by a change in Egyptian policy. I wish to emphasise, however, that the protagonist perceives – or at least expresses – such a state of affairs within the outline of a preconceived pattern. We must identify the 'grid' represented by this pattern in order to reconstruct the kernel of historical reality in its true configuration.

A true ending, a true conclusion is lacking, since the pattern is by its very nature always anchored in the present, it is dynamic but does not evolve. The future always remains the future; it never becomes the present and is never realised. Moreover a resolution of the kind usually found in wisdom literature is missing. There is no liberating intervention by god. That would be just an artificial 'happy ending', a literary materialisation of psychological hopes that is intended to lower the emotional tension of the audience. And there is no psychological evolution of the 'righteous one', who through suffering becomes wiser, more conscious, and better able to acknowledge the inscrutability of god, or to admit the possibility of his own fault, of a – perhaps involuntary and unknown – 'sin'.

Rib-Adda undergoes some psychological evolution during his final crisis, when his fear of isolation is realised in the form of political 'death', and is coupled with the onset of a physical illness – another sure sign of abandonment by god. He was probably truly ill, but what matters is that he felt ill, that is, that he considered his physical state to be connected with the course of events. 'There is hostility against me and against Sumura. Behold, now the *rābiṣu* has died, and I am ill' (EA 106: 21–23). In his last letters the disease is brought to the fore. 'I am old, and a serious disease is in my body. Let the King my lord know that the gods of Byblos departed (?), and my disease is great, and I confessed my sins to the gods. Therefore I cannot enter into the presence of the King my lord' (EA 137: 29–35; the free translation by Oppenheim 1967: 132, changes the logical connection). The relation between sin and disease (with 'confession' as a means to eradicate it), between behaviour and fate, is clearly established. The righteous one, who is always so sure of his own justice and therefore astonished at divine abandonment, finally reverses his usual way of reasoning. If I am sick, it means that the gods are angry with me; and if they are angry, it means that I offended them with a sin. Although the illness is only used as a pretext for not going to Egypt – yet, at one time Rib-Adda had longed to reach the distant god and thus be at peace! – it partakes of the normal diagnostic procedures of the time and follows the usual mental routine. It is not transferred to the political situation, which remains without development or outcome. At the political level it is significant that in the same letter (and also in letter 138, written in the same situation) Rib-Adda still insists on his incomprehension of Pharaoh's attitude and his hope for a change in the future – a hope now passed on to his sons, since no future is left in Rib-Adda's lifetime. After the final crisis, Rib-Adda feels that death is near. He alludes more than once to death, as if his mind were attracted by the idea of it.

The coherent application of the pattern of the 'righteous sufferer' to the vicissitudes of Rib-Adda's life poses the question of how conscious it was. Did it refer to a literary model? I do not think we can give an affirmative answer to such a direct and simplistic question. It is possible, however, that Rib-Adda and his court circle (especially the scribal milieu) knew Mesopotamian wisdom literature which, at precisely this time, became fully formulated and reached the palaces and the palatial scribal schools on the Syrian coast.[26] It is possible that a text like *Ludlul bēl nēmeqi* (Lambert 1960: 32–62) was known at Byblos. In it the protagonist proclaims his justice and loyalty (ii 23–30), complains about illness (i 47–48, 71–76, ii 49–81) and civil misfortunes (ii 55–70, 77–83), notices his abandonment by friends and relatives (i 84–94), and calls upon the intervention of a god who does not answer (i 4–5, 112–113). Similar texts could have been known, and indeed probably were known, since the similarities in pattern with the Rib-Adda letters are too systematic and precise to be completely coincidental. Even if we do not accept that there was a direct influence of Akkadian wisdom texts on the composition of the Rib-Adda letters (and I do not), we can nevertheless establish some connections between the two groups of texts.

First, there is a chronological connection. It is now firmly established that the main phase of creativity and systematisation of Mesopotamian wisdom literature was the Kassite period (Lambert 1960: 13–19), a period that coincides with the Amarna archive. Even if the cultural history of the ancient Near East is still poorly understood, it seems obvious that a concentration of wisdom compositions in the fourteenth and thirteenth centuries should go back to a cultural feature of that time, to some stream of thought or some generalised existential experience.[27] In this perspective it is indeed significant that Rib-Adda's correspondence belongs to the same cultural period as Akkadian wisdom literature, even if we leave aside possible specific connections. Second, and most importantly, a link between Babylonian wisdom literature and the political correspondence of Rib-Adda can be identified in the social setting from which both originated. The expectations and existential problems of this social group are reflected by both. The setting is a court setting. The nucleus that gave rise directly to wisdom literature – that is, the scribal nucleus – forms part of the palace organisation. As administrative officials, the scribes are part of the palace setting as a whole, they belong to the circle of the 'king's men'. Their experience of life is of the court, of administrative office, of bureaucratic careers, and of political activity. That experience is reflected in the wisdom literature. They are concerned about not losing

---

[26] The discovery at Ugarit of some fragments of Mesopotamian wisdom texts (Nougayrol 1968: 265–300) proves a spread of those literary works into the Syro-Palestinian scribal and palatial milieus of the Late Bronze Age. It is through this channel that the links with Old Testament wisdom need to be studied: cf. Gray 1970.

[27] The pessimistic character – proper of an 'age of crisis' – of Middle Babylonian wisdom literature could perhaps be connected with the contemporaneous final crisis of Bronze Age civilisation. This crisis was only secondarily technological, and primarily social, political, and moral.

the king's favour, about the envy and slander of colleagues, loyalty to their own offices, and the denunciation of others' treachery. More generally, the problems in the social circles where wisdom literature originated include experience of human relations and the knowledge of correct behaviour and of one's proper position in the surrounding world. This set of problems is encountered in wisdom texts. It shows that these texts do not deal abstractly and artificially with the solution of generic human problems, but deal historically and concretely with the daily experiences of their authors.

While the palace and court setting of wisdom literature has been studied in general terms,[28] another positive result could be achieved by pointing out wisdom features in professional and technical texts that originated from the royal court. Literary texts situate their wisdom perspective in imaginary, literary situations. Rib-Adda's correspondence situated it among real facts, in present life. Therefore, I would not seek the origin of Rib-Adda's epistolary models in the wisdom texts. On the contrary, I would look to the existential conditions that Rib-Adda experienced for the origin of wisdom compositions centred on the problem of the 'righteous sufferer'.

After all, is it really true that a large gap separates the two genres of texts? How much autobiographical material, how many allusions to personal cases are to be found in wisdom compositions of a literary character? And how much atemporal, preconceived material is to be found in the letters? Perhaps the only difference is that Rib-Adda's letters were addressed to a single, real person, while the literary texts were addressed to a more impersonal and wider 'audience' of colleagues, and to posterity.[29] But was the addressee of Rib-Adda's letters – the distant god who is indifferent and never answers (the writer being aware beforehand that he will not answer) – the actual addressee of Rib-Adda's complaints? Sometimes we get the impression that the king of Byblos was writing more to vent his frustrations than to obtain an answer, just for the sake of writing rather than in order to be read.

---

[28] The court setting of wisdom literature in the ancient Near East is well known, especially in Old Testament studies: see, e.g., Duesberg 1966: 59–95, 147–176; Dubarle 1969: 248–9.

[29] Consider also the wisdom character of some Mesopotamian 'Letters to the god', on which attention has been focused by Jacobsen 1946: 205–6; van Dijk 1953: 13–17; Kraus 1971. Some Biblical psalms also have the appearance of 'Letters to the god' with a clear wisdom tone, such as that of the 'righteous sufferer', see Mowinckel 1955.

6

Aziru, servant of two masters[*]

INTRODUCTION

Rib-Adda's bane was the royal house of Amurru, the state inland from Byblos in Syria and the northernmost Egyptian vassal. He griped constantly about the hostile acts of Abdi-Ashirta and his sons, especially Aziru. While much in his complaints was empty rhetoric to gain Pharaoh's attention as was pointed out in the previous chapter, the leaders of Amurru were not the reliable vassals they proclaimed to be in their own letters to Egypt. Pharaoh suspected foul play and demanded that Aziru come to him to explain himself, a trip the latter wanted to avoid. The form and contents of Aziru's letters regarding this matter are the subject of this chapter.

Amurru was unusual in the Syro-Palestinian region in that it was not a kingdom focused around a central city, and did not have an old dynasty. Abdi-Ashirta had recently established himself as a ruler of the region and only under Aziru had the house been accepted as royal. There was also a strange overlap between the name of the state and that of the larger province the Egyptians had organised in northern Syria. The province was administered from the city of Sumura on the coast, a city that had been destroyed and was abandoned by the Egyptian governor. Its rebuilding was one of Aziru's tasks but also here he was reluctant to proceed. Because of the absence of Egypt's governor he could act as if he were ruler over the entire province of Amurru rather than just over the kingdom.

Aziru ended up going to Egypt, but was able to exonerate himself and return home. Probably soon afterwards he concluded a vassal treaty with the Hittite king Shuppiluliuma (Beckman 1996: 32–7) and openly abandoned the Egyptian sphere of influence. Amurru remained a Hittite vassal for some 150 years. The primary basis for the study of Aziru's career is the Amarna correspondence, recent translations of which can be found in Moran (1992) and Liverani (1998–99). The letters from Amurru were studied in a special monograph by Izre'el (1991).

★   ★   ★   ★

[*] Originally published as 'Aziru, servitore di due padroni', in *Studi Orientalistici in Ricordo di Franco Pintore*, eds. O. Carruba, M. Liverani, C. Zaccagnini (Pavia 1983), 93–121.

1 EPISTOLARY TECHNIQUE

1.1 I AM (NOT) COMING!

In the small group of twelve Amarna letters written to the court of Egypt by Aziru, four are strictly contemporary with one another. They are sent in rapid succession, if not written at the same time, and are entrusted to one and the same messenger. Yet they are addressed to different people: Pharaoh (EA 165), the officials Dudu (EA 164), Hai (EA 166), and an unnamed person (EA 167; perhaps this letter was also written to Pharaoh). The letters contain correspondence regarding a visit by Aziru to the Egyptian court at Amarna; a visit that was requested by the Egyptian side and deliberately delayed by the king of Amurru. Additional letters may be linked to the same issue, either because they contain hints of a possible delay (EA 162: 42–45; cf. already EA 161: 4–6; EA 168) or because they refer to the actual visit of Aziru to Egypt (EA 169–171). Thus half of the correspondence between Egypt and Amurru in the time of Aziru deals with this question, especially in the last part of his reign. As is well known (cf. Klengel 1964), during his visit to Pharaoh, Aziru was so clever as to dispel Egyptian doubts about his political behaviour, and to obtain permission to go back to Amurru.[1] But immediately after his return, Aziru became a vassal of the Hittite king, Shuppiluliuma (Freydank 1960, line I 24'; cf. below, §2.3), definitively shifting his allegiance and showing how well founded Egyptian doubts about his loyalty were.

The clustering of several letters dealing with the visit to Egypt emphasises, even more clearly than the contents of the documents themselves, how crucial this visit was in the framework of the political relations between Pharaoh and Aziru, as well as the difficulties in the diplomatic relations between the two. The case is simple: Aziru wants to reply to Pharaoh that he will *not* go to Egypt. Were he to state this openly and abruptly, it would show clearly that he pays no regard to Pharaoh's invitation, which is in reality a command. Aziru's problem is to arrange his message – which is basically unpleasant, and contrary both to the general behavioural code governing relationships between the two partners, and to the specific expectations of the addressee (cf. Liverani 1971a: 259) – so that it will be taken as innocently as possible. The solution is to answer 'I am coming', but to indicate 'I am not coming'. Such a solution is quite commonplace and regularly used by all of us in interpersonal relationships.

---

[1]   The general opinion in Syria on the result of Aziru's visit is stated by the king of Nuhashe in EA 169: 19–28: 'When will (Pharaoh) release him (= Aziru) from Egypt? ... Never will Aziru leave Egypt!'

To answer 'I am not coming' would be more direct and immediately effective as far as the transmission of factual information is concerned. But such an answer would have broader implications than the sender wanted, and those would not be to his advantage. The answer 'I am not coming' would imply, in ascending sequence, 'I do not want to come', 'I am disobeying', 'I want to disobey', and 'I am not part of the political system led by you'. These extreme implications would not suit Aziru's interests or his intent, at least at the moment when the letters were written. And even if they did, it would be more convenient for him to hide them. Therefore Aziru manages to disguise his disobedience by understating it, to such a degree, as he hopes, that it will pass unnoticed. He explains himself in positive terms in order to keep within the limits of a system that he may seem at first glance to subvert. First, Aziru takes care to send assurances that he does indeed belong to the political system led by Pharaoh: 'Hatib came and brought the fine and good words of the King, my lord, and I rejoiced very much. Together with my country and my brothers, servants of the King, my lord and servants of my lord Dudu, we rejoiced very much when the breath of the King my lord reached me' (EA 164: 1–14); 'Now I and Hatib, we are good servants of the King' (EA 164: 41–42); 'I and Ba'luya, we are your servants. I protect the land of the King, my lord, and my face is turned to the service of the King my lord' (EA 165: 8–12); 'I am a servant of the King, a very good one' (EA 165: 26–27); 'I, my brothers, and my sons, we are servants of the King my lord, forever' (EA 165: 43–45); 'I, my sons, and my brothers, we are all good servants of the King, my lord' (EA 166: 9–11); and 'I am a servant of my lord' (EA 166: 20).

Secondly, Aziru takes care to send messages that state 'I want to obey', or 'usually, I do obey': 'From the words of my lord, my god, my Sun, and from the words of my lord Dudu, I do not deviate' (EA 164: 14–17); 'From the words of my lord I do not detach myself, nor from your (i.e., the Egyptian official Hai's) words' (EA 166: 17–19 and parallel passages, cf. §2.2 below).

Thirdly, Aziru states that he is obeying also in the specific matter of his visit to Egypt. The visit is even a cause of the utmost satisfaction to him. Obviously, he would go willingly, even enthusiastically: 'My lord, my god, my Sun: what do I most desire? The beautiful face of the King, my lord, I desire forever' (EA 165: 4–8; EA 166: 6–8; EA 167: 8–9) and 'In peace I shall see the beautiful face of the King, my lord' (EA 165: 12–13). So he will certainly and obviously come. Indeed, he is already on his way, as he confirms again and again in every letter:

EA 164: 'we come' (20: *ni-il-la-ak*), 'I come' (25: *i-il-la-ak*), 'indeed, I come' (34: *lu-ú a-al-la-ak*), 'I come to you' (*al-la-ka-ak-ku*).

EA 165: 'we come' (15: *ni-il-la-ak*), 'I am arriving quickly' (17: *ka-aš-da-ku i-na ḫa-mut-iš*), 'I come' (25: *a-al-la-ak*), 'I am arriving' (31: *ka-aš-da-ku*).

EA 166: 'we come now, quickly' (13–14: *ni-il-la-ka-am i-na-an-na i-na ḫa-mut-iš*), 'I am arriving' (16: *ka-aš-da-ku*).

EA 167: 'we come quickly' (30–31: *i-il-la-ka-am i-na ḫa-mut-iš*), 'I am arriving' (17: *ka-aš-da-ku*), 'I am arriving' (33: *ka-aš-da-ku*).

By adding the adverbs 'now' and 'quickly', by placing the verb in its stative form, or by adding the verb *kašādu*, which indicates the completion of an action, he causes an action, that has not even begun to be understood as having been fully accomplished. Aziru states 'I am arriving' before he has even left. There is only a difference in time from what Pharaoh expects. Aziru says 'I am coming as soon as possible', which means not immediately. Perhaps it has not been stated explicitly that Pharaoh's command has to be executed immediately, yet this was implicit in the ideology (cf. Posener 1960: 42–3, 48–9), and Aziru is certainly well aware of that. But a simple temporal gap between command and execution cannot in itself be considered as disobedience. In any case, the Egyptian side explicitly acknowledges the time gap. The king of Egypt does so in order to limit the size of this gap, and to avoid the possibility that it will negate the very substance of his command. He makes it into a constitutive element of the injunction: 'Since you wrote "Let the King leave me this year, and I will come next year to the presence of the King, my lord, or else (I will send) my son". The King, your lord, leaves you this year as requested. (But then,) come personally, or send your son, and you shall see the King at whose sight all the lands live. And do not say "Leave me one more year" in order to enter the presence of your lord. Either you send your son instead of you to the King, your lord, or else you come (personally)!' (EA 162: 42–54).

As to the reason for the delay, Aziru takes care to present it as part of his involvement in the Egyptian political system, rather than his disengagement from it. He emphasises that he stays in Amurru for the 'protection' of that country on behalf of, and within the framework of, Egyptian authority, as is his duty as a servant of Pharaoh (cf. below, §2.1). He declares that he is forced against his wishes to delay his response to Pharaoh's order, because he is already much too busy obeying another and more basic pharaonic order. At this point, no charge can be reasonably laid against him from within the framework of the system as a whole.

Another, more specific – but no less adroit – application of the technique of involvement can be detected when Aziru links himself to Egypt's official messenger Hatib, who has arrived to hasten Aziru's visit to Egypt, and to accompany him on his travels. By retaining Hatib, and by linking his own behaviour and intentions to those of Hatib, Aziru can say: 'you know that *we* are *both* faithful and obedient' (cf. EA 164: 41–42), or 'you know that *we both* shall come' (cf. EA 164: 18–20, 25–26; EA 165: 14–15, 25–26; EA 166: 12–14, 30–32; EA 167: 14–15). So

Aziru can claim to his own credit what the Egyptian messenger Hatib will undoubtedly do in the end.[2]

1.2 AMOUNT OF INFORMATION

The most evident characteristic of this group of letters is their redundancy. They transmit the same information at nearly the same time – or at exactly the same time – to addressees who are closely linked, or can even be considered as one from an institutional point of view. Indeed, the letters were filed together in the same archive. They are also internally redundant, repeating the same piece of information over and over again. Beyond a certain point redundancy is no longer intended to ensure a correct transmission of the core message, but instead makes it as unnoticeable as possible. Redundancy becomes a powerful 'noise'. The insistence on an 'empty' message (not a real one) in fact hides an unpleasant reality (cf. Liverani 1973b: 273). Redundancy is applied to secondary elements, which are pleasant and obvious, rather than to important new information, which is both unpleasant and unexpected. The logical chain of information supplied by Aziru can be summarised as follows: (1) I am a faithful servant; (2) I obey; and (3) I am willing to come; but (4) I have to protect the country; therefore (5) I cannot come immediately. Points (1) to (4) are characterised by a high rate of predictability (therefore a low informational content) both because they are stereotypical in the administrative correspondence of the time, and because they fit correctly into the political system of which they are part. Pharaoh is accustomed to receiving positive answers. Point (5), unexpected and unpleasant, is hidden in the surrounding verbiage, but is logically so well linked to the previous points that its unpleasantness and abnormality, if not the very substance of the information, can pass unnoticed.

If we could quantify the informational content[3] of the various sections in a 'typical' letter of Aziru, we could see a diagram running from low levels of positive/pleasant information, to suddenly moving downwards to a high level of negative/unpleasant information:

---

2 To detain a messenger is generally considered a hostile act, to be evaluated negatively. But in this case the Egyptian court is to evaluate it as positive, and as a signal that Aziru will not delay his coming excessively. In fact, once the one-year delay was obtained (EA 162), Aziru did send Hatib back together with his own messenger (EA 168). That letter also plays on the use of the verb *kašādu*, 'to arrive'. When the verb refers to Aziru, it is an illusion and will take place late (5, cf. 14!), when it refers to Hatib it is accurate (7–10).

3 Specific techniques for quantifying the information contained in texts have been suggested many times, but I find it better to make use here only of the very general notion. For an introduction, see De Lillo 1971; for political texts in particular the book by Lasswell and Leites 1965 remains fundamental.

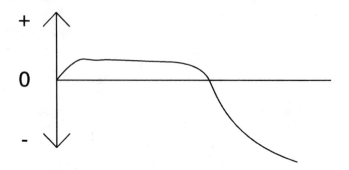

The moment of the negative surge is when the addressee of the letter finally realises that the sequence of 'I obey', 'I come immediately', and 'I am arriving', really means: 'I am not coming'.

Aziru's technique of passing information is certainly a normal 'diplomatic' technique, indeed a common one. Yet in the Amarna archive, not all the correspondents of Pharaoh use it; not all of them show the same cunning. Rib-Adda, the most 'redundant' correspondent of Pharaoh, uses a technique that can be schematised as the opposite of Aziru's:

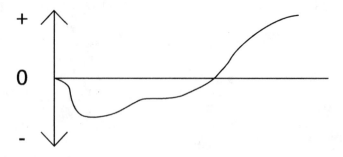

He prefers to give the unforeseen and unpleasant news immediately, even adding unpleasant statements on stereotypical secondary problems ('protection' of the city, supply of 'life/food'). Only from what follows, and after reading the letter as a whole, does it become clear that his critical and recriminatory position toward Pharaoh does not imply a desire to leave the Egyptian political system (see Liverani 1971a for an analysis of EA 126 and EA 130). Rib-Adda's epistolary technique is less 'diplomatic', if diplomatic at all. His use of redundancy produces negative results. In fact, he repeats and emphasises not the pleasant elements in order to hide the unpleasant ones, but the unpleasant elements that further highlight the negative answer. To judge from the available data, one would conclude that these two diplomatic/epistolary techniques produce the most obvious results:

Rib-Adda's technique results in angering and annoying Pharaoh's court, while Aziru is able to obtain approval for the delay he desires.

1.3 REBUILDING SUMURA

Aziru applies the same technique of argument to another problem, which presents analogies to his visit to Egypt; this is the case of the rebuilding of the city of Sumura. The undertaking is also explicitly related to a specific order of Pharaoh, but it contains premises that constitute the basic elements of Aziru's relation of dependence on Egypt. The duty to rebuild Sumura is part of the idea that Amurru has been 'entrusted' to Abdi-Ashirta, Aziru's father, and then to Aziru (cf. §3.2). They have to care for and protect the country on behalf of the Egyptian administration. Until recently Sumura was the seat of the Egyptian governor (*rābiṣu*), and outside of the jurisdiction of the local kings (see Knudtzon 1915: II, 1138–1141; Helck 1962: 258; Klengel 1965–70: III, 9–10). Taking advantage of a moment when the Egyptian garrison of Sumura had military difficulties, Abdi-Ashirta was able to 'rescue' the city and, eventually, to include it in his kingdom. He agreed to rebuild the city in order to enable it again to perform the function it had under direct Egyptian control.[4] The command to restore Sumura is the very basis of Egypt's acknowledgement that Abdi-Ashirta's house is qualified to rule over the area. And since he is taking the place of the Egyptian governor (*rābiṣu*), he will rule from a different position from that of the other local petty kings.

Aziru's reluctance to go to Egypt is easily explained by his fear of being held (cf. n.1) or of being punished (note the guarantees explicitly requested in EA 164: 35–40). I can only offer hypotheses, however, about the real reasons for his reluctance to begin rebuilding Sumura. Perhaps Aziru delays the work because of its costs, and intends to carry it out in a more favourable period, or as late as possible. From a political point of view, the completion of the reconstruction of Sumura would mean the return of the Egyptian governor. So the king of Amurru probably delays it in order to keep his control over this important site, and over Amurru as a whole, without any direct presence and tutelage from the Egyptian side. From Aziru's perspective, the *assignment* to rebuild Sumura is politically important, while the practical execution of the work is a burden.

---

[4] The basic document on these events is EA 62, sent by Abdi-Ashirta. He relates the attack by the city of Shehlal on Sumura, its rescue, which is described in terms of 'protection' (cf. also EA 60 and EA 371), and its reconstruction, which is described in terms of 'entrusting'. The relationship between Amurru and Sumura should be reconsidered, in my opinion. We should distrust the information supplied by Rib-Adda, king of Byblos, who is obviously biased by his attitude against the state of Amurru, and by his cyclical concept of events. I am not convinced by Altman 1978: 104–7, on the location of Shehlal.

Be that as it may, Aziru once more needs to clothe his actual disobedience in statements of general obedience. He uses the same techniques of persuasion: (1) his negative conduct is shown as being momentary, as simply a delay, while his obedience is stated to be valid on a general level; (2) the delay is caused by the more important need to protect the country, thus by his striving for a general goal of which the rebuilding of Sumura is only a part. We see again the same details, such as the one-year delay (EA 160: 27–28), the use of 'now, quickly' (EA 159: 43–44; EA 161: 39–40), and the involvement of the Egyptian official Hatib (EA 161: 38). Last but not least, the political and military reasons are also the same: a threat from the land of Nuhashe needs to be faced first of all. Just as Aziru cannot leave for Egypt because the Hittite army is in Nuhashe (cf. §2.1), he cannot rebuild Sumura because the kings of Nuhashe are hostile (EA 160: 24–26; EA 161: 36–39). He locates the hostile forces in Nuhashe not only because of the real political and topographical situation, but also to make the Egyptian addressee realise that beyond Nuhashe is Hatti. Thus Aziru is preoccupied by problems that are not his own, but those of interest to Pharaoh himself. They are problems at the level of 'Great Kings'. Amurru is the northernmost element in the Egyptian political system, and Nuhashe the southernmost in the enemy's political system. Aziru makes it clear that the protection of the boundary between Amurru and Nuhashe, of which he takes care, must be considered by Pharaoh himself as important for safeguarding Egyptian territory as a whole.

2 THE CODE OF MOVEMENT

2.1 CONDITIONED DISPLACEMENTS

Aziru's explanation to Pharaoh in relation to his visit to Egypt – which is also evident in connection with the reconstruction of Sumura – is completely based on physical and mechanical elements, on movement and stasis, and on a bi-directional balance and opposition. In the letter EA 164 the pattern is as follows:

- Just as Hatib came (*alāku* 164: 4) and stayed (*uzuzzu* 164: 19) in Amurru // so the king of Hatti came (*alāku* 164: 22) to Nuhashe.
- If the king of Hatti moves away (*paṭāru* 164: 24) // then I will come (*alāku* 164: 25).
- As long as the king of Hatti remains (implicit) // I cannot come (*lā le'û* + *alāku* 164: 23).

In the letters EA 165–167 the pattern is even clearer:

- The king of Hatti is staying (*ašābu* 165: 19; 165: 39; 166: 22; 167: 12; 167: 21) in Nuhashe // I am staying (*ašābu* 166: 26; 167: 22; *uzuzzu* 165: 23; 166: 29) in Amurru.
- If the king of Hatti leaves (*paṭāru* 165: 24;[5] 165: 41; 166: 29; 167: 12; 167: 24) // I will come (*alāku* 165: 25; 166: 30; 167: 15; *kašādu* 167: 24).
- If the king of Hatti comes (*alāku* 165: 21; 166: 24;[6] 167: 26) or attacks (*šaḫāṭu* 165: 40; 166: 26) // I will... (the result is censored! He just states 'I am afraid') (*palāḫu* 165: 40; 166: 27; 167: 27).

Note that other letters by Aziru in addition to the group EA 164–167 used here as the focus of analysis contain patterns of conditioned and oppositional movement, always in contexts related to the political location of Amurru between the two 'blocks' of Hatti and Egypt. Thus in EA 157, Aziru wishes for Egyptian military intervention (*ana rešūti nadānu* 31–32) to oppose a possible hostile 'coming' (*ana nukurti alāku* 29) of the king of Hatti to Amurru, so that a defensive balance (*naṣāru* 33) would be achieved. In EA 161 Aziru, accused of entertaining the Hittite messenger and not the Egyptian one (47–50), defends himself in two ways: (a) while Aziru 'stayed' (*ašābu* 12) in Tunip, the Egyptian messenger Hani 'arrived' (*kašādu* 13) in Amurru. So Aziru 'came' (*elû* 15) to him, but did not 'reach' him (*kašādu* 16). When Hani will 'arrive' (*kašādu* 17) in Egypt, he can testify that Aziru's brothers 'stayed behind' (*uzuzzu* 20) to meet him. (b) When Aziru will 'go' (*alāku* 26) to Egypt, Hani will 'go' (*alāku* 27) and welcome him. Therefore, when Hani went to Amurru, it was obviously in Aziru's interest to welcome him. Lastly, all of EA 170, a letter written by Aziru's relatives to Aziru in Egypt, is also built on a play on the opposition between standing and moving.

Returning now to the focus of my analysis (EA 164–167), the movable elements are on the one hand Aziru himself, and on the other hand the Hittite king and his troops. As Aziru is staying in Amurru, so the Hittite troops are staying in Nuhashe. If the Hittite troops were to move away, departing from the boundary Nuhashe/Amurru, then Aziru too could depart and go to Egypt:

---

5 It is also possible to keep *li-tu₄-ur* (from *târu* 'to return'), but I think it better to restore *li-<ip>-tu(m)-ur*, on the basis of parallel passages, since Aziru's lexicon is limited and repetitive.

6 Here too it is possible, and perhaps better, to keep *i-la-am* (from *elû* 'to go up' in the West-Semitic sense of 'to come'), or to emend to *i-la-<ka->am* on the basis of parallel passages. In any case, my analysis is not affected by this alternative, nor by the one discussed in n.5.

But should the Hittites remain, then Aziru too must stay where he is, obviously in order to face them; therefore he will have to renounce his visit to Egypt.

A third possibility is merely alluded to as something to 'fear', because the Hittite troops are only two days' march from Tunip (EA 165: 39; 166: 26; 167: 22). The Hittites could proceed in his direction, and invade Amurru. In this case – since the rules of symmetry are not optional – Aziru should go against or towards them:

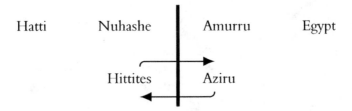

'Against' or 'toward'? – that is the question! We have to keep two levels of reading apart. There is an explicit level, expressing a physical/military view. Aziru states that he cannot move because he 'fears' (*palāḫu*, cf. above) an invasion or attack by the Hittites. He is therefore assuming an Egyptian point of view. He means that his physical-symbolic *approach* to Egypt – his visit to Pharaoh – will take place once the threat is over, once the *departure* of the rival king is accomplished. Otherwise, his very faithfulness to Pharaoh keeps him engaged on the frontier. In this frame of reading, it is clear that if there were to be a Hittite attack Aziru would go 'against' the enemy. But there is also a level of reading that we could define as 'unintentional', expressing a political/institutional view. Aziru's possibility of movement between Egypt and Hatti, his personal movement as conditioned by other movements (the Hittite troops), is also a move on the political chessboard. Aziru cannot openly confess this, but he knows perfectly well that, if the Hittites invade Amurru, he would have to *side with the Hittites*. Therefore he cannot go to Egypt unless he renounces his throne. As long as he does not know what will happen, it is wiser to wait. If the Hittites were to withdraw from Nuhashe and respect Egypt's rule over Amurru, it would be confirmed that Aziru belongs to the Egyptian sphere of influence. Then Aziru would go to Pharaoh and reassert his submission. But, if there were a Hittite attack, Aziru would defect and go 'toward' the Hittite king, in order to submit to him.

So the political reading is linked to the physical one, but it is also its complete opposite. Pointing out a hidden political reading implies that Aziru's insistent use of verbs of motion and stasis is not only an unavoidable consequence of the topic, but is also a true expressive code, one I call the 'code of movement'. His insistence on using verbs of motion or stasis functions as a sign of the hidden preoccupation, of his basic political problem: his position between two power blocks, and the possibility of changing position, by 'moving' to the other side.

2.2 DISOBEDIENCE AS SEPARATION

In the attempt to quantify the relevance of the 'code of movement' in Aziru's letters (EA 156–161, 164–168), I have sorted the verbal forms into four groups:

- A: verbs of motion and stasis;
- B: verbs of causing motion (to give and to take, to send and to bring, to leave and to prepare, etc.);
- C: verbs of saying, hearing, seeing, and knowing;
- D: various verbs unconnected with motion (to do and the like; to fear, to wish, etc.; to be and the like).

As a comparison, I have analysed equivalent samples of Rib-Adda letters (EA 68–77) and samples of letters from Palestinian rulers (EA 260–284). The percentages have merely an indicative value, not only because of the limited size of the sample, but also because of the difficulty and arbitrariness in assigning some verbs to one of the four groups. With these provisions, here are the percentages obtained:

	A	B	A+B	C	D	C+D
Aziru	38.8	21.1	59.9	19.6	20.5	40.1
Rib-Adda	19.4	26.9	46.3	24.4	29.3	53.7
Palestine	19.8	30.7	50.5	31.1	18.4	49.5

The greater percentage of verbs of motion as a whole (A+B) in Aziru's letters is evident, and not accidental. This high percentage is due primarily to the numerous verbs of motion and stasis narrowly defined (that is, pertaining to displacements of persons, group A), and to a lesser extent to verbs of caused motion (mainly pertaining to displacements of goods, group B). The percentage of group A in Aziru's letters is twice that of both other groups of letters.[7] Moreover, a more

---

[7] There are also minor differences in the other two groups. The Palestinian letters, being shorter

or less fixed quota of verbal forms belongs to stereotypical formulae (address, greetings), so that the imbalance will be even greater in the remaining sections, those that contain the specific message.

The use of the 'code of movement' is not limited to contexts where there was real physical displacement, even if the insistence on these may itself be a sign of the excessive political importance attached to them. The 'code of movement' is also employed where it is completely extraneous, as a pure metaphor. Aziru repeatedly states: 'From the words of my lord I do not detach myself' (EA 157: 8; 158: 33–35; 159: 5–6; 164: 14–17; 166: 17–19; 167: 5–6; the verb is always *paṭāru*), an expression that belongs to the 'code of movement'. Egyptian vassals normally express that idea in an 'auditory code': 'I listen to the words of the King my lord' (EA *passim*). This more common way to express one's obedience is an obvious metaphor, endowed with a direct physical basis. Pharaoh's words are indeed 'listened to' by the vassal, when the message is read to him. Only the actual execution of the orders belongs on a purely political level.

The metaphor of 'not detaching oneself' from the King's words is not at all self-evident. It implies that disobedience will indicate a shift in political dependence, and therefore a displacement (in the sense defined in §2.1). It is no accident that the use of the verb *paṭāru* with a political meaning, outside the letters of Aziru is attested only in those of Akizzi of Qatna (EA 52: 46; 55: 6; 56: 11). Akizzi was the protagonist of another noteworthy political displacement, having shifted allegiance from Mitanni to Egypt under the pressure of the advancing Hittites. One, different and isolated, attestation of the 'code of movement' in a Rib-Adda letter (EA 109: 7–8) hints also at a possible movement between Mitanni and Egypt.[8]

It seems that the use of the 'code of movement' in the sphere of obedience depends on the author's position on a geopolitical border. In a marginal position, disobedience is possible and full of political consequences, because it is based on, and results in, a shift to another sphere of influence. For obvious geographical reasons such movement is impossible for those rulers who were well within the Egyptian sphere. Therefore they use the 'auditory code', which is static in its implications, just as the code of movement is dynamic. The only possible alternative for the 'inner' vassals is not to listen: but this was an option without outcome, a kind of passive resistance or even suicide. It is not a move that initiates an alternative strategy. At the very moment when the possibility of 'not

---

and more stereotyped, inflate especially groups B (displacement of goods, their main topic) and C (related to the epistolary mechanism itself).

8   Rib-Adda generally describes political change with the expression *nēpušu ana* ('to become', literally 'to be made into', based on an Egyptian expression, see Liverani 1979b), viewing it not as movement (code of movement, group B) but as self-modification (group D).

listening' is expressed, it is also denied and rejected as unbelievable, through the use of rhetorical questions and humiliating similes ('Who is the dog who does not listen to the words of the King?' EA 319: 19–21; 320: 22–25; 322: 17–19; 324: 16–19). The only option for the inner vassals is to hear and to obey. For the vassals on the border, there is an option of 'moving away' from the king and his orders, obviously coming closer to another king and to other orders.

To sum up, I suggest that Aziru uses the 'code of movement' rather than other codes because it fits the political situation of his kingdom particularly well, and because it is symptomatically expressive of hidden worries and of wishes that cannot be stated, and constructs what can be termed a 'politics of movement'.

2.3 THE INTERNATIONAL SCENE

Applying the 'code of movement' to political relations is not exceptional in the juridical and political literature of the time. Countries and communities are said 'to enter' and 'to leave' the borders delimiting political spheres. They are also said to have been 'brought into' or 'caused to enter' such spheres. It is as if the borders are viewed as fixed, immovable, and the political and territorial elements as movable entities (cf. Liverani 1990, §I.5). This is the complete opposite of reality, and it is clearly a point of view of the 'Great Kings', located at the center of a political sphere. They consider the existence of such a sphere as a definitive and unchallenged fact, with its borders toward other (equally definitive) spheres. On the other hand, they consider the minor states to have only casual pertinence to any one of them.

Yet in the Aziru letters we see something else. Not only is there the use of the metaphor that reveals a variation in political relations, beneath the terminology of physical movement. We notice also a particular insistence that portrays a movement (Aziru's displacements, the moves of the Hittite troops, the position of the messenger) that was simply physical as important, worrying, and meaningful. That movement would not be given such attention if it were not the sign of a quite different 'movement', namely a political one.

This dynamic, 'motional' view of the political situation characterises border areas and periods of change in the international scene. Some years earlier, there was 'movement' in Ishuwa and Kizzuwatna, which involved the spheres of influence of Hatti and Mitanni in the belt stretching from Cilicia to the Upper Euphrates. 'In the past, at the time of my father's father, the Kizzuwatna land belonged to Hatti. Then the Kizzuwatna land detached itself (*paṭāru*) from Hatti and turned itself (*saḥāru*) to Hurri... Now Kizzuwatna has detached itself from Hurri and has turned itself toward the Sun' (Weidner 1923: no. 7, Vs I 5–7, 30–32; for an analysis of the 'code of movement' in this text see chapter 3). In the Amarna period, movement is located in central Syria, and involves a redefinition of the Hittite and Egyptian spheres. Amurru and Nuhashe, as well as Qatna and Qadesh, located on both sides of the border, are the sites where movement takes place, and where the use of the 'code of movement' with a political function is consequently more frequent. 'The city of Qatna with its goods and everything, I caused to enter into (*erēbu* Š) the Hatti land… All those people with their land and everything – the Hittite king Shuppiluliuma is speaking – I caused to enter into the Hatti land… All those lands I plundered and caused to enter into the Hatti land, from the Lebanon to the Euphrates I returned them (*târu*) to my border' (Weidner 1923: no. 1, Vs 37, 45–47).

As for Amurru, the process of 'coming out' of the Egyptian political sphere and 'going into' the Hittite system is marked by the personal movements of Aziru. At first, he goes to the Hatti king (EA 165: 29–32); then he goes to Pharaoh; finally, as soon as he comes back from Egypt, he runs and throws himself at the feet of the Hittite king Shuppiluliuma. So his new and definitive dependence is symbolised by a strong enacting of the 'code of movement': '(Aziru) came from the gate of Egypt, and at the feet of my Sun, the Great King, he knelt down' (Freydank 1960: i 24).

3 BUILDING A KINGDOM

3.1 'I AM DOING AS THE OTHERS DO'

Another recurring and insistent theme in Aziru's letters is the emphasis on his acquiescence to Pharaoh's requests, especially about the supply of goods. He emphasises specific supplies (cf. EA 160: 14–19, 44; 161: 54–56), but also formulates his willingness in general terms. He states, for instance: 'As to the wish expressed by the Sun, my lord: I am your servant forever' (EA 156: 4–7); 'Every wish of my lord, I shall supply' (EA 157: 17–19); 'Whatever may be your wish, write to me and I shall give you what you want' (EA 158: 17–19; cf. *ibid*. 5–9); or 'Whatever the King my lord wants, I am preparing, and whatever comes out of the mouth of the King my lord, I am preparing' (EA 160: 9–13). He also uses statements such as 'my house is your house' (EA 158: 16; cf. 161: 51). The more these statements are stereotypical and conventional, the more they are indicative of the fact that Aziru is not simply communicating a piece of information. He is also, and more importantly, pointing out his own behaviour to the addressee. His message is not so much 'I am obeying', as rather 'You can see that I am obeying'. The same holds true for a statement like 'I am not sinning' (EA 157: 13–16), which becomes meaningful only if compared to other passages related to charges or slanders against him, and disdainfully rejected by him in letters by Aziru himself (EA 158: 20–31; 160: 30–32; 161: 7–9; 165: 42–43) and in a letter from Pharaoh to Aziru (EA 162: 33–38). It seems that Aziru is preoccupied with emphasizing the normality and correctness of his conduct, and in blaming any doubt about his loyalty on hostility and malice.

A key to understanding this recurrent emphasis lies, in my opinion, in two passages where Aziru explicitly states that his conduct is correct, because it is like that of the other vassal-kings of Pharaoh. 'Whatever the (other) *ḫazānus* give, I am also giving to the King my lord, my Sun, I am giving forever' (EA 157: 37–41), and 'I am your servant like all the previous *ḫazānus* who resided in his city' (EA 162: 8–9). Aziru's main concern is to be recognised and legitimised in his position as king. At least in one passage the logical link 'I am supplying what you request – therefore let me reign' is stated explicitly: 'As to the wish expressed by the Sun, my lord: I am your servant forever and my sons are your servants. Now I gave you two boys, the sons of X, who are to do what the King my lord orders; and (so) let me remain in Amurru!' (EA 156: 4–14). It is hardly necessary to recall that the royal house of Amurru, established under Abdi-Ashirta (who was not yet given the title of king), acquired stability only under Aziru, both in practice (Aziru became his father's successor, after a period when he shared power with his brothers) and in the opinion of others (Aziru was awarded the title of king; cf. Klengel 1964: 65–6; Liverani 1965a: 268–9). And it is hardly necessary to recall how tenaciously this process of forming a new royal house had been opposed by the surrounding kings. Their attitude is exemplified by Rib-Adda, who considered Abdi-Ashirta and his sons as *ḫabirus*, dogs, and traitors, and tried to disqualify them in the eyes of Pharaoh in every way possible (see chapter 5). We are faced with the difficult process of the legitimisation of a 'new' kingship, whose origins were 'irregular', and 'illegitimate'. This was an ideological translation of the trouble caused in real terms by adding one more occupant within a limited territory. The technique of legitimisation used by Aziru is not unusual for the time; it consists of showing that a real legitimacy is a *de facto* one. Aziru is a legitimate king, because he really reigns. He does so in an effective and normal way, 'as the others do' – both in the spatial sense (= like the nearby kings, as in EA 157: 37–41) and in the temporal sense (= like previous kings, as in EA 162: 8–9).

The syndrome of the usurper and the legitimisation through analogy are found in famous apologies of 'new' kings in the same historical period. Consider the statement by the king of Alalah, Idrimi: 'I made my throne like the throne of kings, I made my brothers like the brothers of kings, my sons like their sons, my comrades like their comrades... I made my cities like as before, as (in the time) of our fathers' (Idrimi 81–84, 87).[9] And consider the statement by the Hittite usurper Hattushili III: 'Those who were on good terms with the kings my

---

[9] Cf. Oller 1977: 15–16, 107–113. On Idrimi as usurper see chapter 7.

predecessors, they entered into good relations with me too. They sent me messengers, they sent me gifts; and the gifts they sent me they had not (even) sent to any of my fathers and forefathers... Even those who were enemies of my fathers and forefathers, they came to terms with me' (Goetze 1925: 36–7: iv 50–9). Finally, consider the statement of the Palestinian equivalent to Aziru, Lab'aya: 'I am a faithful servant of the King, I am not a sinner, I am not a culprit, I have not refused tribute, I have not refused the wishes of the governor' (EA 254: 10–15). The statements by Aziru belong to this kind of self-legitimisation. It is true that Idrimi and Hattushili made this address 'downward', to their subjects, while Aziru and Lab'aya spoke 'upward', to the suzerain. Yet the substance of their messages is the same: a new kingship achieves legitimacy by the very fact of functioning 'normally', or still better than before, better than the others. What does it matter to Pharaoh whether Aziru and Lab'aya are new men or descendants of old houses? What really matters is that they are doing what a small king is expected to do: to supply what is asked for, to pay tribute, and to ensure stability and protection in his land.

Once again the different character of the conduct of Rib-Adda, who was a member of an old royal house, is evident. While Aziru emphasises his similarity to the other kings and wants it to be acknowledged, Rib-Adda emphasises his difference and refuses to be compared or assimilated to the others.[10] This is true even at the level of detail. While Aziru emphasises his willingness to supply what is requested, Rib-Adda sometimes seems tenaciously to emphasise his refusal or his inability to satisfy the request (Liverani 1971a: 260–1).

Aziru	Rib-Adda
wants to be alike	wants to be different
emphasises supply of goods	refuses to send goods
avoids contacts	seeks for too much contact
offers to protect	aspires to be protected
reigns together with brothers	rivalry against his brother
new kingship	old kingship
seeks substantive autonomy disguised as submission	seeks formal autonomy under Egyptian tutelage

[10] Cf. EA 88: 42–45 ('Byblos is not like the other cities, Byblos is a city faithful to my lord from of old'); EA 138: 25–27 ('I am a servant of the king, there is no (other) *ḫazānu* like me for the king, I would die for my lord'); or EA 125: 31–38 ('Why is the king comparing me to the (other) *ḫazānus*?'). See chapter 5 for more passages.

3.2 ANOMALY IN ORIGIN, ANOMALY IN OUTCOME

On a couple of occasions Aziru asks Pharaoh to 'leave' (*wuššuru*) him in Amurru, that is, as a king: 'Let (the King) leave me in the land of Amurru' (EA 156: 13–14); 'My lord, long have I wished to serve the King my lord, but the 'great-ones' in Sumura did not allow me to do so' (EA 157: 9–12); and, with an allusion that is not clear: 'Since the King my lord did not allow me to protect his land' (EA 165: 36–37).[11] This topic, which is presented as a logical outcome of the one examined in §3.1 ('I am doing as the others do'), is clearly connected with another key theme and key term in the Amarna correspondence, that of 'entrusting' (*paqādu*; cf. Campbell 1976: 45–54). The verb is used in a precative form, therefore with a future perspective, in the letters of the 'new' kings Abdi-Ashirta (EA 60: 30–2 'Let the King my lord entrust me to Pahamati my governor', that is, the governor who has jurisdiction over me) and Lab'aya (EA 253: 32–5 'Let the King my lord entrust me to his governor, in order to protect the city of the King'). It is used in the narrative form, therefore as an already completed and stabilised process, in the letters of a king such as Abi-Milki of Tyre, who employs it frequently (EA 148: 20–2; 148: 28–9; 149: 9–10; 151: 6–7; 155: 49–50).

The shift from *paqādu* to *wuššuru* reflects the passing of time. The relationship between Pharaoh and the Amurru kings is still developing at the time of Abdi-Ashirta, and requires an explicit act of 'entrusting'. In the time of Aziru the relationship is sufficiently consolidated to require only a 'maintaining' of the *status quo*. But the consolidation was not yet definitive. It could still be threatened, as the verbal forms in Aziru's correspondence show (precative in one case, recriminatory in the two other cases). Abdi-Ashirta's concern (*paqādu*) and Aziru's concern (*wuššuru*), are those of an emerging royal family. They cannot yet rely on the institutional inertia that the old families exploit. Instead they have to rely on explicit and active acknowledgements by Pharaoh. Another statement by Aziru that contains a different terminology is also significant: 'This is the land of my lord, and the King my lord placed me (*šakānu*) among the *ḫazānu*s' (EA 161: 51–53). The two demonstrative ways of reasoning 'I am King, since I am acting so' (§3.1) and 'I am King, since you decided so' (§3.2) contribute in this case among others to the establishment of a new kingship.

When Abdi-Ashirta, Lab'aya, and Abi-Milki, use the term *paqādu*, there is a certain amount of ambiguity, as well as a shift in the concept of entrusting, on the logical rather than the chronological level. There is a different combination of the

---

11 In Pharaoh's letter to Aziru, EA 162: 42 *wuššuru* is used when he quotes Aziru's request for one year to be 'left' to him before he will come to Egypt. The verb is used here in a more specific context. Yet it is just as symptomatic of Aziru's worry about being removed from the throne. Notice that Pharaoh answers with *ezēbu*, also 'to leave' but not a verb of motion.

four constitutive elements of the theme: entrusting (*paqādu*), Egyptian governor (*rābiṣu*), protecting (*naṣāru*), and city *(ālu)*. In the first and normal conceptual stage, the local king is entrusted to the governor in order to protect the city; in the following stage the city is entrusted directly to the local king, who therefore becomes a more autonomous protagonist and no longer an object of the entrusting. In the case of Abi-Milki, for instance, the difference is only formal because the city involved, Tyre, is his city, where he reigns in any case under the control of a *rābiṣu*. But in the case of Abdi-Ashirta, and then Aziru, the difference is substantive, because the city to be protected, Sumura, had been the seat of a *rābiṣu*, not of a local *ḫazānu*. In such a case there is quite a difference between being entrusted to a *rābiṣu* and receiving in trust the very seat of a *rābiṣu* (cf. §1.3). Through expressing the wish to be properly integrated into the Egyptian political-administrative system, which belonged to the first stage, the king of Amurru tries to get himself acknowledged as supervisor, or even as protector, of the entire region of Amurru in its widest sense. He exploits the situation of Sumura, the problem of its rebuilding, the absence of the residing *rābiṣu*, and so on. Abdi-Ashirta and Aziru also seem to take advantage of the ambiguity of the term Amurru. Amurru designates all the territories on the mid-northern Syrian coast under Egyptian control, with Sumura as its administrative centre, next to the areas named Ube/Abina, with its center in Kumidi, and Kinahniu, with its centre in Gaza (cf. Helck 1962: 258–60). But Amurru also designates the smaller area corresponding to the kingdom ruled by the house of Abdi-Ashirta. The king of Amurru attempts – and is successful – to rise from being chief of the sub-area to being chief of the entire homonymous super-area. At the formal/verbal level he plays on homonymity, at the substantial/political level he uses his military pre-eminence in the area.

Aziru inherited the situation in its 'second' stage. The reconstruction of Sumura, entrusted to him and solicited from him by Pharaoh, was the clearest hint regarding a situation that is ambiguous and therefore dynamic. Aziru will accomplish the rebuilding of Sumura on behalf of the Egyptian administration in order to make it his own residence (or one of his residences). But at the same time the status of Sumura as centre of the wider whole will be useful to Aziru in his attempt to ascend to a higher level in relation to the other kings of the area – who remain only chiefs of their respective sub-units. The 'small kings' of the neighbourhood are aware of the tendency of Abdi-Ashirta and Aziru to act as 'great kings'. At least Rib-Adda is well aware of it, and he insistently asks Pharaoh: 'Who do they think they are, the sons of Abdi-Ashirta, the servant and dog? Are they perhaps the king of Kashshu (= Babylon) or the king of Mitanni, that they take the King's land for themselves?' (EA 104: 17–24 and parallel passages). The act of 'taking the king's land for themselves' is not attacked in absolute terms, but because it is in conflict with the status of a 'small king'. Aziru is acting illegally as only a 'great king' could act legally.

Thus the kings of Amurru follow a coherent policy in exploiting the ambiguity in the terminology of entrusting and maintenance. Under an apparent connotation of 'stability', evolving and dynamic aspects of the political picture are concealed. By asking for nothing more than firm integration into the Egyptian system, the kings of Amurru engage in a rapid shift in status. From a status of 'non-kings', being simply tribal or military chiefs, who are not acknowledged by their neighbours and even despised by them, they aim rapidly to gain the status of kings, and eventually even seek autonomy from the 'great Kings' of Egypt and Hatti. The final failure of their attempt cannot conceal the fact that it was planned and carried out up to a certain level, to be eventually subverted and overturned by a sequence of events of major importance.

3.3 HORIZONTAL AND VERTICAL MOBILITY

Like Harlequin, Aziru has to act as 'a servant of two masters' at once. To achieve this he has to use a great deal of physical mobility and verbal ambiguity. Harlequin's aim is 'to get two salaries and to eat double rations'. Aziru's aim is to free himself from the tutelage of both masters.

The great mobility of Aziru is well known. He has no fixed capital city, and moves between the cities Tunip and Sumura, as well as the highlands from which he originates. He is unavailable to the Egyptian messenger because he is speaking with the Hittite one, and probably vice-versa on occasions whose record is lost. He goes to meet the Hittite king when he is still formally an Egyptian vassal. Then he goes to Egypt when he has already decided on the substance of his agreement with Hatti. As soon as he is back from Pharaoh's court, he rejoins the Hittite king Shuppiluliuma for his definitive submission. His mobility between the two 'great kings' is the translation of his political project into physical terms. He avails himself of the international protection that derives from his belonging to the Egyptian sphere, in order to avoid having Hittite troops in Amurru. And he avails himself of the advances of Shuppiluliuma in order to free himself, at least partly, from Egyptian overlordship. His politics of movement, of wedging himself between the two opposing political blocks, clearly aims at achieving a rise in status, a condition of *de facto* independence from both great kings. At the same time he also aims for the status of great king by establishing asymmetrical relations to his own advantage with the surrounding kings. He is actively involved from Ugarit to Byblos, from Tunip to Arwad, and even to the Qadesh area. He uses military action (cf. Klengel 1964: 67–9), offers a type of protection that was rather a protectorate, and ambiguously assumes the function of the Egyptian *rābiṣu* in Sumura.

It would be unfair to label Aziru as 'servant of two masters', because he longs to be no one's servant. His double dependence is part of a stage that he conceives as transitional and instrumental in the development of his own policy. He seems never formally to renounce his dependence on Egypt – or couple it with dependence on Hatti – before his last and manifest change of sides. Throughout the entire period covered by his Amarna correspondence, there are ambiguities, suspicions, charges of treachery, accusations, and self-defence. His 'double game' was evident, not only to the small kings nearby, but also to the distant Pharaoh. The latter's letter to Aziru (EA 162) repeatedly asks the ironic question 'If you are really my faithful servant...' (EA 162: 15, 19, 25–26, 32). Pharaoh does not demand anything specifically, but his letter shows a perfect knowledge and correct evaluation by the Egyptian court of the state of affairs in Amurru. Only the Amarna archive gives us information on this state of affairs. Aziru's 'double game' would have been even more evident if we had records, for instance, of his exchanges with Hittite ambassadors – while the Egyptian messenger was waiting in vain for an audience. But even with this documentary bias, the 'double game' in Aziru's policy is quite clear.[12]

Verbal ambiguity is an obvious element in this policy. On the conscious level it consists of addressing both partners in a suitable manner. What Aziru says to one party is probably the opposite of what he says to the other partner. He conceals what is useful to conceal, emphasises and even invents whatever makes him look good in their eyes. But underneath this conscious ambiguity, another one becomes evident. This latter is quite involuntary and unconscious, and is the opposite of the first. The worries and the unstated goals of Aziru come to light in his speech, in the form of almost obsessive insistences – notably in the 'code of movement' – and of lexical usages that are ideologically reversed. Unwillingly, Aziru lets us perceive just what he would have liked to conceal completely, and gives us the 'signals' of his bad conscience. Since we know the end of the story, we easily notice these 'signals' of Aziru's hidden purposes. Did Pharaoh also notice them?

---

12 The picture of Amurru as totally dependent on Mitanni, as reconstructed by Kestemont 1978: 27–32, on the basis of a limited selection of the evidence (and on an inadequate control of the bibliography) is unacceptable. The very fact that it could be proposed, however, confirms the striking ambiguity in the political situation of Amurru.

PART FOUR

Hebrew Bible

7

*The story of Joash**

INTRODUCTION

The biblical story of Joash (in 2 Kings 11 and 12) suggests that in the late ninth century the rule of the house of David over Judah had been interrupted. King Ahaz had died as the result of wounds he suffered in battle, while his son, Joash, was an infant. Athaliah, the mother of Ahaz, became regent and massacred the rest of the royal family, but Joash was saved by an aunt, who hid him in the temple of Yahweh. Seven years later the high priest, Jehoiada, recognised Joash as the true king, installed him on the throne, and killed Athaliah.

In this chapter Liverani reads this brief narrative as an example of the apologetic texts that are written by usurpers to the throne in order to justify their rule. He compares it to two well known apologies of the second millennium: the inscription on Idrimi's statue (chapter 4 here), and the explanation given by the Hittite king Hattushili III after he seized the throne from his nephew Urhi-Teshub (for a recent translation, see van den Hout 1997). The Joash episode becomes then a fictional explanation from the hand of the high priest who *de facto* took charge by placing a seven-year-old boy on the throne. It is like the text of a staged theatrical performance where the recognition of the young boy is the event that removes the disruption in the rule of the house of David. The comparison with other apologies is done on the basis of a structural analysis that identifies themes and their sequence within the narrative, which are the same for the three texts. Moreover, in other types of documents, primarily treaties between the Hittites and their vassals, parts of the sequence can also be found in the so-called historical introductions. A recent translation of those has been published by Gary Beckman (1996; Shattiwaza = no. 6, Mashhuiluwa = no. 11, Benteshina = no. 16).

★ ★ ★ ★

★ Originally published as 'L'histoire de Joas', *Vetus Testamentum* 24 (1974), 438–53.

1 THEATRICALITY AS A FORM
OF POLITICAL PROPAGANDA

The biblical story of the murder of Athaliah and the enthronement of Joash (2 Kings 11) possesses a remarkable dramatic quality that has inspired famous tragedies, such as Racine's *Athalie*. It is worth asking the question whether the stage-like effects of the story are present already in the biblical text – perhaps not in the text we have, but rather in previous literary formulations that are reflected in it – or even in the way the events were originally acted out. 'Events' considered in purely mechanistic terms cannot be qualified as 'theatrical' or otherwise, yet they can become so when they are used to express human relationships.

In other words, the dramatic features in the Joash story could be the result of a cunning 'staging' of the event by the protagonists, or else they could have originated at a slightly later point, when the episode was first told to an audience. Since the episode had great political significance for the kingdom of Judah, its theatricality should in any case be a function of a political purpose. The *coup de théâtre* at the dénouement of the story could have been exploited to get the attention of the whole community – the audience of a plot developing not in the realm of fiction, but in that of reality. This reality was of course not at all a matter of chance, but was manipulated by those who were in a position to do so, at the level of action and/or of its presentation.

If the theatricality was unintentional, its constituent elements should not follow in a structured sequence. But if it was the result of a clever manipulation of events for a specific aim, it is reasonable to expect the same type of narrative to be used in other cases where the political situations and propagandistic purposes were similar. A search for documents that exhibit the same pattern as the Joash story is therefore a fundamental step in analysis.

2 JOASH AND IDRIMI

A precise correspondence can be pointed out between the stories of Joash and of Idrimi, king of Alalah in the early fifteenth century BC.[1] To be sure, the two stories have come down to us in texts of different types. The Idrimi story is recorded in an inscription on the statue of the king himself. It has a celebratory and specifically apologetic aim. The protagonist, who commissioned the inscription, had a direct responsibility for the precise terms in which the story is related.

---

[1]   For the text of Idrimi's statue, see Smith 1949. A translation by A. L. Oppenheim can be found in Pritchard 1969: 557–8. The narrative themes in the first part of the inscription are studied in chapter 4 here.

By contrast, the Joash story is part of a continuous historical narrative with obvious and well known problems relating to the sources and the distance in time from the events narrated. It is clear that a more direct comparison could be established between the Idrimi inscription and an inscription whose redaction might have been ordered by Joash – or by Jehoiada on his behalf – to celebrate his enthronement. But such an inscription, which, as we shall see, we can strongly suspect did exist, is lost forever. Moreover, about 650 years of time separate the two stories and they were written in places 500 kilometres apart, even if in the context of a rather coherent and conservative culture. Lastly, the languages are different: Idrimi's Akkadian is a literary language, learned by a scribe who spoke Amorite or Hurrian, while the Joash story is written in the local native language, Hebrew. Needless to say, the historical data too are different in many respects. These preliminary differences make the substantially identical structure of the two stories the more significant. That identity is displayed in the following table:

	Idrimi	Joash
1.	Revolt in the father's house; flight to Emar.	Murder of Ahaz; his entire family is massacred by Athaliah; Joash escapes.
2.	For 'seven' years Idrimi keeps hidden in Ammiya, while someone (a usurper) reigns in Aleppo.	For 'six' years Joash keeps hidden in the temple, while the usurper Athaliah reigns in Jerusalem.
3.	Idrimi is recognised as the son of their lord by the refugees (who will eventually act as troops to retake the throne).	Jehoiada causes Joash to be recognised as the king's son by the Carites and the guards (who will eventually act as troops to retake the throne).
4.	'In the seventh year' Idrimi retakes the throne by force of arms.	'In the seventh year' Joash (helped by Jehoiada) retakes the throne by force of arms.
5.	The people are happy.	The people are happy.
6.	Pact between Barattarna and the new king, in the presence of the people.	Pact between Yahweh and the new king, in the presence of the people.
7.	Cultic reforms.	Cultic reforms.
8.	The reign lasts 'twenty' years in total.	The reign lasts 'forty' years in total.

Features of the same narrative pattern can be identified in other stories – although in a less systematic sequence – and always relate to an irregular succession to the throne. Similar themes can be detected in the framework of a longer and more complex narrative in the Apology of Hattushili III (Goetze 1925: 1930).[2] King Muwatalli dies (analogous to theme no. 1), and for 'seven' years, during which Urhi-Teshub reigns, Hattushili is in a marginal position (no. 2). In a dream all the dignitaries receive a divine revelation about the royal destiny of Hattushili (equivalent to no. 3). The text is cunningly evasive about the armed usurpation (no. 4). Also in Hattushili's case the favour of the people of Hattusha (no. 5) is emphasised, as well as the help of the divinity (Shaushka) and the king's dependence on her (no. 6). Finally, the text mentions his pious attitude when he becomes king and institutes reforms in the cult (no. 7).

Other stories from Syria and Anatolia, although incorporated into different specific contexts such as vassal treaties, reveal the same narrative structure. The Mitannian king Shattiwaza (Weidner 1923: nos 1–2) escapes from the massacre of his family in which his father dies (no. 1), and finds asylum with the Hittite king, Shuppiluliuma, while Artatama reigns in Mitanni (no. 2) until Shattiwaza retakes the throne by force of arms (no. 4). The theme of recognition (no. 3) is replaced here by his lawful designation as successor (cf. Liverani 1962). The theme of the pact with the great king (no. 6) is emphasised by the very nature of the text as a treaty, while themes nos 5, 7, and 8 are absent because they are not relevant. More simply, Benteshina, king of Amurru (Weidner 1923: n.9), loses the throne (no. 1), finds asylum with Hattushili (no. 2), and retakes the throne (no. 4). Mashhuiluwa of the Anatolian kingdom of Arzawa (Friedrich 1926–30: I, no. 3)[3] is driven away by his brothers (no. 1), and is received by Shuppiluliuma (no. 2), who eventually (re)instates him on his father's throne (no. 4). By their very nature the last two texts stress theme no. 6 (pact with the great king). These stories are so typical of the Hittite world that they are summed up in the astrological omen that states: 'The king's son, who had been driven away, will come back and retake his father's throne' (*KUB* VIII 1: ii 7–8).[4]

3 USURPATION AND LEGITIMATION

The Idrimi and Joash stories, as well as related examples, are characterised by two usurpations: a first usurpation (no. 1) in which the protagonist is the victim, and a second one (no. 4) through which the protagonist attains power. Usurpation is an act that can be defined and evaluated morally in different, even opposing ways,

---

2   The relevant passage is iii 38–iv 40. On the propaganda themes in the Hattushili text, see Archi 1971 (but I disagree with the comparison tabulated on p. 189). See also Wolf 1967.

3   On political 'death' and 'resurrection' in texts like those of Benteshina and Mashhuiluwa see Wijngaards 1967.

4   Translated by Friedrich 1925–26: I, 27; Archi 1966: 77–8. It is significant that the detail on the expulsion and return is a Hittite addition, not present in the Akkadian prototype of this omen.

according to the point of view of the narrative and to the act's relation to previous events. It is morally ambiguous, but always highly significant. In this, it differs from ordinary succession according to the simple mechanisms of the time, whereby the king designates as his heir one of his sons, who then succeeds him after his death (cf. Liverani 1974c: 335–8). In this way the transfer of power is not salient: the identity of the ruler changes, but the son assumes the role of the father, within the framework of family continuity centred on inheritance, and retains the appropriate possessions and powers. Confronted with an ordinary succession, public opinion does not react, it is not troubled, and undergoes no crisis. By contrast, where there is usurpation, public opinion perceives a change not only in the person, but also in the family line. The traditional role of a single family is appropriated by people who were outsiders before. One might say that public opinion is not disturbed by a change of person within a role, but by a change of role within a person.[5] In order to deal with the perturbation of public opinion, the usurper always needs some justification or legitimation, which the natural heir does not need.[6] This need stimulates the production of apologetically coloured royal autobiographies like those of Idrimi and Hattushili.

As we know them, each of these stories aims to justify the 'second' usurpation, the more recent one, the one whose instigator is the protagonist, and which is currently troubling public opinion. The 'first' usurpation is not necessarily linked to the second one in the real course of events; what matters is that it is cited as a justification for the second one, that it is utilised in order to legitimise the protagonist. Indeed, the only way in which the protagonist can transform his own usurpation – a fact that is in itself negative – into a legitimate action is by showing that it was really not a usurpation but a restoration. Since the past situation provides the model of what is correct, a single departure from its pattern can only be viewed negatively; but two departures, the second being opposed to the first one, will result in the re-establishment of the proper situation (cf. Liverani 1973a: 187–8; 1973b: 287–90). Two views of the same event are possible: (1) The antagonist will identify the ideal past with his own reign and consider the protagonist's usurpation as a lapse from good to evil, a phase of disturbance. (2) The protagonist, by contrast, will identify the ideal past with the reign of his father, the antagonist's usurpation being the phase of disturbance and lapse from good to

---

5   In the ancient Near East, the reversal of a person's role is a stereotypical motif indicative of trouble. Suffice it to recall the recurrent statement: 'the wealthy will become poor, the poor will become wealthy', which spread from Egypt (Wilson in Pritchard 1969: 441: ii 4–5) to Babylon (Biggs in Pritchard 1969: 607: iv 15), or the blame that is always attached to the enthronement of a 'son of a nobody'. On the overturning of a man's destiny, see Fensham 1971.

6   It should be noted that the 'people of the land' do not intervene in political events, except where there is an irregular succession or a dynastic crisis: cf. de Vaux 1964: 169–70; Tadmor 1968: 65–6.

evil. His own action will finally re-establish the ideal situation in a re-conversion from evil to good (cf. Bremond 1966, esp. chart a on p. 61).

If the second usurpation is to be presented as eliminating the first one, the persons involved should be the same but in reversed roles. The victim in theme no. 1 should be the usurper in theme no. 4, and the usurper in theme no. 1 should be the victim in theme no. 4. This necessary chiasm cannot always be embodied in one and the same individual, but it is important that it be realised within the same family, in the father–son sequence. The most frequent case is that of the protagonist's father being the victim of the first usurpation and the protagonist retaking, through the second usurpation, the 'father's throne' that belongs to him by inheritance but was denied him until then.[7]

The central problem is to ensure that events fit the pre-established sequence into which they are to be inserted. The connection of the first usurpation to the second can be real or artificial (with all the subjectivity involved in this distinction). Those who wish to legitimise their position, by transforming an usurpation into a re-establishment, can use two strategies: either theme no. 1 can be linked to theme no. 4 through a pseudo-recognition; or else one and the same role can be split into two, by giving to one person the merits and rights that really belong to someone else. An analysis of these two possibilities will help us to evaluate the reliability of the interpretations given by Idrimi and Joash in their stories.

4 HIDING AND RECOGNITION

The central theme in the plot is no. 3, which can be defined as 'recognition'. On its basis the second usurpation comes to be considered a reversal of the first one. The recognition identifies the victim of the first usurpation with the instigator of the second one – who can also be his direct and legitimate heir. The opportunity for 'role-playing' is offered by the previous, inseparable theme, which can be defined as 'hiding'. Hiding has various forms: flight, disappearance, or death. In all cases it is a mechanism whereby the victim of the first usurpation disappears from the stage and is eliminated from action in the eyes of the 'audience', that is, of public opinion. Recognition cancels out the hiding and presents the entire development of the plot anew in strictly theatrical terms.[8] A hero coming from a distance (Idrimi), or a child coming out of a hiding-place (Joash), is recognised as

---

7   The inheritance of roles is the reason for physically eliminating all the members of the deposed king's family. The usurper wishes to ensure that no heir could in turn reverse the cycle through another usurpation/restoration.

8   Note the importance of recognition in Aristotle's theory of drama: cf. Wehrli 1936, esp. 35–45, 114–7. I am grateful to Prof. L. E. Rossi for his valuable advice on this point.

someone whose death was taken for granted as having occurred – in a physical or at least in a political sense – and who is now able to vindicate his rights.

Even where narrative and historical facts truly correspond to each other, this theme is not without ideological implications. Indeed it effectively detaches the hero from the troubled phase, so that he is uncontaminated by the evil prevailing after the first usurpation. He can put an end to the negative phase because he is not responsible and returns from afar innocent and fit at once to transform evil into good.[9] It can also be observed that the hiding phase always involves the female line of the hero's family, either through members of older generations or through marriage.[10] Idrimi finds shelter with his mother's relatives, Joash is hidden by an aunt (but a paternal aunt, since the antagonist's side enlisted the mother's family), Shattiwaza and Benteshina marry the daughters of their protectors, and so on. The sociohistoric reason for this pattern is evident: in a patrilocal society a disturbance in the hero's household eliminates (as victims) all the members of the paternal branch, and the hero finds refuge through the solidarity of maternal relatives residing elsewhere. Moreover, the feminine character of the sphere in which he hides helps to shape the phase as a second upbringing or even a rebirth. The hero, who is politically – if not physically – 'dead' after the first usurpation, is reborn through hiding, which is characterised as a physical gestation and moral upbringing and is consequently entrusted to a woman. Only through the 'recognition' does the hero fully recover – or acquire – his personality, freeing himself from the family and feminine protection and confronting his own fate.[11] If the hero is already an adult – or has already reigned – at the time of the first usurpation, then the hiding acquires a matrimonial character, but an uxorilocal one (contrary to the customs of the time). It is unbalanced in the sense that it accords increased prestige and power to the wife's family, with the father-in-law assuming a directive role and some features of the hero's father, who was eliminated by the first usurpation.

---

[9] This is why the king issues edicts and actual measures, rectifying a situation of disorder, either at the beginning of his reign, as soon as he is in a position to take steps (as in the '*mīšarum*' edicts issued in their first years by Old Babylonian kings), or when the king has returned after a long absence (as in the Tudhaliya edict studied by von Schuler 1959), or as soon as the king is informed of disorder (as in the typical opening of the Egyptian *Königsnovelle*: 'One came to inform His Majesty that ...'; cf. Hermann 1938: 12–13; Grapow 1949: 61–3). In all these cases the king has no responsibility for the evil, either because he was not yet king, or because he was unaware of it. As soon as he knows, he cares: the connections between evil and the king's absence, and between good and the king's presence, are assured.

[10] On this point, our stories fit precisely the motif, found in Greek literature and mythology, studied by Gernet 1932; cf. esp. 20 on a genre story which is identical to ours, and generally on the fact that the child is entrusted to the mother's family.

[11] On the initiatory character of stories about (re)capturing the throne, see chapter 4; Gernet 1932: 24.

The psychological and sociological implications are valid, whether or not the narrative corresponds to the actual events. But the main value of the sequence hiding-recognition lies in its suitability for some deliberately equivocal strategies that enable the narrative's propagandistic force to be exploited – a force not immediately detectable in the course of the events themselves. In the case of Idrimi, the recognition seems to be beyond suspicion: the 'second' Idrimi, the hero who conquers the throne of Alalah, is really the same individual as the 'first' Idrimi, the child who escaped from Aleppo with his family. The recognition is split into two phases: Idrimi is first recognised by the exiles, then by his brothers. Thanks to the latter testimony it is difficult to imagine that there was any impersonation, since that would have been generally known. Nevertheless, the recognition of Idrimi as the son of the former king of Aleppo is used equivocally and with bias, in order to legitimise Idrimi's position on the throne of Alalah. It is evident that Idrimi did not re-establish the ideal situation that had existed before the first usurpation, he merely re-established his own royal position. The instigator of the first usurpation retained the throne of Aleppo, since he was a different person from the king of Alalah, who was the victim of the second usurpation. If the latter had survived, he would have certainly considered Idrimi's action to be a 'first' usurpation, a disturbance of the proper state of affairs. He would not have accepted the logic of Idrimi's argument, which is based on events in which he did not participate.

In the case of Joash, the situation is different and, frankly, appears distinctly suspect. No one could truly recognise the child Joash, who was newly born when he was hidden and a boy only 'seven' years old at the time of his recognition. First the Carites and the guards, and then the entire people, do not 'recognise' someone who was already known, they simply accept the testimony of Jehoiada. But the latter is the direct beneficiary of the identification, thanks to which he will in reality reign in the name of the boy Joash. If one views the matter from the perspective of Jehoiada, the artificial character of the recognition becomes evident. Jehoiada wants to usurp Athaliah's throne, but his usurpation would be considered illegitimate, since he has no claim at all to the kingship. He does not possess the means in his own person to transform the usurpation into a restoration. Athaliah's character, however, is well suited to such a transformation, since she attained power through a massacre, and so has all the characteristics of an evil antagonist. So Jehoiada decides to split his role into two persons, himself retaining the active part in the 'second' usurpation and the benefits of power, while allotting to another person the legitimising link with the 'first' usurpation. He produces a boy, 'seven' years old, presents him as the legitimate heir of Ahaz, and so gives legitimacy to his own action. No one can check the personal identity of the young Joash, whose concealment would remain transparently artificial even if it had taken place in reality.

5 ROLES AND CHARACTERS

The case of Jehoiada introduces the problem that the same role may be distributed over more than one person. What is important for our analysis is to determine what the fixed roles in the narrative are, the 'functions' in Propp's terminology (Propp 1966, esp. 85–9 on the splitting of functions among characters and their clustering into 'spheres of action'). The narrative model to which Idrimi and Joash adapt themselves requires three basic roles: the protagonist-hero, the antagonist-usurper, and the protector – as well as the people, with its chorus-like function of approval or disapproval.

Examples of a protagonist who is personally the victim of the first usurpation and the instigator of the second one are not very frequent. This is the case, for example, with Benteshina, king of Amurru, who loses his throne to the advantage of Shapili (at the behest of the Great King Muwatalli) and recovers it at the expense of the same Shapili (at the behest of the Great King Hattushili). Here the theme of hiding (by the protector Hattushili) is present, and is important for keeping the protagonist outside the negative phase; but there is no recognition, which would be unnecessary since the protagonist had already reigned and was known to everyone as the legitimate king. This enables us to realise that the theme of recognition is the signal of a problematic situation. The case of Benteshina is, however, exceptional. More often the role of protagonist is split between father and son: the father succumbs in the first usurpation, and the son recovers the throne in the second. This is the case with Idrimi, and also with Shattiwaza and Mashhuiluwa. The role of the son as heir to his father is clear and obvious. Yet we must note that there are (or may be) several sons, while there is only one heir. Now we have no proof that Idrimi or Shattiwaza were the heirs designated by their respective fathers. Moreover, Idrimi's insistence on his having been the youngest son demonstrates his low standing in his family's hierarchy of authority and responsibility. As for Shattiwaza, it is revealing that he asks to be designated as heir by the usurper himself (Artatama): clearly he could not claim to have been designated by his father. Finally, the role of protagonist in Joash's story is more complex: Ahaz plays this role in theme no. 1 (as victim of the first usurpation), Joash in themes no. 2 and no. 3 (hiding and recognition), and Jehoiada in theme no. 4 (as instigator of the second usurpation). In this case, correspondence to the narrative pattern is achieved through a very marked manipulation of the historical events, a manipulation that must be ascribed to Jehoiada.

The role of antagonist can also be transmitted by inheritance from father to son. In the story of Shattiwaza, Artatama is the instigator of the first usurpation and his son Shuttarna is the victim of the second one. Shattiwaza clearly intends to attach all the negative aspects of the role to Shuttarna, thus freeing Artatama, for political reasons that we can only partly understand.[12] The role can, however, also be unitary, as in the story of Benteshina, who loses and retakes the throne, both times in relation to Shapili. It is interesting to note also that the opposition between Benteshina and Shapili is replicated at a higher level of authority by the opposition between Hattushili and Muwatalli. The higher level interferes here in the sphere of the antagonist, as it more usually does in that of the protagonist (through the protector). In the Joash story, the role of the antagonist is basically unitary, in the person of Athaliah; yet Jehu, the murderer of Joash's father, also plays a role. In the case of Idrimi, on the contrary, the function is sharply divided between two persons who are neither related by blood nor otherwise connected (so far as we know); the artificial character of Idrimi's account is therefore evident. The instigator of the revolt against Idrimi's father in Aleppo plays the role of antagonist in theme no. 1, while an unknown king driven out of Alalah by Idrimi plays the role in theme no. 4. The complete silence of Idrimi about this second antagonist's identity implicitly proves that the 'revenge' took place at the expense of an unworthy person.

The relevance of the role of 'protector' is evident in the texts about Shatti-waza, Mashhuiluwa, and Benteshina – all of them Hittite in redaction – which were issued only because the protector needed to emphasise his role in the action. Benteshina's protector is Hattushili in a unitary way, although with possible appropriation of Urhi-Teshub's merits (cf. Klengel 1969: 241–2 n.123). Shatti-waza's protector is Shuppiluliuma, but the latter's son Piyashili carried out some practical (military) actions. In both cases – and in the case of Mashhuiluwa – the protector is also the father-in-law of the protagonist, who contracts the marriage tie while hidden. He is also the 'Great King', that is, the representative of the higher level of authority, the arbiter of events. Idrimi, by contrast, has neither protector nor father-in-law: heroically, he accomplishes the entire process alone and unaided. The Great King Barattarna exercises the function of higher arbiter of the events, but he appears on the scene as an adversary rather than as a protector. Finally, the hider/protector of Joash is obviously Jehoiada, while the function of higher authority is transferred to the divine level (Yahweh), as also in Hattushili's Apology where it is the goddess Shaushka.

The varied configuration and partition of theoretically unitary functions among several persons is a direct result of adapting to a preconceived plot events that have their own historical shape and are complicated by a varied network of political and personal relationships. The texts aim to link these different relationships in the most appropriate way, in order to make them fit the purpose of propaganda to the protagonist's advantage.

---

12 Shuppiluliuma had previously stipulated a pact with Artatama, and he seems still to have felt to some extent bound to it.

6 POLITICAL ACTION AND PROPAGANDA

I have emphasised sufficiently the 'theatrical' features in stories of this kind, especially in that of Joash. The stage is set in the father's house, the hiding is offstage, and the recognition is a return to the stage. The time is self-contained (with a precise beginning and end), and subdivided into three 'acts' characterised respectively as good, evil, and good, with dramatic breaks from each one to the next (the two usurpations), and the final triumph of justice. Roles and characters are fixed in their actions and in their moral worth. The final solution emerges through a *coup de théâtre* (the recognition) functioning as a *deus ex machina*. It is no coincidence that many of these features constitute the typical structure of classical drama (cf. n.3 above). To be sure, this theatrical character has no 'ludic' function; the audience does not choose to play its part as audience for a strictly limited time; it is not ready to leave when the 'play' is over.[13] The theatrical character of these stories has instead a political function; and the audience, for whom the *mise-en-scène* is intended, is the political community as a whole, which needs to be convinced not for a fixed and limited time but throughout its life. The coincidence of political action and drama springs only from the elementary character of archaic techniques of persuasion. The theatrical character of these stories is simply the way in which they are presented for propagandistic purposes.

Already in the case of Idrimi, the deceptive nature of the propagandistic presentation is evident: he usurps the throne of Alalah and tries to legitimise his action through the memory of his father, who had been driven out of Aleppo. The 'seven-year'-long opposition of Barattarna, the very need to address his subjects in an apologetic text, and finally the need – or psychological 'complex' – he feels to be considered the equal of other kings,[14] all these elements prove that Idrimi's action had produced negative opinions and reactions. He therefore decides to propose *a posteriori* a propagandistic account of events that were not in any way 'theatrical' in their original occurrence.

The case of Joash is different, even though the propagandistic purposes are similarly evident. The true 'protagonist' in the political action is Jehoiada, who, well aware that he could not legitimise his position *a posteriori*, finds a way to legitimise it while achieving it, by manufacturing the figure of a legitimate heir, who escaped from a massacre and suddenly reappeared. The theatricality is not just in the way the facts are presented in 'literary' fashion after having being accomplished. The theatricality is the very way in which the political action is

---

[13] Compare Huizinga 1964: 29 ff.: the game as isolated in space, time, and rules from ordinary life; 209–11: ludic character of theatre.

[14] Lines 81–84, where I think we can speak of an 'inferiority complex' of the new king, with his doubtful legitimacy, toward other kings who are already established and confident in their positions.

performed. The *coup de théâtre* of presenting an unknown child – first to the guards and then to all the subjects – as if he were the heir to the throne, did indeed take place at the critical moment of the action.

The aims of political propaganda also explain the interaction of three superimposed levels of political action and evaluation. The Great King or God belongs to the uppermost level; the protagonist and antagonist belong to a middle level; the common people belong to the lowest level. The protagonist has to establish his position toward both the uppermost and the lowest levels. He uses the support of the people in order to convince the Great King or God, and the favour of the Great King or God in order to convince the people. The texts of these stories are basically written in order to convince the lowest level, but they retain vestiges of both aims. Theme no. 5 (the population is happy) proves legitimation from below, and is immediately followed by theme no. 6 (the pact with the Great King or God) which proves legitimation from above. It is not an accident that the pact is enacted in the presence of the people, who are provided with an additional reason for being convinced.[15] But it should also be noted that – by a slightly less coarse propagandistic device – theme no. 5, popular favour, is emphasised in order to convince *the people itself*, in order to incorporate into the community's memory a favourable reaction that may not have been apparent when the events took place.

The propagandistic aims of the Joash story seem clear enough, as do the points of precise literary contact with similar presentations (Idrimi and Hattushili). It is then perhaps not too speculative to conclude with the hypothesis that an inscription (or whatever kind of text would have been destined for popular diffusion)[16] also underlay the biblical text. In this inscription Jehoiada would have legitimised Joash's ascent to the throne by reworking the facts according to the well-known story of the young prince who escaped from a massacre, was hidden, recognised, and finally put back on the throne that legitimately belonged to him. As we have seen, already in earlier centuries such stories were surely known at a popular level and from time to time entered the official literature. They could have been familiar to the people of Jerusalem in the ninth century, and thus have

---

15 On the conditioning of Syro-Palestinian kingship from above and below, see Liverani 1974c: 336–44. It should be noted, with Tadmor 1968: 61 (cf. also Malamat 1965: 36–37), that only twice in the history of Israel was a pact established between king and people, namely for the enthronement of David and of Joash: 'In the first case the Davidic dynasty was established, in the second it was restored'. Yet in the second case too it was a matter of establishing a new dynasty. On the problem of Joash's double pact with Yahweh and with the people, see Kutsch 1973: 163ff.

16 2 Kings 11 (together with the chronological data in 12.1–2) would derive its content from the hypothetical royal inscription which I postulate here. Chapter 12, on the relations between Joash and Jehoiada, has a different origin.

constituted the emotional grounds for granting the figure of the young Joash sympathetic support.[17]

★ ★ ★

Two historical consequences seem worth noting. First, the continuity of the 'House of David', which was extraordinarily significant for the royal ideology of Judah, can reasonably be considered to have been interrupted by the massacre ordered by Athaliah. We have no reasons to believe that the unknown child used by Jehoiada for his goals was really one of Ahaz's sons. Second, we cannot accept that the chronology of the reigns of Athaliah and Joash is recorded in the biblical passage. The 'seven' and 'forty' years attributed to them by the text, and accepted – as such, or with some arbitrary corrections – by all scholars,[18] are not reliable. They clearly spring from time measurements of a fictional and non-historical character, as is typical of this kind of story. It is a literary motif to state that 'during six years he (= Joash) remained with her, hidden in the temple of Yahweh, while Athaliah reigned over the land. But in the seventh year...' (2 Kings 11:3–4). It is used to point to a change in status, and also occurs in the Idrimi inscription and in Hattushili's Apology, at the same functional position in the plot (cf. Liverani 1967b). As for the figure of 'forty' years for the reign of Joash, it is certainly a round number, meaning one generation, and can be compared to the 'twenty' years of Idrimi. Such an indication would be inconceivable in chronicles or similar sources that were used by the redactor of the book of Kings. But we can easily imagine it to occur in a propagandistic inscription, one written even before the end of the protagonist's reign (when its length was still unknown!). The purpose then was simply to state that 'he lived happily ever after' (that is, his entire life), as in a fairy tale.

---

[17] The problems studied here can be compared in general with the more numerous studies on the narrative of David's succession (2 Sam. 9–20; 1 Kings 1–2). See in particular the fairy tale motifs (which are also propaganda motifs) that have been pointed out in this narrative, and its relation to the Egyptian *Königsnovelle*. On this set of problems I restrict myself to quoting the critical analysis by Whybray 1968.

[18] Compare the synoptic chart of Thiele 1951: 254: everyone assigns 6 to 7 years to Athaliah and 40 years to Joash (except Albright and Lewy, who 'correct' the number to 38).

8

Messages, women, and hospitality: inter-tribal communication in Judges 19–21*

INTRODUCTION

Two stories at the end of the biblical book of Judges are usually considered to be appendices, as they do not mention any of the Judges. Their insertion there was probably due to the fact that they are said to deal with the 'days when there was no king in Israel'. The second story, told in chapters 19 to 21, is quite long and complicated. While a mundane retelling does not do it justice, it may help the reader to follow the discussion in the chapter here. A Levite from Ephraim has been abandoned by his concubine, who returned to her father's house in Bethlehem. The Levite goes to reclaim her and after leaving his father-in-law's house with the woman, has to spend the night at Gibeah in Benjaminite territory. Only an old man, who himself is from Ephraim, is willing to talk to the Levite and puts him up in his house. That night the men of Gibeah demand that they be allowed to have sexual intercourse with the Levite, who offers them his concubine instead. After she is abused all night long, she dies.

When the Levite finds her the next morning, he takes her home and cuts the body up into twelve pieces, sending one to each of the tribes of Israel to summon them. At their assembly the tribes decide to demand that the men of Gibeah be surrendered, and when rejected they attack the Benjaminites at Gibeah. They win by leading the main body of the Benjaminite army into an ambush, taking the city behind their back, and burning it down. They massacre the men of Benjamin. Moreover, they swear an oath never to give brides to the remaining Benjaminites.

The survival of that tribe is thus in danger, and in order to obtain women the people of Jabesh-Gilead are attacked and slaughtered but for 400 virgins who are given to the Benjaminites. As this number does not suffice, and the oath that no woman should be given to Benjamin cannot be broken, an arrangement is made whereby the Benjaminites can seize girls at the annual festival of Shiloh and thus obtain brides.

* Originally published as 'Messaggi, donne, ospitalità. Comunicazione intertribale in Giud. 19-21', *Studi Storico-Religiosi* 1979/III, 303–41.

The chapter translated here was originally published in 1979, long before a feminist approach became fashionable in biblical studies. It discusses many topics that have become the concern of later feminist scholarship, such as the anonymity of the concubine, her rape, and her dismemberment (eg., Exum 1993; Stone 1995). Unfortunately, the Italian article is rarely acknowledged, so its republication will serve a purpose. Liverani uses this story to discuss a wide array of other topics, including hospitality, reciprocity in the exchange of gifts and women, interior and exterior spaces, and manners of communication. He has continued to study those in his subsequent work, and they are most elaborately discussed in the book he published in 1990 entitled *Prestige and Interest*.

★ ★ ★ ★

1 NON-VERBAL COMMUNICATION IN JUDGES 19–21

1.1 TWELVE PIECES OF A CORPSE

1.1.1 One of the strangest and crudest features in the harsh story of Judges 19–21[1] is the manner in which the Levite summons an assembly of the twelve tribes of Israel:

> Back in his home (the Levite) took a knife, and seizing (the corpse of) his concubine he cut her, limb by limb, into twelve pieces, and sent her throughout all the territory of Israel. He gave order to his messengers saying: 'Behold what you have to say to all the Israelites: has such a thing ever been seen, since the day Israel came out of Egypt and until this day? Consider, take counsel, and pass judgement'. And all people who saw said: 'Never such a thing happened, nor has been seen, since the day Israel came out of Egypt and until this day!'   (Judges 19: 29–30)

A passage in the book of Samuel shows that we are not dealing with an unprecedented message, whose decoding is left only to the shrewdness or imagination of the addressee, but with a recurring symbolic procedure. In order to summon the tribes to the aid of Jabesh of Gilead, Saul makes use of a similar procedure:

> He took a pair of oxen and cut them into pieces, and sent them through messengers in all the territory of Israel, with these words: 'Whoever will not march behind Saul, his oxen will be dealt with in this way!'   (1 Sam. 11: 7)

---

[1] Within the book of Judges chapters 19–21 constitute a narrative unit, with a stratification of its own. This can be summarised as the presence of 'old' materials, basically unitary in chapter 19 and twofold in origin in chapters 20–21, with a late, post-deuteronomistic redaction. Beside the standard commentaries (starting at least with Burney 1918: 442–58), see especially Noth 1930: 162–170; Fernandez 1931: 297–315; Besters 1965. Schunk 1963: 67–8 suggested a different reconstruction (the basic tradition plus four layers of redaction).

The agreement between the two passages makes clear that this was a specific procedure for summoning Israel's tribes on the occasion of a military mobilisation. It can easily be assumed that the normal procedure (if it was normal at all) was Saul's, that is, the use of animals. In the other case, the use of a human corpse adds a special connotation of seriousness and uniqueness, causing the people that are summoned to assume some elements of impiety and horror in the episode that provoked the convocation itself.

A symbolic message of this kind certainly possesses a plurality of meanings. It can be decoded differently, and adapted to different events. Yet the basic structure of the message is related especially to a correspondence between 'pieces' delivered and addressees.[2] As the twelve pieces of the animal or the human corpse constitute parts of a unit, so the twelve tribes, which are the addressees of the message, constitute parts of a unit (the 'tribal league') and have to come together. Each tribal delegate, perhaps holding the 'piece' received as convocation, goes to the meeting in order to reconstitute the complete organism. The distribution of 'pieces' is therefore a procedure for summoning an organism, which in theory forms a unit, even if it is spread, in fact, over the territory.

1.1.2 Saul's 'object-based' convocation is accompanied by a verbal message decoding its symbolism. The verbal message establishes a threatening parallel between the oxen used for the message and the oxen belonging to the individual tribes. The message thus becomes not a mere convocation, but a threat in case the convocation is not accepted. The verbal decoding is secondary and accessory: it is an additional simile, not at all essential, and only aimed at further stressing how urgent and important the convocation is. But it would be incomprehensible in itself, if the primary meaning of the message were not that of calling an assembly. The verbal addition presumes that the addressee immediately understands that the ox delivered is a call to foregather.

The same holds even more for the passage in Judges 19. Here the added verbal message is only meant to emphasise the exceptional gravity of the affair, by qualifying it as 'never before seen'. In both cases we can say that the informative content is entrusted to the object-based part of the message, while the verbal part has a purely connotative function.[3] As supplementary element in the object-based message, the verbal message has only an accessory position. But it also effectively emphasises that the recourse to an object-based message is not

---

2   Compare also the explicit correspondence between the twelve tribes and the twelve pieces of Ahijah's mantle in 1 Kings 11:30–31. Gaster 1969: 443–4 based a contrary opinion on commonplace and irrelevant evidence. See also Crown 1974: 253–4; Grottanelli 1979: 30 and *passim*.

3   Note that the text says 'Never has such a thing been *seen*…', emphasising the object-based nature of the message.

due to the absence of verbal channels. Indeed, the messenger's words accompanying the delivery of the object demonstrate that a verbal channel is available. Therefore the recourse to an object-based message must have a value of its own. It certainly gives a greater solemnity and significance to a symbolic message when compared to the banality of common language. Yet there is probably a further purpose. It avoids any need for the messengers to enter into the content and the details of the case, which are to be discussed in the assembly, and cannot be anticipated in the call for convocation. This is especially true because (as we shall see in detail later) the use of verbal communication is reserved for the people who accepted the convocation, and not those who refused. Only people who accept the call to assemble will eventually be addressed through speech, while the convocation has to be kept at an allusive and strictly symbolic level.

It should be noted that the Levite is to explain the 'unprecedented crime' only at the opening of the assembly. Up to that moment the tribal delegates formally ignore the matter (even if informally the news must have been passed on through many channels). Strictly speaking, what is defined as 'never before seen' by the messengers and those who are summoned is the manner of convocation itself – namely, the use of a human body instead of that of an animal – not the case which produced it. But obviously a horrifying convocation presupposes a horrifying event.

1.1.3 The integration of verbal and object-based messages is normal in the ancient Near East. Since the verbal messages themselves are lost forever (cf. Liverani 1978), the most abundant and richest documentation is provided by letters. There are letters sent in order to accompany gifts, gifts sent in order to accompany letters (cf. Zaccagnini 1973), messengers charged with adding words of clarification and emphasis to letters (Oppenheim 1965: 254; in general Nielsen 1954: 29–30), and letters of greeting so short and stereotypical that the messenger could easily have done without the written support, were it not for its symbolic value (compare, e.g., the Ugaritic letters in Herdner 1963: 51 and 52).[4] We could say that a letter, a written message, which should be considered as the support for long-distance transmission of a verbal message – and so identical with the message – becomes a sort of object-based message. It does so because of its physical character (as is especially true of clay tablets), and because decoding of written texts was neither generalised nor direct, and necessitated recourse to a highly

---

[4] There is a popular aetiology in Mesopotamia of the letter as a means to overcome the difficulty in memorising a lengthy message (Kramer 1952: 36–7: ll. 503–505). This is neither historically accurate (the first letters were very short administrative messages) nor anthropologically exhaustive.

specialised interpreter.[5] The written message was in itself unreadable and highly obscure, if it were not accompanied by words: the words of the scribe reading the letter, or the interpreter translating it, or the messenger adding comments and explanations, and emphasising important points.

In general we have the impression that the transmission of a purely object-based message, unaccompanied by words, or the transmission of a purely verbal message, unaccompanied by objects, would be considered simplistic and impolite, devoid of connotative relevance. This is quite clear in the case of gifts and letters: a gift without a letter or accompanying words is useless, since it is ineffective in initiating the personal and social contacts that are the very aim of gift-exchange. The gift could be effective as a simple trade item, provided for merely mercantile or financial reasons. Conversely, a message unaccompanied by gifts is ineffective in maintaining contacts or in obtaining answers, because of its implicit coarseness and hostility. If it is the custom to accompany letters with gifts, the absence of a gift expresses a precise message, one of hostility, or at least of tension (cf. Nougayrol 1955: 6).

What is evident in the exchange of gifts and letters of a diplomatic nature, can also be the case with other kinds of communication, like the convocation to an assembly. A purely verbal convocation would be defective, because it would be considered coarse, banal, or 'feeble'. A purely object-based convocation would run the risk of remaining equivocal. Through the integration of the two, a convocation is issued, that is simultaneously comprehensible and endowed with the necessary significance and connotative relevance.

1.1.4 The use of a human corpse as the support for a message is not exceptional in Israel and the ancient Near East in general. It mostly has two precise purposes: either as a proof of somebody's death or as a public warning (the 'propaganda of terror'). In the first case, the head is mostly used as the part of the body that can be recognised and identified. Ishbaal's head is brought as demonstration of his death to King David. But the executioners, who expect a reward, themselves are killed, and their bodies are exposed with hands and feet cut off (2 Sam. 4: 7–8; and see n.9 below). The head of Sheba is cut off and thrown over the city walls in order to prove that he was executed (2 Sam. 20: 21–22). The Elamite king, Umman-Haldash, sends to Ashurbanipal the corpse of Nabu-bel-shumate (covered with salt in order to preserve it during the trip) together with the head of the groom who killed him. Ashurbanipal has the head cut off from Nabu-bel-shumate's corpse, in order to 'make him more dead than before' (*ARAB* II 815).

---

5   Compare the different but relevant considerations on the prestige of the epistolary message by Longo 1978: 523–31.

When corpses and heads are numerous, it is no longer the identification of a single person that matters, but the general effect of horror. The heads of Ahab's 70 sons are brought to Jehu in order to prove both that they were punished and that Samaria had submitted (2 Kings 10: 7). But Jehu arranges the same 70 heads in two piles outside the entrance as an explicit denunciation of the Samarians' responsibility – I killed your lord, but you killed 70 more persons! – and as an implicit threat for the future. This episode introduces us to the other and more widespread use of corpses, that of horror. The motif of terror appears frequently in the Neo-Assyrian royal inscriptions (cf. Saggs 1963: 149–150). Piles of severed heads (*ARAB* I 221, 445, 447, 463, 480, 559, 605; II 254, etc.), impaled heads and bodies (I 472, 478, 480, 499, 585, 605, 776; II 830, 844, etc.), or skins spread over the walls (I 441, 443; II 773, 844), all are stereotyped threatening messages to potential enemies and possible traitors. When addressed to the Assyrian public rather than to enemies, the message of horror becomes one of exultation. The severed head of the Elamite king, Teumman, is paraded around in order to announce the 'good news' (*a-na bu-us-su-rat*) of his death to the Assyrians (Streck 1916: 312–13; also Piepkorn 1933: 74), exactly like the severed head of Saul announced the 'good news' (*le-baśśēr*) of his death to the Philistines (1 Sam. 31:9–10).[6] The horrifying or admonitory – or else triumphal – exhibit was not limited to Assyria. Famous examples come from different areas and periods, from the Mari kingdom[7] to Tuthmosid Egypt.[8]

I do not think it is an accident that the punitive/admonitory exhibiting of corpses – which brings about some kind of dismemberment and is the opposite of burial[9] – is mostly related to cases of treachery. The traitor overturned the 'natural' sociopolitical hierarchy, therefore he cannot claim a regular burial and

6   On this term see McCarthy 1964: 26–33; Fisher 1966. An etymological connection between *bśr* 'to announce' and *bśr* 'flesh' is generally denied; this does not rule out the possibility of word plays and allusions.

7   In *ARM* II 48 the head of a prisoner was cut off and 'marched around so that people would be afraid' (19: *li-sa-ḫi-ru aš-šum ṣa-bu-um i-pa-al-la-aḫ*) and 'that they would assemble immediately' (20: *ar-ḫi-iš i-pa-aḫ-ḫu-ra-am*). The exhibition of a corpse in order to obtain a military gathering and its obvious decoding 'whoever does not gather will be dealt with in this way' are a good parallel to the decoding of 1 Sam. 11: 7, presented above; cf. Wallis 1952.

8   *ARE* II 797: Amenophis II sacrificed seven Asiatic rulers and, for celebratory purposes, had six of their corpses exposed on the walls of Thebes, and one on the walls of Napata in Nubia.

9   There is no need to insist on this point, which is quite clear in the texts. I would note only that, besides the head, also hands and feet were considered as identifying parts and were therefore the objects of a symbolic burial. Compare 2 Kings 9: 35 ('They went to bury her [= Jezebel] but only her skull, hands and feet were found', the rest having been devoured by dogs) to Herodotus I 119 (Astyages shows Harpagus the head, hands and feet of his son, whose flesh he gave him to eat. Harpagus buries these remains). Cf. also *ARM* VI 37: a corpse is thrown into the river, but the head is cut off and buried in the normal fashion.

his corpse can be butchered in any way possible, including the typical anti-burial consisting of becoming food for dogs and pigs (a common curse against transgressors of oaths: Wiseman 1958: 63–6: vi 451.484). The case of the Levite's woman in Judges 19 is certainly different. It affects the victim and not the perpetrators of treachery, but perhaps in this case too the communicative use of the body hints at treachery.

So the object-based message organised by the Levite may seem to be an unusual message, but it becomes comprehensible through a wide range of allusions and equivalences located at different levels of consciousness. The twelve pieces indicate a 'summon for a military mobilisation'. There is an implicit equivalence 'woman = sacrificial victim' and a hint at 'treachery'. The news about the 'bloody deed' is obvious, while the 'unprecedented event' needs verbal decoding. All these elements together built up a picture not too different from the event they are meant to signify.

1.2 SIGNS, CONVENTIONS, POSTURES

1.2.1 The message of the corpse cut into pieces is not the only non-verbal message in the narrative of Judges 19–21. A virtual pattern-book of types of communication can be found there. Another visual and formalised message, also a part of normal conventions in antiquity (not only in the Near East), is the smoke signal on the occasion of the taking of a city, in this case Gibeah:

> There was this agreement (*môʿēd*) between the Israelite troops and those in ambush. When the latter made a smoke signal (*maśʾat ʿāšām*) rise from the city, the men of Israel engaged in battle should turn backwards… When the signal, a smoke column, began to rise from the city, the Benjaminites turned around and saw that their entire city was rising in flames to the sky. The men of Israel turned back and the Benjaminites were seized by panic, realising that their ruin was imminent.
>
> (Judges 20:38–41; on the topography see Rösel 1976)

There is a precise parallel for this case too. The same stratagem is said to have been used by Joshua while taking 'Ai (Josh. 8; see Rösel 1975). Not only the stratagem of the smoke signal, but also the battle and siege tactics as a whole are the same in the two episodes. They partake in a widespread literary motif and – why not? – in actual tactics of war as is shown by parallels from Classical anecdotal literature of *stratagemata* (quoted by Malamat 1978: 15–19).

The interest of the smoke signal rising from the captured city lies in its twofold value, as far as meaning and addressee are concerned. The agreed communicative function, addressed to friends, is a temporal definition (Hebrew *môʿēd* often has this meaning; cf. *THAT*, I, 742–6), in order to coordinate action between two parts of the army that are too distant to communicate by speech.

The decoding of the message is consequently as follows: we have taken the city; this is the moment for a counter-attack. The meaning is not too complicated, but it requires a previous agreement on how it should be decoded. It is a message in the full sense, agreed upon within the circle of addressers and addressees. The function as a temporal sign leaves free – or could do so – the choice of combustible material: an artificial fire would work just as well (cf. Frontinus III 10: 5, quoted by Malamat 1978: 18–9). But a second communicative function, not agreed upon (yet predicted), is addressed to the enemies. The information in this case is not transmitted in a symbolic way, but in the real one. It is: the city is burning, therefore it has been taken. The panic that spreads among the Benjaminite troops comes from the fact that their battle technique is based on rapid and direct sorties from a protected site, where they can find refuge if needed. Once their refuge is eliminated, they know that they are lost, even if they win the actual battle.[10] The success of the stratagem lies in the cumulative effect of both communications, in the synchronism not only between the two parts of the federal army, but also between their action and the Benjaminite panic – a panic due not to the encircling tactics but to the capture of their refuge.

1.2.2 To burn down a city in order to issue a signal is rare, even paradoxical. Yet, in a sense, it can be said that every burning city issues a significant message to men and gods.[11] On the other hand, it is worth recalling that in antiquity smoke (during the day) and fires (at night) are among the most usual forms of message (see, esp. Longo 1976). While different from the object-based messages that are endowed with a specific social and procedural prestige, smoke and fire messages have a purely technical advantage: that of immediate visibility from a distance. These signals by their very nature 'rise' (Hebrew *nś'*, Akkadian *našû*),[12] and so become visible. Their reach can be increased by making use of a chain of stations, covering an entire region or linking distant sites in a short time (cf. Longo 1976; Crown 1974). But smoke or fire messages cannot remain exclusive, previously agreed on by a small group. Unavoidably, such messages simultaneously reach both friends and enemies (or at least outsiders). When they are issued, one has to

---

10 As is well known, battles in antiquity were mostly decided by a sudden collapse of one side by panic or loss of morale. Casualties were limited and equally spread over the two parties up to that moment; then a massacre followed. Cf. Bouthoul 1970: 154–6.

11 See Güterbock 1964: 2 for an explicit example. In Thureau-Dangin 1912 the same expression is used for burning bushes as signals (150: *qi-da-at ab-ri*) and for the fire of the Haldia temple 'like a bush' (279: *ab-ri-iš a-qu-ud*).

12 Hebr. *maś'ēt* 'rising' (of fire), in the meaning of 'signal', is also used in Jer. 6: 1 and in the Lachish ostracon 4: 10, as well as in our passage Judg. 20:38.40. On Akkadian *našû* said of torches, smoke and fire signals, or the like, see *AHw* s.v. *našû(m)* I 1c; *CAD* N/2 s.v. *našû* A1b; Dossin 1938: 176 and 178.

take into account the agreed reactions of the friends and the predictable reactions of the enemies.

The main disadvantage of smoke or fire signals lies in their lack of flexibility. If there is no way to arrange for intermittent emissions of smoke or fire, which can create a more complex, or even very complex, code, the signal can transmit only a binary code of information: 'yes or no', indicated by its presence or absence (Longo 1976: 123 n.8, 130–1 n.27). Since the absence of smoke is the normal situation and its presence the abnormal, the kindling of fire and smoke naturally announces the beginning of an unusual situation. The message transmitted is therefore mostly a simple 'attention!' or 'mobilisation!' – and is decoded as such in some of the Mari letters.[13] We are not dealing with 'mysterious' fires kindled at night,[14] but with unequivocal and trite signs of alarm that possess all the usual complications of noise and redundancy in the transmission of information.[15] Indeed, when there is a case of a special danger, as when a fortress is under siege (Lachich ostraca), it is the absence of signals that is worrying. Apart from other pre-arranged meanings the smoke signal has the meaning 'we are still alive', or 'we still resist' (cf. Lemaire 1977: I, 113–7, 142).

1.2.3 Even the bodily pose of a person transmits a message. This does not even require a gesture, just a 'posture' or 'attitude':

> The Levite went in and sat down in the city square, but no man took them into his house to spend the night.   (Judges 19:15).

A stranger, a traveller, who sits in the village square at nightfall, clearly shows his intent to stop there (by means of analogy: he sits down) and his request to be hosted (by means of contrast: he stays in the open). He does not speak, he does not ask explicitly, because that is not necessary (his posture was 'telling' enough), and because speaking requires friendly relations that have yet to be established. In such a 'silent dialogue', the absence of an answer implies that the answer is negative. The fact that the people of Gibeah, though they see a stranger sitting in their

---

13 Dossin 1938. Cf. *CAD* D, s.v. *dipāru* e; I/J, s.v. *išātu* 3b. Explicit decodings are attested, as 'Help! Come and help!' (Dossin 1938: 181: 10–12) and as 'attention! The enemy is coming' (*ibid.*, 182: 21–2). Fire signals at the arrival of the enemy are also attested in Thureau-Dangin 1912: 40–1: 249–50 (on the interpretation, see *CAD* D, 157 e; A₁, 63 a).

14 In speaking about 'mystérieux signaux', Kupper (1957: 65) evidently adopted the attitude of the sources themselves (Dossin 1938: 178: 17–18: : *warkāt dipārātim šināti ul aprus*). The decoding seems obvious: the alarm signals when the enemy troops come closer (cf. Kupper himself, 57).

15 Agreement on the answer (Dossin 1938: 178: 16; 183: 11–13; 184–185), misunderstandings (182–183, where a signal interpreted as a request for help is to be corrected by a letter), repeated signals in order to avoid misunderstanding (183: 14–18), blackout (183–184, the remedy is a letter), useless signs (184), especially agreed meanings (185–186: 8–10), and so forth.

square, do not invite him in, does not signify refraining neutrally from being involved in a problem not of their concern. It means refusal: we do not want you. It is clear from the continuation of the story that they do not want to welcome him because he belongs to another tribe. His residence is Ephraim and he is Levite while they are Benjaminites. Only an old man, who is also from Ephraim, is willing to address and host him. He recognises him immediately as 'suitable to be hosted', from the peculiarities of his dress, or from other external appearances.

In this case a non-verbal term of message is used in order to overcome – or to try to overcome – the barrier of communication between outsiders, the members of different tribal groups. We speak to members of the same group, while we can express our needs to strangers only through bodily posture. The specific case of the Levite is more difficult, because in social terms his request is not minor – even if it really is minor in economic terms. Hospitality leads to the irrevocable passing of a barrier of hostility or at least of diversity, for the future as well as for the present. The historical reasons for this episode are partly known (cf. Eissfeldt 1935; Schunk 1963: 70). They have in any case to be assumed if the passage is to be understood. Speaking to an Ephraimite traveller would inevitably lead to becoming his host. It would mean entering into a relationship with him, and not a momentary one (as a simple exchange of words would be) but a comprehensive one (hospitality, as a kind of residence, is also a form of familial assimilation).

It must be said that, by 'entering' (*bw'*) the city square, the Levite in part imposes the relationship. But that is unavoidable and customary. Granting hospitality means allowing someone 'to enter' the house in order to spend the night there. Hospitality can only be obtained by an explicit invitation from the master of the house. It is correct to give hospitality, but incorrect to take it, as is the case with gifts and women. Yet the Levite at first makes a more general passage from 'outside' to 'inside' when he enters in Gibeah by himself. The city is walled, as is clear from the continuation of the story , access is through a gate, and all the houses are arranged like a protective enclosure around a square (*rĕḥōb*, a wide area). By entering this enclosed area, the Levite does not infringe on the space of anyone in particular, but upon communal space. He cannot do otherwise. Initiating communication, even if by posture only, always brings about some coercion or intrusion that is eliminated only by a positive response.

The granting of hospitality by the old Ephraimite goes through two essential and meaningful stages. The first stage is an exchange of words about the economic burden. The stranger states that he has straw, food and drink, that is everything essential. He needs nothing of economic value, only hospitality. The host answers by saying that all the burdens of hospitality, including its material aspects, will be left to him. Such an exchange of statements is to be considered as quite conventional and typical of the situation. This is the way hospitality is offered and requested.[16] Its purpose was to emphasise the mainly social, not economic, value of the relationship that is being created. The second stage is also stereotypical, and consists of placing shelter (admittance into the house), washing, food, and drink at the guest's disposal. These four are needed for survival (cf. chapter 1), and are therefore symbolic of hospitality, in addition to being effective. Hospitality is initiated with a ceremony that is partly verbal (invitation, negotiations), partly non-verbal (washing, feeding), after which a more informal and relaxed phase can follow. One can talk in an unstereotyped way and, above all, one can sleep.

1.2.4 In the narrative of Judges 19–21 we encounter many more communicative elements, some of which I will analyse below. These range from the excited knocking on the door by the evil-minded men of Gibeah (Judg. 19:22) to a complete set of intertribal institutional communications (oracle, oath, drawing of lots, etc.; see below, §4.1.2–3). The communicative value can even be involuntary, as in the case of the posture of the dead woman when she is discovered by her husband:

> The next morning the husband awoke, opened the door, and went out in order to go on his way. But the woman, his concubine, was lying down at the entrance of the house, with her hands on the threshold.   (Judg. 19:27)

The position of the corpse, with its hands on the threshold – a dividing element between 'inside' and 'outside' – constitutes an involuntary, but very strong message. The house has been hospitable to the husband but not to the woman. Nevertheless, she too approaches the house while dying, even if her husband himself had taken her out of the protected area ('The man seized his concubine and let her go out, to them', Judg. 19:25). We could say that this message is a charge against that house and that man – yet the message does not come from the woman, who is dead, but from the position of the corpse, reflecting the sequence of events.

The stress on 'with her hands on the threshold' is by no means necessary for the understanding of the passage. It reveals that the author of the story has a specific interest in elements endowed with communicative value. Indeed, through the specific episode it relates, the story as a whole is concerned with human

---

16 The dialogue between Abraham and Ephron on the sale of land in Gen. 23:3–16 is equally paradigmatic. The economic aspects, formally neglected and understated, are in fact the most relevant. In gift exchange among kings a similar game is played, between 'self-sufficiency', which was essential at the economic level, and the desire to interact, which is essential at the sociopolitical level (see Zaccagnini 1973: 104–5).

relations: inter-tribal relations as a visible topic, and inter-personal (especially sexual) relations as a hidden topic. Relationships between social groups are a problem of communication and exchange (exchange of messages, of goods, of women, according to Lévi-Strauss's formulation). The story is consequently interwoven with communicative facts, with special attention paid to the semantics of words, of gestures, of postures, and of silence.

2 THE WOMAN AS MESSAGE

2.1 THE ATROPHIED ISSUER

Throughout the story, the Levite woman, who, by an objective evaluation, is the protagonist (the main facts 'happen' to her), never speaks:

(a) she does not speak when showing dislike for her husband: she simply goes back to her father's house;
(b) she is not asked nor is she able to express her opinion when the husband comes to take her back;
(c) she never speaks at home or during the journey (while even the servant speaks);
(d) she does not speak in Gibeah, and in, particular, she obviously is not asked nor is she able to express her opinion when taken out of the house;
(e) she does not speak the next morning, when the husband calls her, because she is dead.

Note that the last case is the only one where the husband addresses her – when she is already dead! And the words the husband addresses to her do not require a verbal answer, only an action:

'Awake – the husband said – we are leaving.' No answer. So the man took her on the donkey and left and went to his place.   (Judg. 19:28)

The posture of the woman 'speaks' enough. But the husband turns out to be 'deaf' to the message, which requires some attention and sensitivity (during the night the man has probably slept). He understands only when his order is not carried out.

The woman therefore never issues a verbal message. In general, she has nothing to communicate – or at least this is implied by the 'social logic' into which she is inserted, or by the 'narrative logic' expressing it. If she has something to communicate, she has to make use of non-verbal channels, of physical behaviour. She departs from her husband's house (only to go back to her father's house) when she decides she cannot live with him any longer.[17] She 'departs' completely – that is, dies – when she undergoes the violence that she cannot and does not wish to endure. It is significant that the only way in which she shows unease is by going away and by removing herself instead of removing what makes her uneasy.[18] And it is even more significant that the only message she has to communicate is intolerable unease. Until she is at ease, or while her pain remains tolerable, she had no need to send messages. Her passive insertion into the social system suffices to let her live. When her unease passes the threshold of what she can tolerate, when the social context no longer guarantees the minimum conditions for living, she cannot protest through the verbal code, which has become atrophied. A non-verbal channel is then employed, one of simply disappearing from the scene.[19]

2.2 THE REBELLIOUS MESSAGE

2.2.1 While the woman never speaks or issues a message, and seldom is addressed, she is a channel and a material object for messages. She does not speak, but she is 'spoken with'. She is used as the material for communication after her death, when her corpse is cut into pieces in order to summon the tribal assembly. While dying she has already used her body, the posture of her body, as an involuntary message. But above all she has been used when alive as an item of exchange between male partners, so that she has been a significant message.

In the correct relationship between the Levite and his father-in-law, the woman has been a medium for positive communication. The marriage relationship (whatever kind of marriage was entered into)[20] between the Levite and the woman was essentially a link between two men. When the woman interrupts the communication between father and husband, by going back to her father's house

---

17 The reason for the woman's flight (19: 1 *wattizneh 'alāw*) is a philologically vexing point in the text, which has been emended and interpreted in ancient and modern times (partly in order to make the woman guilty). But we can leave the text as is, and understand that 'she hated him', with Driver 1947: 29–30.

18 The sequence 'to hate' → 'to go away, to flee' (cf. Hebr. *znh* → *hlk*) is well attested in Akkadian (*zêru* → *alāku/nābutu/ezēbu*; cf. *CAD* Z, s.v. *zêru* 1a). For instance, in juridical texts such as the laws of Eshnunna (§30: 'If a man hates his city and his king, and flees...') and of Hammurabi (§136: 'since that man hated his city and fled ...'; §193: 'if an (adopted) son hates the adoptive father or the adoptive mother and goes away to his father's house...'). Cf. also Landsberger 1937, tablet 7: ii 49 – iii 3.

19 Similarly in socioeconomic conflicts in the ancient Near East, the slave's protest or hatred toward his owner (or the enslaved debtor's toward his creditor, etc.) can find expression only in flight; cf. Renger 1972; Liverani 1965b.

20 The woman's status as *pilegeš*, usually translated as 'concubine', in any case was a formalised relationship between the Levite and the father-in-law, and has no negative implication for the woman.

by her own free will, the problem arises of how to re-establish this communicative relationship. The Levite goes to talk to the father-in-law, not to the woman. What matters is re-establishing the link between the men, where the woman is a constitutive element, a medium for message, not the issuer or the addressee. Her behaviour is anomalous at the moment when she tries to affirm her own will. It is the behaviour of a message rebelling against its issuer. But the rebellious message has no escape. It can only go back from addressee to issuer, from the husband's house to the father's house.[21] There is no properly female space, no closed space or shelter, that does not belong to a male (husband or father). The male monopolises responsibility for socioeconomic management, as well as communicative activity.[22]

The woman is used as a medium also in the incorrect relationship between the Levite and the men of Gibeah. While the transfer of the woman from her father to the Levite is the substance of a friendly relationship, her transfer to the men of Gibeah is the culmination of a hostile one. In this case too the 'dialogue' takes place between men; the woman is only used. Indeed, the dialogue takes place between the men of Gibeah and the Levite's host. The Levite runs the risk of also being used as a medium in a relationship between other people. The woman functions as a substitute, and consequently renders the case less aberrant, eliminating the specific anomaly of using a man (issuer/addressee) in place of a woman (medium). From our modern perspective, the substitution of the woman for the husband is the greatest aberration, but this is because we are outside the value-system of that period's sociocultural milieu.[23] In that milieu substitution does in fact lessen the tension, for two reasons. First, it allots to a woman a passive, 'feminine' sexual role, while saving the man. Second, it takes the form of a 'transfer' of the woman from men to men (even if under coercion), as a caricature of the correct procedure in the exchange of women.

In this case too the woman as message rebels against both the issuer and the addressee. She does so in a way similar to her previous rebellion, namely by departing, in this case by dying. This rebellion is unforeseen (in the morning the Levite departs saying 'Awake, we are leaving'). Had the woman not been dead, presumably the case would not have been considered 'unprecedented'. By dying, by withdrawing herself from her use as a means of communication, the woman is

---

21 The flight toward an open, non-structured, space was only accessible to men, who could 'become *ḫabiru*', that is hide themselves in woodlands. Even when rebellious, women can only go from the house of one man to that of another.

22 The term *ba'al/bêlu* defines this role aptly, since it is used in relation both to goods (*b'l.byt* 'master of the household') and to women (Ugaritic *b'l.att* 'husband', lit. 'master of a woman').

23 We now appreciate different values, especially of an individualistic character (focused on the concept of the 'person' and on personal responsibility), according to which only a voluntary substitution is morally positive (as a self-sacrifice). We reject a forced substitution.

able to point out the aberrant character of the message, which would otherwise have remained almost unnoticed. The medium 'rebels' by becoming a selective and evaluative filter of the messages running through it.

2.2.2 In the last analysis the only difference between the 'correct' and 'incorrect' use of the woman lies in the voluntary nature of her transfer – voluntary from the point of view of the man (father, husband), not of the woman herself. Similarly, a gift and a robbery are different terms of the circulation of goods: it would be absurd to take into account the will of the object transferred from one person to another. What matters is that the transfer takes place by will of the donor, in the case of gift or marriage, and by the will of the receiver, in the case of robbery or rape. Moreover, the will of the receiver is consequent on that of the donor ('obligation to receive' in Marcel Mauss's terms). Therefore in a correct relationship, the coincidence of wills is realised, in the incorrect one, a divergence.

Thus, the story defines the conventions of marriage as a relationship between partners who are on good terms, and as taking place through the will of the donor. There are two rules: (1) women are given (and consequently accepted), they cannot be taken; (2) women are given to those with whom one 'speaks'. The two rules define the woman as a message most efficiently: clearly the message is transmitted by the issuer, it cannot be assimilated by the addressee if the issuer refuses to transmit it. And the message cannot but be accepted by the addressee, once it has been issued.

The story of the woman is indeed strictly parallel to the story of the dialogues. The Levite speaks to the father-in-law, who transfers his daughter to him as wife. They institute an exemplary relationship, including the exchange of women, messages, and gifts (hospitality). This correct and positive relationship is even faulty by its excess, as we shall see below: the father-in-law transfers the woman too often (twice), speaks too much with the Levite, and hosts him for too long (cf. below, §3.2.2). The men of Gibeah, by contrast, do not entertain any relation with the Levite: they never speak to him – neither when they see him in the city square, nor when they surround the house of his host, when they speak only to the latter. They do not host him, and they do quite the opposite of 'transferring a women' since they want to 'take the man'. The remedy of sending the woman outside turns out not to be the best solution of the problem. The woman, a message from an issuer who is not willing to issue, to an addressee who is not willing to receive, is an anti-message. In fact, she dies.

2.2.3 There are many parallels in the ancient Near East that can contribute to a better understanding of the values involved in the double transfer undergone by the protagonist of the story. They exist both for the correct transfer, which establishes or consolidates social relations, and for the incorrect one, which is made to escape from a 'siege'. The material at our disposal, mostly concerning royal persons, is certainly affected by political implications that modify the nature of procedures and set them apart from common life. But, it is the best known documentation, the most detailed, and the only one from which it is possible to reconstruct values and behavioural models.

It is not necessary to discuss at length the 'correct' transfer of women in Near Eastern court circles of the fifteenth to thirteenth centuries, the period that provides the most abundant and detailed documentation, since F. Pintore (1978) published an insightful and original study of the topic. The main features are well established. They include the 'male' dialectics between giving and receiving, between refusing and taking, the aggressive model of the pretender (pp. 60–61) as against the accommodating model of the giver (pp. 58–60), and the passive and 'dumb' role of the woman (pp. 61–62, 96), who has a tendency to disappear once she arrives at her destination and the communicative function is accomplished. Perhaps more relevant are the parallels, even if they are not direct, between the aberrant story of Judges 19–21 and other equally aberrant stories. These include the Ehli-Nikkal story, with the anti-model sequence of rape and repudiation of this Hittite bride at the court of Ugarit, and the story of the 'daughter of the *rabītu*, a princess from Amurru who is sheltered in her father's house and sought by her husband, the king of Ugarit, not for reconciliation but for capital punishment (Pintore 1978: 76–8, 83–7).

It is more useful here to cite some parallels with the transfer of women in order to escape from a siege, because such cases have not so far been accorded any special attention. I have in mind episodes like Sennacherib's siege of Jerusalem:

> Hezekiah the Judean... I shut him into Jerusalem, his royal city, as a bird in a cage. I heaped up ramparts against him... Hezekiah was overwhelmed by the terrible splendour of my kingship...in addition to 20 talents of gold and 800 talents of silver...his daughters... I let be brought to me at Nineveh, my royal city.
> (*ARAB* II 240; cf. also 284 and 312).

The description of the siege of Tyre by Ashurbanipal is quite similar:

> I marched against Ba'lu king of Tyre, who dwells in the midst of the sea, because he did not obey my royal orders and did not listen to the words of my mouth. I heaped up ramparts against him... I let him submit to my yoke: a daughter, seed of his loins, and the daughters of his brothers, he brought to my presence, in order to serve me as concubines...   (*ARAB* II 547; cf. also 779)

More examples from Assyrian inscriptions could be added, related to Babylon (*ARAB* II 270), Arwad (II 780 and 848), Tabal (II 781), Hilakku (II 782), and other polities. We find the same in literary texts like the Ugaritic Keret poem or

Homer's *Iliad*. In all of these the threat of a total sack of the city is avoided by an agreement that reduces the tension. The besieged king agrees to transfer goods and women, in this way conferring on the relationship some semblance of the 'correct' model.

The two groups of episodes are not as far apart as appears at first sight.[24] There is a sort of chiastic opposition between them, between the substantive and the ceremonial levels. The latter has the function of mitigating a dramatic reality, by way of a reversal. In the case of dynastic marriages, the substantive goodwill of the donor is contrasted to the aggressive role of the pretender (cf. Pintore 1978: 58 'conflitto cerimoniale'). In contrast, in the case of a siege, the substantive physical violence by the besieger, or at least the threat thereof, results in an agreement and a formally voluntary transfer of women by the besieged. The difficult balance between agreement and conflict shows that marriages are located in a dangerous territory in between families or (in case of dynastic marriages) polities, in a state of tension and competition that could explode into reciprocal oppression or annihilation. The tension has to be reduced through a link that would forever retain a trace of the aggressiveness it serves to dissipate. The woman, the 'object' of marriage relations between males, like the trade goods, object of a material exchange, has to play a silent and passive role in this mechanism. Her speech and action risk interrupting an already difficult communication between partners who remain in potential conflict even after the agreement has been reached.

2.3 RITUALISATION OF THE ANTI-MODEL

2.3.1 The particular tension connected to the use of women as media for messages derives not only from their possible 'rebellion', but also from the great importance attributed to their exchange. To consider the transferred or received woman as a 'message', as a symbolic element in a relation between partners, is a rather paradoxical formulation, since the very subject-matter and purpose of the relation is the woman herself, that is her reproductive functions which enable a community to survive. Therefore, after having established the rules of correct communication, one must not be overwhelmed by the rules themselves, to the point of forgetting the final purpose of the transfer of women, namely the possibility of reproducing a community through time.

In the story of Judges 19–21 it is clear that the episode of the Levite's woman, at the beginning, is connected to the problem of the women to be allotted to the

---

[24] A case like EA 99 is located halfway between a violent imposition and an inter-dynastic transfer, cf. Liverani 1972b: 314–15; Pintore 1978: 13–15. I have even suggested (Liverani 1977: 284) that dynastic relationships (including marriages) may have functioned as an outlet or sublimation for political rivalries.

Benjamin tribe in order to avoid its extinction, at the end (and as a culmination) of the story. The connection is not cumulative but organic in character: in other words, we are not simply dealing with two segments of the same narrative sequence, but with two homologous segments. We could say that the very same segment is repeated from two different points of view. The first episode is located at an inter-personal level, the second at an inter-tribal level, but the meaning is the same. The obvious premise is that there is a correct way of maintaining relations. But something is introduced that risks halting relations completely: a rule, a prohibition, an agreement, or a wish. The oath 'Cursed be the one who gives a woman to Benjamin!' runs the risk of causing that tribe to become extinct. The wish of the Gibeites not to host the Levite and then to have homosexual relations with him – that is, negative relations from the point of reproduction – brings about an interruption of relations. In order to avoid the extinction of a tribe, an 'anti-model' is introduced at this point. It is the opposite of the 'correct' model, and therefore needs to be supported by a ritualisation and a mythical foundation. Its function is to obtain the final and essential result, namely reproduction and the survival of the community. The 'anti-model' is violence, rape. If the woman is not given, then she is to be taken by force. One cannot tolerate the ending of all circulation of women, which would result in annihilation.

2.3.2 This reading of the story could be defined as 'the ritualisation of misbehaviour'. The anti-model takes the place of the correct model, in order to ensure the necessary end result through any possible means. This reading seems obvious for the final part of the story. It is less obvious for the beginning, especially because the relationship between the Gibeites and the Levite woman (a heterosexual but violent relationship) ends not in reproduction, but in death. Nevertheless, such a reading – and in any case a reading of the first episode as a 'first draft' of the final part of the story – entails a re-evaluation of the conduct of the Levite, within the logic of the story itself. By sending out the woman instead of going himself, he chooses the lesser of two evils. He chooses the anti-model, and avoids an absence of relations. He prefers violence to sterility. Two things go wrong. First, the woman 'rebels' – she dies, as we have seen.[25] Second, the Levite himself sends out the woman and can be charged with the crime that the tribal league is able to prevent through the stratagem of the Shiloh festival:

> Be grateful to them, to have taken each his woman in battle. Otherwise you had to give them to them (by yourselves), and in this case you had committed a sin! (Judg. 21:22)

---

25 The girls who are ritually kidnapped by the Benjaminites in Shiloh are implicitly solicited (by the narrative logic) not to rebel or 'escape', as the Levite's woman did.

Someone who wishes to act correctly can even tolerate the anti-model if the reasons for doing so are strong enough, but he cannot be its very perpetrator.

2.3.3 Between the model of transfer and the anti-model of rape, a solution within the segregated tribe itself is not even imagined.[26] Note that the massacre of the Benjamin tribe eliminates first of all the fighters, and then all the males in the villages. Only the Benjaminite women survive (Judg. 20:44–46, 48). After the war and massacre, men are lacking in Benjamin, not women. Yet the problem is how to find women! All of the Benjaminite women have been spared, and are obviously intended for non-Benjaminite men. They have been spared in order to let the flow of women to other tribes continue. But it cannot continue in the correct way, because Benjaminite *givers of women* are lacking! No longer incorporated into a regular exchange system, the Benjaminite women presumably (the text is not explicit) are taken as war booty by the other tribes,[27] instead of being given to them. For reasons of symmetry, therefore, the Benjaminites themselves should take women, who cannot be given to them because of the oath 'Cursed be who gives a woman to Benjamin!' The lack of women for the Benjaminites is not the result of the massacre, but its very opposite. It is not women but givers of women who are lacking. Benjaminite givers have been physically eliminated in war, and givers in the other tribes voluntarily eliminated themselves through the oath. The massacre has stopped the flow in one direction, the oath the flow in the other direction. There is an evident redundancy in this double development: strictly speaking, if all the Benjaminite males were killed there would be no need for such an oath. The extinction of the givers of women coincides with the extinction of the receivers of women. But the narrative 'logic' is not affected by such a contradiction. In the logic of the story, the Benjaminites can no longer be partners in correct exchanges – either because they are too few now, or because they are 'sinister'. They have to provide in the incorrect way. If they cannot give and receive women, they have to take women and their women have to be taken. The possibility that each tribe can use its own women for reproduction is not even suggested. Women have to circulate, if possible, in the correct way, and if not in the incorrect way. More generally, tribes have to have relations, if possible friendly relations with one another, but if this is impossible, it is better to have hostile relations than no relations at all. The model is the transfer of women and the anti-model is rape; renouncing relations would mean the end of life.

[26] In the similar story (cf. §4.3.2) of Lot in Sodom, the anti-model adopted in order to prevent extinction, following a lack of hospitality, is in fact endogamy in its extreme form as incest. I do not see the 'irony' suggested by van Seters 1975: 219.

[27] E.g., Diakonoff 1976: 72 n.59 thought that all Benjaminite women were enslaved by other tribes, and that for this reason it was necessary to look for other women for the (few) surviving Benjaminites. This interpretation seems unacceptable.

2.3.4 In speaking of ritualisation and of the mythical foundation of the anti-model, it is clear that I consider the entire story to be a mythical expression of a complex that finds its ritual expression in the Shiloh festival. All the evidence suggests that this festival is the only element that really existed in 'historical' times. During the festival, a ritual rape of the girls from Shiloh by Benjaminites takes place. The name Benjamin means the 'right-handed', but through polarity they are characterised as 'left-handed', that is as the 'sinister', bad ones. They behave in a way that is the opposite of what is correct (cf. Grottanelli 1978: 44–5). The story explains the origin of this ritual rape, which perpetuates through a periodic re-enactment a rape accomplished 'once upon a time'. An explanatory chain links back the Shiloh rape, the massacre of Jabesh, the inter-tribal war, and finally the episode of the Levite woman. Every passage in the tale deepens and makes the preceding one more explicit.

But the entire story, including the Shiloh ritual, is really meant to give a foundation to a view of inter-tribal relations, with its exchange of messages, women, and hospitable gifts. The story especially wishes to emphasise how such a network of relations that was kept in place by a set of conventions and rules – either traditional in character or introduced on specific occasions – exists in order to ensure the physical reproduction of people and to avoid extinction. If the rules and conventions are in contradiction with the final goal, it is necessary not to confuse the means with the ends. The means can be reversed if necessary, but the goal cannot be abandoned. Between curse and survival, survival prevails. The ritualisation of the incorrect manner of acting is effective in reversing the means in order to reach a goal that is normally reached in the correct way. In the dilemma between breaking an oath or extinguishing the Benjamin tribe, a superficial and very formal enunciation states that breaking the oath is more serious than breaking the rules of giving and receiving. But beneath this formal articulation is a very substantive logic, which states that the survival of a tribe is much more important than adhering to the most solemn decision.

3 HOSPITALITY

3.1 AMBIGUOUS TERRITORY AND BINDING ROLES

3.1.1 The story of the Levite in Gibeah is also, and above all, a paradigm of hospitality. Hospitality is a strictly functional institution in a society that does not see itself as homogeneous, but as diverse within the same territory, built up of friends and enemies, or at least acquaintances and strangers. Hospitality makes it possible to travel through the territory, to move from one friendly nucleus to the next, and to pass by the unstable intermediate realm of hostility. The dialectics of friendship vs. enmity, acquaintance vs. hostility, community members vs.

strangers are ordered not on two, but on three levels: those of full cohesion, of complete extraneousness, and of interaction. Complete cohesion brings about an absence of social relations: at home one is not hosted and does not speak to oneself, and women do not circulate within a family (as strict endogamy is precluded). Complete extraneousness also brings about an absence of social relations: groups considered strangers in the strict sense (*nokrî*) are 'other', not as possible counterparts, but as unavoidably different. With these people there is no conversation, no agreement, no trade, no exchange of women,[28] and no hospitality. If the Benjamin tribe does not receive women from the other tribes of the Israelite league, it is doomed to extinction, because it is not even thinkable that it can get women from the 'Canaanites'. The travelling Levite cannot spend the night in Jerusalem, which is a foreign, Jebusite, city. He has to go on to Gibeah or Ramah, which are Israelite cities. Social relationships are created with groups that are not exactly the same but are related. One can transfer women to other tribes of the league, or be hosted in an Israelite village.

The intermediate territory in social relations is the meeting ground of two opposite requirements, meant to avoid two opposite risks: those of external communication and of security. Because of the first requirement, one is forced to go outside the family or kinship group to avoid the risk of extinction, and so protect future generations. Hospitality is granted because one can foresee the need for hospitality in the future. Women are given up in order to have access to those of other groups. Because of the second requirement, on the other hand, the openness toward the outside world cannot be indiscriminate, and is permissible only with formal acquaintances. This requirement avoids risks and attempts against security, and therefore protects the present generation. Formal acquaintance is the explicit agreement that the offering of prestations is reciprocal. One does not grant hospitality to people who would not act as hosts, and one does not transfer women to people who would not do the same.

3.1.2 In this closed mechanism of balanced prestations (or, if one prefers, of reciprocal blackmail), it is difficult to initiate relations. The granting of hospitality can itself function as a decisive element for distinguishing between friendship and hostility. It can reverse relations of cause and effect: instead of granting hospitality to friends, one becomes the friend of his guest. If hospitality were granted to an enemy – because of ignorance, deception, or necessity – the enemy is no longer an enemy, and has to be considered above all a guest. The 'stratagem' used by the

---

28 Recall that the 'foreign woman' (*'iššāh nokriyyāh*) was always evaluated negatively (e.g., in the book of Proverbs), even though Humbert (1937: 1958) showed that an 'outside' woman was in question, not necessarily a 'stranger'. In any case, intermarriage with foreign women was strongly criticised, especially in post-exilic times (cf. §4.3.3).

Gibeonites in order to survive and somehow become assimilated into the Israelite tribes, is an exemplary model of this mechanism.[29]

On the other hand, if one desires not to transfer women to a tribe of the 'league' – that is, to people to whom one should transfer women – the oath bears such symbolic weight that it overrides real needs. In order to cancel or neutralise the oath, specific and equally weighty symbolic devices have to be used. To swear, grant hospitality, exchange gifts, or address in speech, are not only functional but also meaningful acts. If they are carried out, this means friendship, and the actors become (or recognise themselves as) friends. If they are absent, this means enmity, and people who do not act in that way become (or recognise themselves as) enemies.

'Roles' are definitively and irreversibly fixed. At the very moment when he addresses the Levite, the old Ephraimite of Gibeah fixes his role forever. Since he talks to him, he has to host him, and since he hosts him, he has to protect him, even at the risk of complete ruin for himself and his house. At the very moment when the first of the Gibeites crosses the city-square without addressing a word to the Levite, their roles are fixed forever. Since the Levite is labelled as 'not to be hosted', hence as an enemy, hostile relations *have to be* maintained with him. The more they are hostile, the better they play their role. An attempt on his life *has to be* made. After all, he is guilty of having placed himself in a position of institutionalised danger.

3.2 A TIME FOR TRAVELLING, A TIME FOR RESTING

3.2.1 Movements through a territory that has safe, hostile, and dubious zones have also to take into account two different periods of time: day and night. During the day it is possible to move; during the night it is necessary to rest. Hospitality is related to the night. Just as it is not correct to move during the night, it is not correct to rest during the day. The 'interior' space provides a maximum of security but a minimum of communication. The 'exterior' space provides a maximum of communication but a minimum of security. The effect of the opposite time period can either balance the character of the spatial zones, or can fuse them. The dark night is inimical to security: to stay in the open during the night presents a double risk that should be avoided. The practice of moving by day and resting by night allows one to avoid such an excessive risk. But to stay in a closed space during the day is also to be avoided since it wastes security. A maximum of security would be achieved, but at the expense of a lack of communication. Not to communicate is appropriate in the small interior

---

29 On hospitality in the ancient Near East in general, see also Zaccagnini 1973: 51–8, 186–8; Grottanelli 1976–77; Xella 1978.

group, but not in the ambivalent, yet fertile, territory of exterior relations, which involve the calculated risk of a loss of security to the advantage of communication.

As with all ambiguous zones, the shift from day to night is full of risks. The evening is the critical moment, when it is necessary to take special care. Still travelling when evening arrived, the Levite can choose between resting at the correct moment but in the wrong place (Jebusite Jerusalem), or continuing too long in order to reach an Israelite village with darkness already approaching. He decides to continue, but he will not find security. The timing of his journey was compromised by a late start. At the moment of the transition from day to night, he has to face the passage from the exterior to the interior zone. In this way he combines two risks and is unable to overcome the attendant difficulties. Perhaps the Gibeites would have hosted him if they had seen him arriving at the right moment; but they cannot host him when he arrives as darkness approaches. It is impossible to inspect him and there is no time to see whether he is fit for hospitality, so they do not host him.[30]

3.2.2 The conduct of the Levite in his father-in-law's house is correct, so that we can deduce the proper rules of behaviour from it. The guest has to stay 'three' days. That is neither too short – it would have been a purely utilitarian exploitation of hospitality to leave as soon as he obtained the woman – nor too long – which would have created an economic gain for the guest and a corresponding burden for the host. Arriving on the evening of the first day, the Levite remains in the company of the father-in-law throughout the second day, and wishes to leave early on the third. But his father-in-law, who shows an excess of hospitality, detains him. The same thing happens on the morning of the fifth and sixth days. The father-in-law acts generously, he wants to show that his feelings toward the Levite are friendly, which makes sense considering the purpose and premise of the visit. Yet he breaks the customary rule of the third day. The tragic outcome of the story makes it clear that one of its purposes is to warn against excessive hospitality. Had the father-in-law not detained the Levite beyond the appropriate time, the latter would not have suffered the incident in Gibeah.

Excessive hospitality is incorrect, because it alters the very nature of the institution. Instead of a sheltered rest that allows for movement in dangerous territory, excessively prolonged hospitality becomes assimilated to a stay at home. Intermediate space risks becoming interior space, at the expense of communicative action. Whoever continues to stay cannot travel. Moreover, a guest who is too

---

[30] This 'explanation' is additional and therefore contradictory (according to a certain kind of unambiguous logic) in comparison with the explanation that the Gibeites do not host because they are different and 'sinister'. But both explanations are clearly inherent in the narrative logic (which is never unambiguous).

much 'at home' becomes unsuitable for the exchange of women or for any other interaction between parties that know each other, while remaining separate.[31]

In our story, not only does the father-in-law *host the Levite too much*, presumably he also *speaks too much*. What else could they have done, for all those days, besides eating and drinking? In any case, he *transfers the woman too much*, since he transfers her twice. The first transfer is certainly correct, but after its bad outcome it would have been wiser perhaps not to insist on it. In fact, the result turns out to be tragic. Similarly, while it is correct to host for a first set of three days, it seems incorrect to double this period. Relationships in an ambiguous social space are to be measured carefully. It is risky to abstain, and risky to abuse. We are not dealing here with absolute values, which can be meritoriously increased as much as possible. We are dealing here with balanced arrangements.

3.2.3 The shift in timetable produced by the excess in hospitality on the part of the father-in-law leads the Levite to face the lack of hospitality on the part of the Gibeites. Inter-tribal solidarity does not work, so only its tribal and local forms are left. Relations are maintained between the Levite who resides in Ephraim and the Ephraimite who resides in Gibeah, and between the latter and the Benjaminites of Gibeah. The Ephraimite acts as a middleman between the Levite and the Benjaminites, and allows for the development of the story by hosting the wayfarer in a village that does not wish to host him. It should be noted not only that the Benjaminites do not host the Levite – when he was seated in the village square 'no-one welcomed them to spend the night in his house' – but also that there is no exchange of words between the Levite and the Benjaminites. The latter only address the old Ephraimite. The Levite does not even see the Benjaminites, both while staying in the Ephraimite's house and while leaving the next morning.

Obviously this is not only a matter of lack of hospitality. There is also an active anti-hospitality, an opposite treatment. This treatment entails letting the guest 'go out' from the house where he has 'gone in' to spend the night. Hospitality provides shelter in an enclosed space to overcome the dangerous period of night. The act of casting someone out into the open space and darkness is as anti-hospitable as possible. Moreover, hospitality takes the form of supplying a guest with services. Here the Benjaminites want to receive services from the guest. In an excess of irony, the anti-hospitable treatment the Benjaminites want to apply to the Levite is expressed by the verb 'to know' (*THAT*, I, 682–701):

31　Compare the difficulties experienced by Jacob, who stayed too long with Laban – in his case two time-cycles, of seven years each, required for a double transfer of women – before detaching his household and patrimony from that of his father-in-law. On the dialectics of endogamy vs. exogamy, see de Geus 1976: 144–8.

Let the man who is in your house go out, and we will 'know' him!

(Judg. 19: 22; cf. Gen. 19:5)

Hospitality is a relationship between people who are known. The Benjaminite anti-hospitality is an absence of hospitality, but also a desire for excessive and unnatural knowledge.[32]

4 THE TOPOGRAPHY OF SOCIAL COMMUNICATION

4.1 PIVOTAL PLACES FOR COMMUNICATION

4.1.1 The setting of the story in Judges 19–21 is provided not only by a series of topographically precise places – the itinerary of the journey and the description of the battle could be verified on the spot – but also by a social setting that suits a qualitatively diverse territory. Three kinds of territory are interwoven: 'our' territory, where we are quite safe; enemy territory, where we do not even venture; and the intermediate territory of the kindred tribes, where we move with caution and according to conventional rules. In this third territory the dialectic between protective closure and communicative opening is acted out. It is basically a dialectic between the security of the actual existence and the security of its transmission down the generations.

In the intermediate territory, some situations are ambiguous. An Ephraimite is found in the Benjaminite village of Gibeah, a Levite in Ephraim, while his wife is from Judah (Bethlehem). A certain amount of mixing, mainly but not entirely the consequence of intermarriage,[33] is superimposed on a theoretical coincidence of domicile and kinship. Mixing produces, and at the same time is the consequence of, the very possibility of communicating, moving, and having relations.

4.1.2 The difficult process of communicating usually takes place within a network of contacts and activities of individuals. But it has also its privileged places, its conspicuous forms, and its overall rhythm. The pivotal places of inter-tribal communication are neatly characterised:

(a) Mizpah is the place for gathering the assembly (*qhl*, Judg. 20:1–2).[34] The assembly is summoned in the symbolic way analysed above (§1.1.1). It decides

---

[32] See Grottanelli 1976–77: 190–4 on inverted hospitality: the guest is eaten instead of being fed.

[33] The fact that the protagonist is a Levite, a member of a non-territorial 'tribe', would bear closer examination about the cohesive and communicative role of the Levites, and the function of asylum cities (not analysed here, because they are not mentioned in Judg. 19–21).

[34] The separation of roles between Mizpah and Bethel is conditioned by a stratified redaction of the

by acclamation (Judg. 20:8 'All the people rose as one man, saying...'), and the decision takes the form of an oath (*šbʿ*) that is binding upon everyone: 'No-one among us shall go to his tent, no-one shall go back home!' (Judg. 20:8); 'No-one among us shall give his daughter as wife to Benjamin!' (Judg. 21:1). The operative procedure is through casting lots (*ʾlh bĕgôrāl*, Judg. 20:9–10; cf. Lindblom 1962; Dommershausen 1971; *TWAT*, I, 991–8), with progressive decimation. A solemn oath condemns to death those who do not attend the assembly (like Jabesh of Gilead; Judg. 21:5; cf. 21:8), and such a decision is carried out in the form of an anathema *(herem, 21:11)*.

(b) Bethel is the place where the oracle of Yahweh is consulted (Judg. 20:18: verb *šʾl*; see Westermann 1960: 9–14, 27–8; von Rad 1952: 2). There are cultic installations of a more or less temporary character (the ark, Judg. 20:27, an altar built for the purpose, Judg. 21:4). First of all a census takes place (*pqd* hitp., Judg. 20:17 and 21:9; cf. Fürst 1965: 18, 25; *TWAT*, II, 472–3; Speiser 1958), which is necessary for military activities. But the main purpose of the Bethel gathering is to consult Yahweh, who does answer (Judg. 20:18, 23, 27; 21:2, 4). The consultation follows procedures of progressive escalation. The oracle is consulted three times about military tactics: the first time people simply ask; the second time, they weep and ask; the third time they weep, sit down and fast, offer sacrifices (of the holocaust and communion types), and finally ask. The oracle is consulted twice about the survival of Benjamin: the first time people sit, weep and cry, and then they ask; the second time they build an altar, offer sacrifices (of the holocaust and communion types), and finally ask. Only requests preceded by sacrifices obtain an answer and have an outcome that is correct and final.

(b₁) In Gibeah the Benjaminites also gather *(ʾsp)* and count themselves (*pqd* hitp.) in order to fight, but of course by themselves (Judg. 20:15). The 'sinister' Benjaminites do not consult oracles, so obviously they are destined to succumb.

(c) Shiloh is perhaps a military encampment (*mahăneh*, Judg. 21:12), but this information is possibly due to a late insertion. It is certainly also the place of the feast of Yahweh (*hag -YHWH*, 21:19; cf. *TWAT*, II, 730–44). The ritual rape of the girls by the Benjaminites alludes to the battle of Gibeah in a reverse way, since it is an 'ambush' (*ʾrb*, Judg. 21:20 for the feast; Judg. 20:33, 37 for the battle) by Benjaminites, who were the victims of an ambush during the battle.

---

text, cf. §4.3.3–4. The role of Bethel is believed to belong to the final (post-exilic) redaction, and to diminish the role of Mizpah in the basic text. Cf. Besters 1965: 20–41; a contrary opinion is given by Dus 1964: 227–43. My suggestion about the 'pivotal places for communication' removes the problem of a central sanctuary of the 'league' (as a historical assumption), on which see Anderson 1970: 135–51; Orlinski 1962; Irwin 1965; Besters 1965.

(d) The 'Rimmon rock' (Judg. 20:45) is a place of asylum (in the desert: *midbar*, Judg. 20:42), where escapees can be safe. They remain there for four months, until peace is proclaimed.

4.1.3 Thus, the tale as a whole gives a real textbook of significant communication: oracle, oath, anathema, acclamation in the assembly, lot casting, sacrifice, and object-based convocation. The network of communicative acts is effective in making and transmitting relevant decisions. It is therefore effective in ensuring the functioning of the community as a political body. Formal acts of communication seldom take place outside the pivotal places, being limited to sending emissaries (*šlḥ*), either just to summon a gathering (Judg. 19:30) or to contact a tribe that has dissociated itself explicitly from the rest (Judg. 20:12; 21:13).

In normal circumstances there is communication during a gathering, and lack of communication during dispersal. We could say that the alternate rhythm of 'gathering vs. dispersal' allows for an exchange of information, for common decision making, and for required actions. The single groups – tribes, clans, households – undertake the symmetrically balanced actions of 'gathering' (*'sp, qhl*) and 'dispersing' (*hlk* hitp.):

> All the sons of Israel went out, and the assembly gathered as a single man – from Dan to Beersheba and the land of Gilead – to Yahweh of Mizpah. (Judg. 20:1)

> Then all the sons of Israel went away from there, everybody to his tribe and to his clan, they went out from there, every man to his household. (Judg. 21:24)

The rhythm of 'gathering vs. dispersal' is mainly, but not exclusively, viewed as a rhythm of 'going out vs. going in'. People 'go out' (*yṣ'*, Judg. 20:1) from their protected, nuclear places (house, city, tribe, patrimonial estate) to go to the assembly; and hence they '(re)enter' (*swr*, used in Judg. 20:8 for tribes going back to their respective houses, and in 19:11–12:15 for an individual going back to his city). Or they 'go back' (*šwb*, Judg. 21:23) or simply 'go away' (*hlk* hitp.) to the respective locations of their dispersed settlements.

These movements take place between a normal residence, protected and dispersed into small closed units suitable for production and reproduction, and an occasional gathering, in a common and open space, suitable for communication and action. Such 'dimorphic' behaviour (in the sense of M. Mauss, cf. Liverani 1997) is linked to occasional, yet mainly seasonal, events (feasts, but also wars). Its prerequisite is the possibility of movement, which is also technologically based. Its background is perhaps a broad dimorphic pattern, connected with horizontal transhumance from and to villages that continue to be based mostly on agriculture.

4.2 COHESION, FRACTURES, AND SANCTIONS

4.2.1 Formal communications have a binding effect. The great significance of words forces people who swear an oath to keep it, even if the reasons for swearing seem no longer to be valid, or even if other concerns seem to overrule the object of the oath. The oracular decision is obeyed, even if it appears to lead to disaster. It is mandatory to summon people: a count is made, and death is sworn to whoever is absent. The inhabitants of Jabesh of Gilead are guilty (and can be exterminated) because they did not go to the assembly. The Benjaminites become enemies when they do not want to 'listen' (*šmʿ*, Judg. 20:13) to the proposals of the other tribes. In a situation where political relations are expressed through the verbal/aural code, the word needs to be considered binding, as otherwise the entire system collapses. All these elements built up a 'topography of communication' as the only topography of political power that is present in a social territory of this kind: the formalisation of differentiated codes for communication (verbal and 'pregnant' with people already in agreement; non-verbal if agreement is still to be ascertained), the network of privileged locations for communication, and the rhythms of opening vs. closure and of gathering vs. dispersal. The picture is neat in terms of the features that compose it, and still more so in those that it lacks. Indeed, the absence of any element of a 'topography of the control of production' is quite evident – yet elsewhere during the same period this was the most salient element in the topography of political power. Here we find no central administration, no system for centralising surpluses, no social stratification, and no differentiation of labour. There is no royal palace or provincial seat of government. There are neither storehouses nor garrisons, neither specialised workshops nor customs posts.

The picture of the elements of sociopolitical cohesion found in Judges 19–21 is diametrically opposed to the picture I would suggest for a kingdom like Ugarit, in second millennium Syria. They are so opposed that I suspect that the two realities could be superimposed one upon the other, and could coexist without significant consequences. In the case of a kingdom like Ugarit, the stratification and consequent organic interlocking of the productive forces makes it obvious that the territory has a unified political conduct. Vertical solidarity is less evident, because the organic connection is the result of the exploitation of some members by others. In the case of the tribal 'league' the tensions are horizontal instead. Any segment can detach itself whenever it wants, because solidarity with the other segments is not organic but cumulative (cf. Liverani 1976a: 281–302, using E. Durkheim's terms). Therefore it is more important to foster cohesion, which is very weak but is indispensable, ensuring that there is a broad enough basis for matrimonial exchanges to avoid the risk of extinction.

A community, focusing on the development of production, generates a topography of political power centred on significant locations of economic activity (production, centralisation of surplus). A community that focuses on safeguarding reproduction generates a topography of political power centred on significant locations of communicative activity.

4.2.2 Within this system, the only possible transgression is a lack of solidarity – including an excess of solidarity, or the difficult choice between two incompatible solidarities, one protecting the small group and the other incorporating it into a wider grouping. The sanction is always death (*môt yūmāt*, Judg. 21:5), even annihilation (*ḥerem*, Judg. 21:11) Whoever is directly responsible for murder (Gibeah) is to be eliminated. A group that shows solidarity with the culprits (Benjamin) is to be eliminated. Even people who simply do not attend the assembly (Jabesh) are to be eliminated.

The war of the entire tribal grouping against Benjamin does not cause the 'league' to vanish, on the contrary it *demonstrates* its functioning (I keep here to a literary analysis; on the historical situation, see §4.3.4). In this instance war is used as a tool for social adjustment. The case is, of course, different when the war is against outside enemies, against those with whom one does not speak, with whom women are not exchanged, and among whom there is no hospitality. In that case war is a kind of 'clearing of the woods' (cf. Josh. 17:17–18), an operation for creating living space by eliminating a 'different' element with which no relation is possible. But war as a tool for social adjustment, used within the 'league', aims at a maximum development of the groups involved as a whole. The total elimination of one group can in theory be planned, if that group poses a danger to the authority of the rules of interaction. But in practice, a partial destruction would be preferred, taking care that a 'remainder' will ensure the survival of the culprit group, which is no longer guilty after it has been punished. Minor massacres have the function of achieving a better balance: all the inhabitants of Jabesh are killed except the girls, who are allotted for the survival of the entire tribe of Benjamin. There was a rationality – a hallucinatory one, for that matter – in this planning for survival, for the maximum probability of survival.

Sanction, like the ritualised anti-model (§2.3.1), is strongly oriented to pursuing the ultimate task of reproducing the community through time. Through progressive adjustment, infringed rules, overturned decisions, and cancelled sanctions, this ultimate task is always pursued. Social interaction is made up of alternate imbalances, which in the long run produce a balance. Gift exchanges and the transfer of women will always result – if one keeps exact accounts – in there being debtors and creditors. But only when imbalance becomes entrenched and excessive, when the very procedures of adjustment and interaction are threatened, there is recourse to a more drastic adjustment: war. War is not the antithesis of intermarriage or hospitality; it is a drastic substitute for them. There is fighting against Benjamin just because he is a part of the community, and at the same time there is concern for his survival. By measuring out war, massacres, and intermarriage, the aim is to achieve a balanced development of one tribe in the context of all others.

4.3 ACTUALISING REINTERPRETATIONS

4.3.1 The 'league of the twelve tribes of Israel', as it had been enacted, recorded, remembered, imagined, or dreamed of – readers can choose the verb according to their exegetic tastes – by the author of the story in Judges 19–21,[35] is the constitution of an ambiguous sociopolitical ground, on which the contradiction between a nuclear closure and circulation is located. It is an intermediate space interposed between the villages and the enemy territories. The constitution of such an ambiguous ground protects single villages and single families against the risk of extinction, a risk that is greater the smaller the self-sustaining cell. Women are transferred – their use within the group is renounced – in order to have access to women from all the other groups. Visitors are hosted in order to receive hospitality in all other villages. On a statistical level, the resulting transfers and advantages as a whole are in perfect equilibrium. But as far as availability is concerned, one has access to infinitely more than what one can give; therefore the risk of remaining unprovided for becomes very remote. The system of communications and sanctions, which constitutes the only formal grid on this ground, is instrumental in the exchange of women. Kinship links are the very *purpose* of intertribal relations. People belong to the same tribal confederation in order to become related through marriage. The 'myths of foundation' preserved by tribal traditions – from fictional genealogies to stories like the one analysed here – reverse reality by stating that kinship links are the *cause* of the league's existence, that people are members of the same league because they are relatives. By their very nature 'myths of foundation' reverse matters, legitimising what exists by pointing to a prototypical situation. We must be well aware of this reversal. This avoids mistaking social facts for genetic facts, viewing as a process of segmentation what is a process of cohesion, and looking for origins rather than studying a progressive constructing, as well as a continuous deterioration, of a system of sociopolitical links.

In such a perspective, the 'league' could never in fact have existed, but it was always experienced in terms of its values. The problem of its historical existence

---

35 My reservations (not only mine!) about accepting the 'league' as a historical reality (reservations expressed by the use of inverted commas) do not affect the fact that the post-deuteronomistic redactor of Judg. 19–21 was thinking in terms of a voluntarily constituted league.

cannot be discussed here. In general I consider it to be very unlikely that we can identify, on the basis of archaeology, a phase when there were 'no longer' Canaanite kingdoms, with their topography of political power based on the control of production, and 'not yet' a Davidic kingdom. It seems hardly believable that there was a historical phase of this kind that had an exclusive topography of communication incompatible with any other system. At most, one might imagine a peculiar arrangement that opposes the palace to the tribes.

Therefore I think it is useless to bring into play the overworked criterion of 'plausibility' in order to confirm or deny the historicity of the taking of Gibeah or of those other factual 'events' that are narrated in Judges 19–21 in order to establish community values.[36] Instead, I think it is legitimate to try to locate in time the different phases of construction and reuse of this literary edifice, by pointing out the specific sociopolitical situations in which the problem and values of the story has a real foundation and function.

4.3.2 Such an analysis of redactional stratification has been attempted many times in textual criticism, with varying results. All attempts point out the presence of (1) very ancient (including pre-textual) materials, (2) a rather coherent and unitary redaction, and (3) a late, post-deuteronomistic rearrangement.[37] This is not the place for elaborating on these aspects, but some additional considerations are in order.

The pre-textual materials are identified by their recurrence elsewhere. I refer especially to two motifs: the 'punishment of an inhospitable city' is found also in Genesis 19 (Lot in Sodom) in terms that are quite similar to Judges 19; and the 'stratagem for capturing a besieged town' is also found in Joshua 8 (taking of 'Ai) in terms that are quite similar to Judges 20. Clearly, later authors were aware of the work of earlier ones; although the direction of borrowing is open to debate. But what matters is that certain motifs can be applied to different episodes, because they are typical elements in a repertoire of admonitory/instructive character (punishment of the inhospitable city) or of aetiological/narrative character (destruction of a besieged city), a repertoire that had an oral tradition before being used once or more in literary, written form.

---

[36] Compare however – as one example – the 'euhemeristic' study of Eissfeldt 1935. The historicity of the episode has been commonly accepted, from Noth 1930: 100–6 to Schunk 1963: 58, 68–70.

[37] As is well known, biblical literary criticism (conditioned by the postulate of divine inspiration) normally views the original materials as organic and coherent, and attributes the 'contradictions' to later interventions, to the point of postulating as many interventions or layers as there are contradictions to be regularised. It is better to restrict oneself to pointing out significant interventions that are endowed with a literary and ideological specificity, and hence offer the possibility of an historical setting.

This repertoire by its very nature cannot be 'dated'; it cannot be pinned down too closely in time. It has a fluidity that must be taken into account. Above all, it has no necessary relationship – either chronological or factual – with the specific cases to which it is applied. It does not 'date' and it is not 'dated' by a destruction layer, which could conceivably be ascertained archaeologically in Gibeah – even less so in 'Ai or in 'Sodom'. In terms of its sociopolitical context, it would not be too difficult to de-tribalise it, by introducing a 'king of Gibeah' besieged by another king, by changing the Levite into a merchant, and so on.

4.3.3 At the opposite end of the compositional history of Judges 19–21, the most certain element has been pointed out. There was a pervasive – and none too subtle – redactional intervention, post-deuteronomistic in date, which is characterised by the use of keywords and key-concepts such as *qāhāl*, *'ēdāh*, *ha-'am* (cf. Rost 1938; also Anderson 1970; *THAT*, II, 609–19). The lack of a king and the role of the assembly fit into the historical situation of post-exilic Palestine. The explanation of the confused and dangerous situation resulting from the absence of a monarchy is an expression of the desire to strengthen the political cohesion of the Hebrew community. Above all, the differentiation of territory into 'safe' and 'external' zones, the risk in crossing them, and the ambiguity of relationships that could become quite hostile fit into the condition of the Hebrew nuclei returning from exile. These nuclei intermingled with foreign immigrants, who were fully established and were considered true enemies, as well as with other Israelite groups who had never been exiles and were partly amalgamated with the foreigners. The same situation of ethnic/religious intermingling and contrast (Judeans/Samaritans) was to be expressed a few centuries later in the story of another difficult situation of hospitality, that of Jesus and the Samaritan woman in John 4 (compare also Matth. 10:5; Luke 9:52–53; etc.).

This post-exilic re-reading in terms of the Samaritan problem retrojects into the period of the Judges the problems of (re)constituting the Hebrew community. These include the risky displacements through the area, and especially the problem of intermarriage (suffice it to recall Ez. 9–10), and of the difficult survival of a 'remainder' that could be extinguished forever.

4.3.4 As to the basic redaction of the story, the chronological and political setting remains the fundamental problem. I think we should not underestimate the proposals that link the evident anti-Benjaminite attitude in the story with the situation under Saul, especially the final phase of his reign and its immediate aftermath.[38] The cities that are punished – Gibeah and Jabesh – are positively

---

38 E.g., Burney 1918: 477: 'The whole story of Judg. 19–21 may have taken its rise out of antipathy to the memory of Saul'; cf. Eissfeldt 1935: 23–4.

connected to Saul.[39] The hostility between the north and the south in the critical belt slightly north of Jerusalem corresponds to the phase when David established his power, during the short reign of Ishbaal (Soggin 1965; on the connection between Judges 19–21 and Saul's story, see Grottanelli 1979: 29). This was a time of rapid political consolidation of 'tribal' relations that had previously been rather tenuous and oscillating. It was therefore a phase when the establishment of cohesive values (so important to the author of Judges 19–21) had a political function, which also found other expressions.[40]

The story is of Judean (pro-Davidic) origin. It contains a strong anti-Benjaminite grudge, yet at the same time it supports general pacification.[41] The scenery is obviously that of a past that cannot be defined ('There was in olden times – when there was no king in Israel – a man, a Levite, residing in the Ephraim mountain…'), and it could not be 'rationalised' into a precise historical period. If it is true – and I think it cannot be denied that it is true – that the substance of the 'system of twelve tribes' was reconstructed on the basis of the story in Judges 19–21 (de Geus 1976: 55–6), then we have to acknowledge that it is the reconstruction of a dream, a short dream playing a precise political function at the moment when the Davidic state was constructed.[42]

---

[39] Notice that Mizpah too was linked to the reign of Saul (who was designated as king there, *through a casting of lots*, 1 Sam. 10:17–24, a passage strongly adverse to Saul); then it disappears until exilic (Jer. 40–41) and post-exilic (1 Macc. 3:46–54) times.

[40] The story of the Gibeonites seems analogous in function and setting: an old episode (located in Joshua's times) related to hospitality rights (Josh. 10); its infringement by Saul (2 Sam. 21:2); and a violent punishment and pacification by David (2 Sam. 21:1–14). The recurrent use of š'l, in the story of David's rise to power (1 Sam. 10–30) in a function quite similar to that seen for Judg. 19–21, was noted by Westermann 1960: 11.

[41] Eissfeldt's thesis (1935) in which he singled out the contrast between Ephraim and Benjamin as the historical kernel, and charged the late redactor with a rewriting in pan-Israelite terms, seems to me to be at once minimal and excessive. I would even reject any 'historical kernel' (in such terms), but believe that the unitary values were already present in the basic text, which I consider to belong to Davidic times.

[42] Compare the formulation by de Vaux 1973: 65: 'Le système des douze tribus, qui les unit dans une même liste généalogique ou tribale est la construction idéale, à l'époque de David, d'un 'grand Israel', qui n'a jamais existé comme organisation politique'; 53–4: 'Le système des douze tribus ne paraît donc pas être antérieur à la fin de l'époque des Juges ou tout au début de la monarchie'.

Bibliography

Aarne, A., and Thompson, S. 1928, *The Types of the Folk-Tale*. Helsinki: Suomalainen Tiedeakatemia.

Albright, W. F. 1955, 'Some Canaanite-Phoenician Sources of Hebrew Wisdom'. In H. W. Rowley (ed.), *Wisdom in Israel and in the Ancient Near East*, 1–15. *Vetus Testamentum*, Supplements 3. Leiden: E. J. Brill.

—, 1966, *The Amarna Letters from Palestine*. The Cambridge Ancient History. Revised edition of volumes I & II (Preprints), II/xx. Cambridge: Cambridge University Press.

Altman, A. 1978, 'Some Controversial Toponyms from the Amurru Region in the Amarna Archive'. *Zeitschrift des Deutschen Palästina-Vereins* 94, 99–107.

Anderson, G. W. 1970, 'Israel: Amphictiony: ʿam, kahal, ʿedah'. In H. T. Frank and W. L. Reed (eds), *Essays in Honor of H. G. May*, 135–51. Nashville and New York: Abingdon Press.

Archi, A. 1966, 'Trono regale e trono divinizzato nell'Anatolia ittita'. *Studi Micenei ed Egeo-Anatolici* 1, 76–120.

—, 1969. 'La storiografia ittita'. *Athenaeum* 47, 7–20.

—, 1971. 'The Propaganda of Hattušiliš III'. *Studi Micenei ed Egeo-Anatolici* 14, 185–215.

Artzi, P. 1964, ' "Vox populi" in the el-Amarna Tablets'. *Revue d'Assyriologie* 58, 159–66.

Baikie, J. 1926, *The Amarna Age*. London: Black.

Balkan, K. 1973, *Eine Schenkungsurkunde aus der althethitischen Zeit, gefunden in Inandik*. Ankara: Türk Tarih Kurumu.

Barthes, R. 1972, *Saggi critici*. Turin: Einaudi. Italian translation of *Essais critiques* (1963), Paris: Editions du Seuil.

Beckman, G. 1996, *Hittite Diplomatic Texts*. Atlanta: Scholars Press.

Bernhardt, K. H. 1971, 'Verwaltungspraxis im spätbronzezeitlichen Palästina'. In H. Klengel (ed.), *Beiträge zur sozialen Struktur des alten Vorderasien*, 133–47. Berlin: Akademie-Verlag.

Besters, A. 1965, 'Le sanctuaire central dans Jud. XIX–XXI'. *Ephemerides Theologicae Lovanienses* 41, 20–41.

Bin Nun, Sh. R. 1975, *The Tawananna in the Hittite Kingdom*. Texte der Hethiter 5. Heidelberg: Carl Winter.

Boccaccio, P. 1953, 'I termini contrari come espressioni della totalità in ebraico, I'. *Biblica* 33, 173–90.

Böhl, F. M. T. de Liagre 1959, 'Die Mythe vom weisen Adapa'. *Die Welt des Orients* 2/5–6, 416–31.

Bouthoul, G. 1970, *Traité de polémologie*. Paris: Payot.

Bremond, C. 1966, 'La logique des possibles narratifs'. *Communications* 8, 60–76.

Bresciani, E. 1969, *Letteratura e poesia dell'antico Egitto*. Turin: Einaudi.

Bryce, T. 1998, *The Kingdom of the Hittites*. Oxford: Clarendon Press.

Buccellati, G. 1962, 'La "carriera" di David e quella di Idrimi, re di Alalac'. *Bibbia e Oriente* 4, 95–9.

—, 1972, 'Tre saggi sulla sapienza mesopotamica'. *Oriens Antiquus* 11, 1–36, 81–100, 161–78.

—, 1973, 'Adapa, Genesis and the Notion of Faith'. *Ugarit-Forschungen* 5, 61–6.

Burney, C. F. 1918, *The Book of Judges*. London: Rivingtons.

Caminos, R. 1954, *Late-Egyptian Miscellanies*. London: Oxford University Press.

Campbell, E. F. 1960, 'The Amarna Letters and the Amarna Period'. *Biblical Archaeologist* 23, 2–22.

—, 1964, *The Chronology of the Amarna Letters*. Baltimore: The Johns Hopkins University Press.

—, 1976, 'Two Amarna Notes: The Shechem City-State and Amarna Administrative Terminology'. In F. M. Cross, W. F. Lemche and P. D. Miller (eds), *Magnalia Dei. Essays in Memory of G. E. Wright*, 39–54. Garden City NY: Doubleday & Co.

Castellino, G. R. 1967, *Mitologia sumerico-accadica*. Turin: Società Editrice Internazionale.

Cavaignac, E. 1930, 'Remarques sur l'inscription de Telibinou'. *Revue Hittite et Asianique* I/1, 9–14.

Cazelles, H. 1963, 'Les débuts de la sagesse en Israël'. In *Les sagesses du Proche-Orient ancien*, 27–40. Paris: Presses Universitaires de France.

Coats, G. W. 1970, 'Self-Abasement and Insult Formulas'. *Journal of Biblical Literature* 89, 14–26.

Coogan, M. D. 1978, *Stories from Ancient Canaan*. Philadelphia: Westminster Press.

Cornelius, F. 1956, 'Die Chronologie des Vorderen Orient im 2. Jahrtausend v. Chr'. *Archiv für Orientforschung* 17, 294–309.

—, 1958, 'Chronology. Eine Erwiderung'. *Journal of Cuneiform Studies* 12, 101–107.

Crown, A. D. 1974, 'Tidings and Instructions. How News Travelled in the

Ancient Near East'. *Journal of the Economic and Social History of the Orient* 17, 244–71.

Dalley, S. 1989, *Myths from Mesopotamia*. Oxford and New York: Oxford University Press.

De Lillo, A. 1971, *L'analisi del contenuto*. Bologna: Mulino.

Diakonoff, I. M. 1976, 'Slaves, Helots and Serfs in Early Antiquity'. In J. Harmatta and G. Komoróczy (eds), *Wirtschaft und Gesellschaft im alten Vorderasien*, 45–78. Budapest: Akadémiai Kiadó.

Dijk, J. J. van 1953, *La sagesse suméro-accadienne*. Leiden: E. J. Brill.

Dommershausen, W. 1971, 'Die "Los" in der alttestamentlichen Theologie'. *Trier Theologische Zeitschrift* 80, 195–206.

Donadoni, S. 1959, *Storia della letteratura egiziana antica*. Milan: Nuova Accademia.

Dossin, G. 1938, 'Signaux lumineux au pays de Mari'. *Revue d'Assyriologie* 35, 174–86.

Driver, G. R. 1947, 'Mistranslations in the Old Testament'. *Die Welt des Orients* I/1, 29–31.

Dubarle, A. M. 1969, 'Où en est l'étude de la littérature sapientielle?' In H. Cazelles (ed.), *De Mari à Qumrân. Donum Natalicium I. Coppens*, 246–58. Bibliotheca Ephemeridum Theologicarum Lovaniensium 24, Paris: P. Lethiellet; Gembloux: J. Duculot.

Duesberg, H. 1966, *Les scribes inspirés*. 2nd edition. Tournai: Editions de Mared.

Dus, J. 1964, 'Bethel und Mizpah in Jdc. 19–21'. *Oriens Antiquus* 3, 227–43.

Eco, U. 1971, *Le forme del contenuto*. Milan: Bompiani.

Edgerton, W. F. 1951, 'The Strikes in Ramses III's Twenty-ninth Year'. *Journal of Near Eastern Studies* 10, 137–45.

Eisenbeis, W. 1969, *Die Wurzel ŠLM im Alten Testament*. Beihefte zur Zeitschrift für die Alttestamentliche Wissenschaft 113. Berlin: W. de Gruyter.

Eissfeldt, O. 1935, 'Der geschichtliche Hintergrund der Erzählung von Gibeas Schandtat (Richter 19–21)'. In A. Weiser (ed.), *Festschrift G. Beer*, 19–40. Stuttgart: W. Kohlhammer.

Eliade, M. 1949, *Le mythe de l'éternel retour*. Paris: Gallimard.

—, 1965. *Le sacré et le profane*. Paris: Gallimard.

Exum, J. C. 1993, *Fragmented Women: Feminist (Sub)versions of Biblical Narratives*. Sheffield: Sheffield Academic Press.

Fahlgren, K. H. 1932, *Ṣedākā, nahestehende und entgegengesetze Begriffe im Alten Testament*. Uppsala: Almquist & Wiksells.

Fales, F. M. 1974, 'L'ideologo Adad-šumu-usur'. *Rendiconti dell'Accademia Nazionale dei Lincei*, serie VIII, 29, 453–96.

Fensham, F. C. 1971, 'The Change of the Situation of a Person'. *Annali dell'Istituto Universitario Orientale di Napoli* 21, 155–64.

Fernandez, A. 1931, 'El atentado de Gabaa (critica historico-literaria de Jud. 19–21'. *Biblica* 12, 297–315.

Fisher, R. W. 1966, A Study of the Semitic Root *BSR*. PhD Dissertation. Columbia University.

Forrer, E. 1922–26, *Die Boghazköi-Texte in Umschrift*. 2 vols. Wissenschaftliche Veröffentlichungen der Deutschen Orient-Gesellschaft 41–42. Leipzig: Hinrichs.

Foster, B. R. 1993, *Before the Muses: An Anthology of Akkadian Literature*. Bethesda, Maryland: CDL Press.

—, 1995, *From Distant Days: Myths, Tales, and Poetry of Ancient Mesopotamia*. Bethesda, Maryland: CDL Press.

Freud, S. 1955, *The Interpretation of Dreams*, translated from the German and edited by James Strachey. New York: Basic Books, Inc.

Freydank, H. 1960, 'Eine hethitische Fassung des Vertrages zwischen dem Hethiterkönig Šuppiluliuma und Aziru von Amurru'. *Mitteilungen des Instituts für Orientforschung* 7, 356–81.

Friedrich, J. 1925–26, *Aus dem hethitischen Schrifttum*. 2 vols. Der Alte Orient 24/3, 25/2. Leipzig: Hinrichs.

—, 1926–30, *Staatsverträge des Hatti-Reiches in hethitischer Sprache*. 2 vols. Mitteilungen der Vorderasiatisch-Aegyptischen Gesellschaft 31/1 and 34/1. Leipzig: Hinrichs.

Furlani, G. 1929, 'Il mito di Adapa'. *Rendiconti dell'Accademia Nazionale dei Lincei*, serie VI, 5, 113–71.

—, 1939a, 'Gli Annali di Mursilis II di Hatti'. In *Saggi sulla civiltà degli Hittiti*, 65–140. Udine: Istituto delle Edizioni Accademiche.

—, 1939b, 'L'apologia di Hattusilis III di Hatti'. In *Saggi sulla civiltà degli Hittiti*, 141–186. Udine: Istituto delle Edizioni Accademiche.

Fürst, H. 1965, *Die göttliche Heimsuchung*. Rome: Pontificium Athenaeum Antonianum.

Gardiner, A. H. 1925, 'The Autobiography of Rekhmerē''. *Zeitschrift für Aegyptische Sprache* 60, 62–76.

Gaster, T. 1969, *Myth, Legend and Custom in the Old Testament*. New York: Harper & Row.

Gelb, I. J. 1956, 'Hittite Hieroglyphic Seals and Seal Impressions'. In H. Goldman (ed.), *Excavations at Gözlü Kule, Tarsus*, I, 242–54. Princeton: Princeton University Press.

—, 1965, 'The Ancient Mesopotamian Ration System'. *Journal of Near Eastern Studies* 24, 230–43.

Gernet, L. 1932, 'Fosterage et légende'. In *Mélanges G. Glotz*, I, 385–95. Republished in *Droits et société dans la Grèce ancienne* (1955), 19–28. Paris: Sirey.

Geus, C. H. J. de 1976, *The Tribes of Israel*. Studia Semitica Neerlandica 18. Amsterdam: Van Gorcum.

Goetze, A. 1924, 'Das hethitische Fragment des Šunaššura-Vertrags'. *Zeitschrift für Assyriologie* 2, 11–18.

—, 1925, *Hattušiliš: Der Bericht über seine Thronbesteigung nebst den Paralleltexten*. Mitteilungen der Vorderasiatisch-Aegyptischen Gesellschaft 29/3. Leipzig: Hinrichs.

—, 1928, *Das Hethiter-Reich*. Der Alte Orient 27/2. Leipzig: Hinrichs.

—, 1930a, *Neue Bruchstücke zum grossen Text des Hattušiliš und den Paralleltexten*. Mitteilungen der Vorderasiatisch-Aegyptischen Gesellschaft 34/2. Leipzig: Hinrichs.

—, 1930b, 'Über die hethitische Königsfamilie'. *Archiv Orientální* 2, 153–63.

—, 1940, *Kizzuwatna and the Problem of Hittite Geography*. New Haven: Yale University Press.

—, 1957a, *Kleinasien*. Kulturgeschichte des alten Orients III/1. München: Beck.

—, 1957b, 'On the Chronology of the Second Millennium BC'. *Journal of Cuneiform Studies* 11, 53–61, 63–73.

Gordon, C. H. 1965, *Ugaritic Textbook*. Analecta Orientalia 38. Rome: Pontificium Institutum Biblicum.

Grapow, H. 1949, *Studien zu den Annalen Thutmosis des dritten*. Abhandlungen der Deutschen Akademie der Wissenschaften zu Berlin, Philosophisch-historische Klasse 1947/2. Berlin: Akademie Verlag.

Gray, J. 1970, 'The Book of Job in the Context of Near Eastern Literature'. *Zeitschrift für die alttestamentliche Wissenschaft* 82, 251–69.

Grayson, A. K. 1975, *Assyrian and Babylonian Chronicles*. Texts from Cuneiform Sources 5. Locust Valley, NY: J. J. Augustin.

Grottanelli, C. 1976–77, 'Notes on Mediterranean Hospitality'. *Dialoghi di Archeologia* 9–10, 186–94.

—, 1978, 'Il giudice Ehud e il valore della mano sinistra'. In *Atti del 1° Convegno Italiano sul Vicino Oriente antico*, 44–5. Orientis Antiqui Collectio 13. Rome: Centro per le Antichità e la Storia dell'Arte del Vicino Oriente.

—, 1979, 'The Enemy King is a Monster'. *Studi Storico-Religiosi* 3, 5–36.

Gurney, O. R. 1962, *Anatolia c. 1750–1600 B.C.* The Cambridge Ancient History. Revised edition of volumes I & II (Preprints), II/vi. Cambridge: Cambridge University Press.

—, 1966, *Anatolia c. 1600–1380 B.C.* The Cambridge Ancient History. Revised edition of volumes I & II (Preprints), II/xva. Cambridge: Cambridge University Press.

Güterbock, H. G. 1938, 'Die historische Tradition und ihre literarische Gestaltung bei Babyloniern und Hethitern bis 1200, II'. *Zeitschrift für Assyriologie* 10, 45–149.

—, 1964, 'Sargon of Akkad Mentioned by Hattusili I of Hatti'. *Journal of Cuneiform Studies* 18, 1–6.

Haas, V. 1970, *Der Kult von Nerik*. Studia Pohl 4. Rome: Pontificium Institutum Biblicum.

Haldar, A. 1950, *The Notion of the Desert in Sumero-Accadian and West-Semitic Religions*. Uppsala: A. B. Lund.

Hardy, R. S. 1941, 'The Old Hittite Kingdom: A Political History'. *American Journal of Semitic Languages* 58, 177–216.

Helck, W. W. 1962, *Die Beziehungen Ägyptens zu Vorderasien im 3. und 2. Jahrtausend v.Chr.* Ägyptologische Abhandlungen 5. Wiesbaden: Harrassowitz.

Herdner, A. 1963, *Corpus des tablettes en cunéiformes alphabétiques*, 2 vols. Mission de Ras Shamra X. Paris: Imprimerie Nationale; Geuthner.

Hermann, A. 1938, *Die ägyptische Königsnovelle*. Glückstadt: J. J. Augustin.

Hirsch, H. 1968–69, 'Den Toten zu beleben'. *Archiv für Orientforschung* 22, 39–58.

Hoffman, I. 1984, *Der Erlaß Telipinus*. Texte der Hethiter 11. Heidelberg: Carl Winter Verlag.

Hoffner, H. A. Jr. 1997, 'Hittite Laws'. In Martha T. Roth (ed.), *Law Collections from Mesopotamia and Asia Minor,* 213–41. Atlanta: Scholars Press.

Holmes, Y. Lynn 1975, 'The Messengers of the Amarna Letters'. *Journal of the American Oriental Society* 95, 376–81.

Hout, Th. P. J. van den 1997, 'Biography and Autobiography'. In W. W. Hallo and K. L. Younger, Jr (eds), *The Context of Scripture*, I, 194–204. Leiden: E. J. Brill.

Houwink ten Cate, Ph. H. J. 1970, *The Records of the Early Hittite Empire*. Istanbul: Nederlands Historisch-Archaeologisch Instituut in het Nabije Oosten.

Huizinga, J. 1964, *Homo ludens*. Italian translation. Milan: Il Saggiatore.

Humbert, P. 1937, 'La "femme étrangère" du livre des Proverbes'. *Revue des Etudes Sémitiques* 1937, 49–64.

—, 1958, 'Les adjectifs *zar* et *nokrî* et la "femme étrangère" des Proverbes bibliques'. In *Opuscules d'un hébraisant*, 111–8. Neuchâtel: Secrétariat de l'Université.

Imparati, F. 1964, *Le leggi ittite*. Incunabula Graeca 7. Rome: Edizioni dell'Ateneo.

Irwin, W. H. 1965, 'Le sanctuaire central israélite avant l'établissement de la monarchie'. *Revue Biblique* 72, 161–84.

Izre'el, S. 1991, *Amurru Akkadian: a linguistic study*, 2 vols. Harvard Semitic Studies 40–41. Atlanta: Scholars Press.

—, 2001, *Adapa and the South Wind*. Winona Lake: Eisenbrauns.

Jacobsen, T. 1929–30, 'The Investiture and Anointing of Adapa in Heaven', *American Journal of Semitic Languages* 46, 201–203.

—, 1946, 'Mesopotamia'. In H. Frankfort (ed.), *The Intellectual Adventure of Ancient Man*, 125–219. Chicago: The University of Chicago Press.

Janssen, J. J. 1975, *Commodity Prices from the Ramessid Period*. Leiden: E. J. Brill.

Kammenhuber, A. 1955, 'Studien zum hethitischen Infinitivsystem, IV'. *Mitteilungen des Instituts für Orientforschung* 3, 31–57.

—, 1958, 'Die hethitische Geschichtsschreibung'. *Saeculum* 9, 136–55.

—, 1965, 'Die hethitischen Vorstellungen von Seele und Leib, Herz und Lebesinneren, Kopf und Person, II'. *Zeitschrift für Assyriologie* 23, 177–222.

—, 1968, *Die Arier im Vorderen Orient*. Heidelberg: Carl Winter.

—, 1969, *Altkleinasiatische Sprachen*. Handbuch der Orientalistik I/II/1–2/2. Leiden and Köln: E. J. Brill.

—, 1970, 'Die Vorgänger Šuppiluliumas I'. *Orientalia* 39, 278–301.

Kestemont, G. 1978, 'La société internationale mitannienne et le royaume d'Amurru à l'époque amarnienne'. *Orientalia Lovaniensia Periodica* 9, 27–32.

Kienast, B. 1973, 'Die Weisheit des Adapa von Eridu'. In M. A. Beek (ed.), *Symbolae biblicae et mesopotamicae F. M. Th. de Liagre Böhl dicatae*, 234–9. Leiden: E. J. Brill.

Kirk, G. S. 1970, *Myth: Its Meaning and Function in Ancient and Other Cultures*. Cambridge: Cambridge University Press.

Kitchen, K. A. 1962, *Suppiluliuma and the Amarna Pharaohs*. Liverpool: Liverpool University Press.

Klengel, H. 1960, 'Zu den *šibūtum* in altbabylonischer Zeit'. *Orientalia* 29, 357–75.

—, 1964, 'Aziru von Amurru und seine Rolle in der Geschichte der Amārnazeit'. *Mitteilungen des Instituts für Orientforschung* 10, 57–83.

—, 1965a, 'Die Rolle der "Ältesten" (LÚ.MEŠ ŠU.GI) im Kleinasien der Hethiterzeit'. *Zeitschrift für Assyriologie* 23, 223–36.

—, 1965b, 'Einige Bemerkungen zur Syrienpolitik des Amenophis IV / Echnaton'. *Das Altertum* 11, 131–7.

—, 1965–70, *Geschichte Syriens im 2. Jahrtausend v.u.Z.* 3 vols. Institut für Orientforschung, Veröffentlichung Nr. 40. Berlin: Akademie-Verlag.

—, 1968, 'Die Hethiter und Išuwa'. *Oriens Antiquus* 7, 63–76.

—, 1969, 'Syrien in der hethitischen Historiographie'. *Klio* 51, 5–14.

Knudtzon, J. A. 1902, 'Anordnung der Briefe Rib-Addis'. *Beiträge zur Assyriologie* 4, 288–320.

—, 1907, *Die El-Amarna-Tafeln,* I: *Die Texte*. Vorderasiatische Bibliothek II/1. Leipzig: Hinrichs.

—, 1915, *Die El-Amarna-Tafeln,* II: *Anmerkungen und Register*. Vorderasiatische Bibliothek II/2. Leipzig: Hinrichs.

Korošec, V. 1931, *Hethitische Staatsverträge*. Leipziger Rechtswissenschaftliche Studien 60. Leipzig: Weicher.

Kramer, S. N. 1952, *Enmerkar and the Lord of Aratta*. Philadelphia: The University Museum.

Kraus, F. R. 1960, 'Altmesopotamische Lebensgefühl'. *Journal of Near Eastern Studies* 19, 117–32.

—, 1971, 'Ein altbabylonischer Privatbrief an eine Gottheit'. *Revue d'Assyriologie* 65: 27–36.

Kühne, C. 1972, 'Bemerkungen zu kürzlich edierten hethitischen Texten'. *Zeitschrift für Assyriologie* 62, 236–61.

Kuhrt, A. 1995, *The Ancient Near East c. 3000–330 BC*. London: Routledge.

Kümmel, H. M. 1967, *Ersatzrituale fur den hethitischen König*. Studien zu den Boğazköy-Texten 3. Wiesbaden: Harrassowitz.

Kupper, J. R. 1957, *Les nomades en Mésopotamie au temps des rois de Mari*. Paris: Les Belles Lettres.

Kutsch, E. 1963, *Salbung als Rechtsakt im alten Testament und im alten Orient*. Beihefte zur Zeitschrift für die Alttestamentliche Wissenschaft 87. Berlin: A. Töpelmann.

—, 1973, *Verheissung und Gesetz*. Beihefte zur Zeitschrift für die Alttestamentliche Wissenschaft 131. Berlin: W. de Gruyter.

Labat, R. 1970, 'Les grands textes de la pensée babylonienne'. In R. Labat, A. Caquot, M. Sznycer and M. Vleyra (eds), *Les religions du Proche-Orient asiatique*. Paris: Fayard/Denoël.

Lambert, W. G. 1960, *Babylonian Wisdom Literature*. Oxford: Oxford University Press.

Landsberger, B. 1937, *Die Serie ana ittišu*. Materialien zum sumerischen Lexikon 1. Rome: Pontificium Institutum Biblicum.

—, 1957, *The Series HAR-ra = hubullu. Tablets I–IV*. Materialien zum sumerischen Lexikon 5. Rome: Pontificium Institutum Biblicum.

Laroche, E. 1971, *Catalogue des textes hittites*. Paris: Klincksieck.

Lasswell, H. D., and Leites, N. 1965, *Language of Politics: Studies in Quantitative Semantics*. Cambridge MA: Massachusetts Institute of Technology.

Leeuw, G. van der 1949, 'Urzeit und Endzeit'. *Eranos-Jahrbuch* 17, 11–51.

Lemaire, A. 1977, *Inscriptions hébraïques, I: Les ostraca*. Littératures Anciennes du Proche-Orient 9. Paris: Les Editions du Cerf.

Lévi-Strauss, C. 1944, Reciprocity and Hierarchy. *American Anthropologist* 46, 266–8.

—, 1956, 'Les organisations dualistes existent-elles?' *Bijdragen tot de Taal-, Land- en Volkenkunde* 112, 99–128.

—, 1964, *Le cru et le cuit*. Paris: Plon.

—, 1973, *From Honey to Ashes*, translated from the French by John and Doreen Weightman. London: Jonathan Cape.

Lichtheim, M. 1973–80, *Ancient Egyptian Literature*. 3 vols. Berkeley: University of California Press.

Lindblom, J. 1962, 'Lot-Casting in the Old Testament'. *Vetus Testamentum* 12, 164–78.

Liverani, M. 1962, 'Hurri e Mitanni'. *Oriens Antiquus* 1, 253–7.

—, 1963, *Storia di Ugarit nell'età degli archivi politici*. Studi Semitici 6. Rome: Centro di Studi Semitici.

—, 1965a, 'Implicazioni sociali nella politica di Abdi-Aširta di Amurru'. *Rivista degli Studi Orientali* 40, 267–77.

—, 1965b, 'Il fuoruscitismo in Siria nella tarda età del bronzo'. *Rivista Storica Italiana* 77, 315–36.

—, 1967a, 'Contrasti e confluenze di concezioni politiche nell'età di el-Amarna'. *Revue d'Assyriologie* 61, 1–18.

—, 1967b, '"Ma nel settimo anno…"'. In *Studi sull'Oriente e la Bibbia offerti al P. G. Rinaldi*, 49–53. Genoa: Editrice Studio e Vita.

—, 1970, 'L'epica ugaritica nel suo contesto storico e letterario'. In *La poesia epica e la sua formazione*, 859–69. Quaderno 139. Rome: Accademia Nazionale dei Lincei.

—, 1971a, 'Le lettere del Faraone a Rib-Adda'. *Oriens Antiquus* 10, 253–68.

—, 1971b, 'Συδυκ e Μισωρ'. In *Studi in onore di E. Volterra*, VI, 55–74. Milan: A. Giuffrè Editore.

—, 1972a, 'Partire sul carro, per il deserto'. *Annali dell'Istituto Universitario Orientale di Napoli* 32, 403–415.

—, 1972b, 'Elementi "irrazionali" nel commercio amarniano'. *Oriens Antiquus* 11, 297–317.

—, 1973a, 'Memorandum on the Approach to Historiographic Texts'. *Orientalia* 42, 178–94.

—, 1973b, 'Storiografia politica hittita. I - Šunaššura, ovvero: della reciprocità'. *Oriens Antiquus* 12, 267–97.

—, 1974a, 'Rib-Adda, giusto sofferente'. *Altorientalische Forschungen* 1, 176–205.

—, 1974b, 'L'histoire de Joas'. *Vetus Testamentum* 24, 438–53.

—, 1974c, 'La royauté syrienne de l'âge du bronze récent'. In P. Garelli (ed.), *Le palais et la royauté*, 329–56. Paris: Paul Geuthner.

—, 1976a, 'La struttura politica'. In S. Moscati (ed.), *L'alba della civiltà*, I, 281–302. Turin: UTET.

—, 1976b, 'Il modo di produzione'. In S. Moscati (ed.), *L'alba della civiltà*, II, 1–126. Turin: UTET.

—, 1977, 'Review of E. Edel, Ägyptische Ärtze und ägyptische Medizin'. *Rivista degli Studi Orientali* 51, 28–6.

—, 1978, 'Le tradizioni orali delle fonti scritte nell'antico Oriente'. In B. Bernardi, C. Poni and A. Triulzi (eds), *Fonti orali: Antropologia e storia*, 395–406. Milan: Angeli.

—, 1979a, 'Messaggi, donne, ospitalità: comunicazione intertribale in Giud. 19–21'. *Studi Storico-Religiosi* 3, 302–341.

—, 1979b, 'Farsi habiru'. *Vicino Oriente* 2, 65–77.

—, 1990, *Prestige and Interest: International Relations in the Near East ca. 1600–1100 B.C.* History of the Ancient Near East/Studies 1. Padua: Sargon.

—, 1997, '"Half-Nomads" on the Middle Euphrates and the Concept of Dimorphic Society'. *Altorientalische Forschungen* 24, 44–8.

—, 1998–99, *Le lettere di el-Amarna*. 2 vols. Brescia: Paideia.

Longman, T. 1997, 'The Autobiography of Idrimi'. In W. W. Hallo and K. L. Younger, Jr (eds), *The Context of Scripture*, I, 479–80. Leiden: E. J. Brill.

Longo, O. 1976, 'Il messaggio di fuoco: approcci semiologici all'Agamennone di Eschilo'. *Bollettino dell'Istituto di Filologia Greca, Università di Padova* 3, 121–58.

—, 1978, 'Scrivere in Tucidide: comunicazione e ideologia'. In *Studi in onore di A. Ardizzoni*, 517–54. Rome: Edizioni dell'Ateneo & Bizzarri.

McCarthy, D. J. 1964, 'Vox *bśr* praeparat vocem "evangelium"'. *Verbum Domini* 42, 26–33.

McKenzie, J. L. 1959, 'The Elders in the Old Testament'. *Studia Biblica et Orientalia*, I, 388–406. Rome: Pontificium Institutum Biblicum.

Macqueen, J. G. 1959, 'Hattian Mythology and Hittite Monarchy'. *Anatolian Studies* 9, 171–88.

Malamat, A. 1965, 'Organs of Statecraft in the Israelite Monarchy'. *Biblical Archaeologist* 28, 34–65.

—, 1978, *Early Israelite Warfare and the Conquest of Canaan*. Oxford: Centre for Postgraduate Hebrew Studies.

Mendenhall, G. E. 1962, 'The Hebrew Conquest of Palestine'. *Biblical Archaeologist* 25, 66–87.

Meyer, G. 1953, 'Zwei neue Kizzuwatna-Verträge'. *Mitteilungen des Instituts für Orientforschung* 1, 108–124.

Michalowski, P. 1980, 'Adapa and the Ritual Process'. *Rocznik Orientalistyczny* 41, 77–82.

Moran, W. L. 1950, 'The Use of the Canaanite Infinitive Absolute as a Finite Verb in the Amarna Letters from Byblos'. *Journal of Cuneiform Studies* 4, 169–72.

—, 1960, 'Early Canaanite yaqtula'. *Orientalia* 29, 1–19.

—, 1963, 'A Note on the Treaty Terminology of the Sefire Stelas'. *Journal of Near Eastern Studies* 22, 173–6.

—, 1992, *The Amarna Letters*. Baltimore and London: The Johns Hopkins University Press.

Morenz, S. 1969, *Prestige-Wirtschaft im alten Aegypten*. Bayerische Akademie der Wissenschaften, Sitzungsberichte der philologisch-historische Klasse 1969/4. Munich: Verlag der Bayerischen Akademie der Wissenschaften.

Mowinckel, S. 1955, 'Psalms and Wisdom'. In H. W. Rowley (ed.), *Wisdom in Israel and in the Ancient Near East*, 205–224. Vetus Testamentum, Supplements 3. Leiden: E. J. Brill.

Munn-Rankin, J. M. 1956, 'Diplomacy in Western Asia in the Early Second Millennium B.C.' *Iraq* 18, 96–108.

Nielsen, E. 1954, *Oral Tradition*. Studies in Biblical Theology 11. London: SCM Press.

Noth, M. 1930, *Das System der zwölf Stämme Israels*. Beiträge zur Wissenschaft vom Alten und Neuen Testament 52. Stuttgart: W. Kohlhammer.

Nougayrol, J. 1955, *Le palais royal d'Ugarit, III: Textes accadiens et hourrites des archives est, ouest et centrales*. Mission de Ras Shamra VI. Paris: Imprimerie Nationale; C. Klincksieck.

—, 1956, *Le palais royal d'Ugarit, IV: Textes accadiens des archives sud*. Mission de Ras Shamra IX. Paris: Imprimerie Nationale; C. Klincksieck.

—, 1968, 'Textes suméro-accadiens des archives et bibliothèques privées d'Ugarit'. In *Ugaritica* V, 1–446. Mission de Ras Shamra XVI. Paris: Imprimerie Nationale; P. Geuthner.

Oller, G. H. 1977, The Autobiography of Idrimi. PhD Dissertation. University of Pennsylvania.

Oppenheim, A. L. 1964, *Ancient Mesopotamia*. Chicago: The University of Chicago Press.

—, 1965, 'A Note on the Scribes in Mesopotamia'. In *Studies in Honor of B. Landsberger*, 253–6. Assyriological Studies 16. Chicago: The University of Chicago Press.

—, 1967, *Letters from Mesopotamia*. Chicago: The University of Chicago Press.

Orlinski, H. M. 1962, 'The Tribal System of Israel and Related Groups in the Period of the Judges'. *Oriens Antiquus* 1, 11–20.

Ossowski, S. 1966, *Struttura di classe e coscienza sociale*. Turin: Einaudi.

Otten, H. 1951, 'Ein althethitischer Vertrag mit Kizzuwatna'. *Journal of Cuneiform Studies* 5, 129–32.

—, 1958, 'Keilschrifttexte'. *Mitteilungen des Deutschen Orient-Gesellschaft* 91: 73–84.

—, 1961, 'Das Hethiterreich'. In H. Schmökel (ed.), *Kulturgeschichte des alten Orient*, 311–446. Stuttgart: A. Kröner Verlag.

—, 1966, 'Hethiter, Hurriter und Mitanni'. In *Fischer Weltgeschichte 3: Die altorientalischen Reiche 2*. Frankfurt: Fischer Bücherei.

—, 1968, *Die hethitischen historischen Quellen und die altorientalische Chronologie*. Akademie der Wissenschaften und der Literatur, Abhadlungen der Geistes- und Sozialwissenschaftliche Klasse 1968/3. Mainz: Akademie der Wissenschaften und der Literatur.

—, 1971, 'Das Siegel des hethitischen Grosskönigs Tahurwaili'. *Mitteilungen des Deutschen Orient-Gesellschaft* 103, 59–68.

—, 1973, *Eine althethitische Erzälung um die Stadt Zalpa*. Wiesbaden: Harrassowitz.

Parpola, S. 1970, *Letters from Assyrian Scholars*. Alter Orient und Altes Testament 5/1. Kevelaer: Butzon & Bercker; Neukirchen–Vluyn: Neukirchener Verlag.

Pedersen, J. 1926, *Israel: Its Life and Culture*. 2 vols. London: Oxford University Press.

Perelman, Ch., and Olbrechts-Tyteca, L. 1958, *Traité de l'argumentation*. Paris: Presses Universitaires de France.

Petschow, H. 1963, 'Zur Noxalhaftung im hethitischen Recht'. *Zeitschrift für Assyriologie* 21, 237–50.

Pettinato, G. 1975, 'I rapporti politici di Tiro con l'Assiria alla luce del trattato tra Asarhaddon e Baal'. *Rivista di Studi Fenici* 3, 145–60.

Pieper, M. 1935, *Das ägyptische Märchen*. Leipzig: Hinrichs.

Piepkorn, A. C. 1933, *Historical Prism Inscriptions of Ashurbanipal*, I: Assyriological Studies 5. Chicago: The University of Chicago Press.

Pierce, J. R. 1961, *Symbols, Signals and Noise: The Nature and Process of Communication*, Harper Modern Science Series. New York: Harper.

Pintore, F. 1972, 'Transiti di truppe e schemi epistolari nella Siria egiziana dell'età di el-Amarna'. *Oriens Antiquus* 11, 101–131.

—, 1973, 'La prassi della marcia armata nella Siria egiziana dell'età di el-Amarna'. *Oriens Antiquus* 12, 299–318.

—, 1978, *Il matrimonio interdinastico nel Vicino Oriente durante i secoli XV–XIII*. Orientis Antiqui Collectio 14. Rome: Centro per le Antichità e la Storia dell'Arte del Vicino Oriente.

Pitt-Rivers, J. 1977, *The Fate of Shechem or the Politics of Sex*. Cambridge Studies in Social Anthropology 19. Cambridge: Cambridge University Press.

Posener, G. 1960, *De la divinité de Pharaon*. Cahiers de la Société Asiatique 15. Paris: Imprimerie Nationale.

—, 1963, 'L'apport des textes littéraires à la connaissance de l'histoire égyptienne'. In S. Donadoni (ed.), *Le fonti indirette della storia egiziana*, 11–30. Studi Semitici 7. Rome: Centro di Studi Semitici.

Postgate, N. J. 1971, 'Land Tenure in the Middle Assyrian Period, a Reconstruction'. *Bulletin of the School of Oriental and African Studies* 34, 496–520.

Pritchard, J. B. 1969, *Ancient Near Eastern Texts Relating to the Old Testament*, 3rd edition. Princeton: Princeton University Press.

Propp, V. J. 1949, *Le radici storiche dei racconti di fate*. Turin: Einaudi.

—, 1966, *Morfologia della fiaba*. Turin: Einaudi.

Pugliese Carratelli, G. 1958–59, 'Su alcuni aspetti della monarchia etea'. *Atti dell'Accademia Toscana di Scienze e Lettere 'La Colombaria'* 23, 99–132.

Rad, G. von 1952, *Der heilige Krieg im alten Israel*. Göttingen: Vandenhoeck & Ruprecht.

Rainey, A. F. 1970, *El Amarna Tablets 359–379*. Alter Orient und Altes Testament 8. 2nd edition. Kevelaer: Butzon & Bercker; Neukirchen–Vluyn: Neukirchener Verlag.

Redford, D. B. 1970, *A Study of the Biblical Story of Joseph*. Vetus Testamentum, Supplements 20. Leiden: E. J. Brill.

Renger, J. 1969, 'Untersuchungen zum Priestertum der altbabylonischen Zeit, II'. *Zeitschrift für Assyriologie* 59, 104–230.

—, 1972, 'Flucht als soziales Problem in der altbabylonischen Gesellschaft'. In D. O. Edzard (ed.), *Gesellschaftsklassen im alten Zweistromland*, 167–82. München: Verlag der Bayerischen Akademie der Wissenschaften.

Riemschneider, K. K. 1958, 'Die hethitischen Lanschenkungsurkunden'. *Mitteilungen des Instituts für Orientforschung* 6, 321–81.

—, 1965, 'Zum Lehnswesen bei den Hethitern'. *Archiv Orientální* 33, 333–40.

—, 1971, 'Die Thronfolgeordnung im althethitischen Reich'. In H. Klengel (ed.), *Beiträge zur sozialen Struktur des alten Vorderasien*, 79–102. Berlin: Akademie-Verlag.

Rösel, H. 1975, 'Studien zur Topographie der Kriege in den Büchern Josua und Richter. I: Der Feldzug gegen 'Ai, Jos. 7,2 – 5a,8'. *Zeitschrift des Deutschen Palästina-Vereins* 91, 159–71.

—, 1976, 'Studien zur Topographie der Kriege in den Büchern Josua und Richter. VI: Der Kampf um Gibea, Ri. 20'. *Zeitschrift des Deutschen Palästina-Vereins* 92, 31–46.

Rosenthal, F. 1950–51, 'Sedaka, Charity'. *Hebrew Union College Annual* 23, 411–30.

Rost, L. 1938, *Die Vorstufen von Kirche und Synagoge im Alten Testament*. Beiträge zur Wissenschaft vom Alten und Neuen Testament 76. Stuttgart: W. Kohlhammer.

Roux, G. 1961, 'Adapa, le vent et l'eau'. *Revue d'Assyriologie* 55, 13–33.

Saggs, H. W. F. 1963, 'Assyrian Warfare in the Sargonic Period'. *Iraq* 25, 145–54.

Ščeglov, J. K. 1969, 'Per la costruzione di un modello strutturale delle novelle di Sherlock Holmes'. In *I sistemi di segni e lo strutturalismo sovietico*, 129–31. Milan: Feltrinelli.

Schachermeyr, F. 1928, 'Zur staatsrechtlichen Wertung der hethitischen Verträge'. *Mitteilungen der Altorientalischen Gesellschaft* 4, 180–6.

Schuler, E. von 1957, *Hethitische Dienstanweisungen*. Archiv für Orientforschung, Beiheft 10. Graz: Selbstverlag.

—, 1959, 'Hethitische Königserlasse als Quellen der Rechtsfindung'. In *Festschrift J. Friedrich*, 446–51. Heidelberg: Carl Winter.

—, 1964, 'Staatsverträge und Dokumente hethitischen Rechts'. In G. Walser (ed.), *Neuere Hethiterforschung*. Historia, Einzelschriften 7, 34–53. Wiesbaden: Franz Steiner Verlag.

—, 1965a, *Die Kaškäer: Ein Beitrag zur Ethnographie des alten Kleinasien*. Untersuchungen zur Assyriologie und vorderasiatische Archäologie 3. Berlin: W. de Gruyter.

—, 1965b, 'Sonderformen hethitischer Staatsverträge'. *Jahrbuch für Kleinasiatische Forschung* II/1–2, 445–64.

Schulman, A. R. 1964, 'Some Observations on the Military Background of the Amarna Period'. *Journal of the American Research Center in Egypt* 3, 51–69.

Schunk, K. D. 1963, *Benjamin: Untersuchungen zur Entstehung und Geschichte einer Israelitischen Stammes*. Beihefte zur Zeitschrift für die Alttestamentliche Wissenschaft 86. Berlin: A. Töpelmann.

Seters, J. van 1975, *Abraham in History and Tradition*. New Haven: Yale University Press.

Šklovsky, V. 1976, *Teoria della prosa*. Italian translation. Turin: Einaudi.

Smith, S. 1949, *The Statue of Idri-mi*. Occasional Publications 1. London: The British Institute of Archaeology at Ankara.

Soggin, J. A. 1965, 'Il regno di ´Ešbaʿal, figlio di Saul'. *Rivista degli Studi Orientali* 40, 89–106.

Sommer, F. 1932, *Die Ahhijavā-Urkunden*. Abhandlungen der Bayerischen Akademie der Wissenschaften, Philophisch-historische Abteilung 6. München: Beck.

—, 1938, *Die hethitisch-akkadische Bilingue des Hattušili I*. Abhandlungen der Bayerischen Akademie der Wissenschaften, Philophisch-historische Abteilung 16. Munich: Beck.

Speiser, E. A. 1958, 'Census and Ritual Expiation in Mari and Israel'. *Bulletin of the American Schools of Oriental Research* 149, 17–25.

Stefanini, R. 1962, 'Studi ittiti. 2: Tetti di Nuhassi in XIX 15'. *Athenaeum* 40, 11–19.

—, 1964. 'Haremhab in KUB XIX 15?' *Atti dell'Accademia toscana di Scienze e Lettere 'La Colombaria'* 29, 70–71.

Stone, K. 1995, 'Gender and Homosexuality in Judges 19: Subject–Honor, Object–Shame?' *Journal for the Study of the Old Testament* 67, 87–107.

Streck, M. 1916, *Assurbanipal und die letzten assyrischen Könige*. Vorderasiatische Bibliothek 7. Leipzig: Hinrichs.

Sturtevant, E. H. and Bechtel, G. 1935, *A Hittite Chrestomathy*. Philadelphia: Linguistic Society of America.

Tadmor, H. 1968, 'The People and the Kingship in Ancient Israel'. *Cahiers d'Histoire Mondiale* 11, 46–58.

Talmon, S. 1966, 'The "Desert Motif" in the Bible and in Qumran Literature'. In A. Altmann (ed.), *Biblical Motifs*, 31–63. Studies and Texts 3. Cambridge MA: Harvard University Press.

Thiele, E. R. 1951, *The Mysterious Numbers of the Hebrew Kings*. Chicago: The University of Chicago Press.

Thompson, S. 1936, *Motif-Index of Folk-Literature*, VI. Helsinki: Suomalainen Tiedeakatemia.

—, 1946, *The Folktale*. New York: Holt, Rinehart and Winston.

Thureau-Dangin, F. 1912, *Une relation de la huitième campagne de Sargon*. Musée du Louvre. Textes Cunéiformes III. Paris: Paul Geuthner.

Vaux, R. de 1964, 'Le sens de l'expression "peuple du pays" dans l'Ancien Testament et le rôle politique du peuple en Israël'. *Revue d'Assyriologie* 58, 167–82.

—, 1973, *Histoire ancienne d'Israel*, [2nd volume:] *La période des Juges*. Paris: J. Gabalda.

Vernant, J. P. 1971, 'Hestia-Hermès. Sur l'expression religieuse de l'espace et du mouvement chez les Grecs'. In *Mythe et pensée chez les Grecs*, I, 124–70. Paris: Maspéro.

Wallis, G. 1952, 'Eine Parallele zu Richter 19 29ff. and 1 Sam. 11 5ff. aus dem Briefarchiv von Mari'. *Zeitschrift für die alttestamentliche Wissenschaft* 64, 57–61.

Waterhouse, S. D. 1965, Syria in the Amarna Age. PhD Dissertation. The University of Michigan.

Wehrli, F. 1936, *Motivstudien zur griechischen Komödie*. Zurich-Leipzig: M. Niehans.

Weidner, E. F. 1923, *Politische Dokumente aus Kleinasien*. Boghazköi-Studien 8–9. Leipzig: Hinrichs.

—, 1932–33, 'Der Staatsvertrag Aššurnirâris VI: von Assyrien mit Mati'ilu von Bit-Agusi'. *Archiv für Orientforschung* 8, 17–34.

Westermann, C. 1960, Die Begriffe für Fragen und Suchen im Alten Testament'. *Kerygma und Dogma* 6, 2–30.

Whybray, R. N. 1968, *The Succession Narrative*. London: SCM Press.

Wijngaards, J. 1967, 'Death and Resurrection in Covenantal Context'. *Vetus Testamentum* 27, 226–39.

Wilhelm, G. 1988, 'Zur ersten Zeile des Šunaššura-Vertrages'. In E. Neu and C. Rüster (eds), *Documentum Asiae Minoris Antiquae: Festschrift für Heinrich Otten zum 75. Geburtstag*, 359–370. Wiesbaden: Otto Harrassowitz.

Williams, R. J. 1969, 'Some Egyptianisms in the Old Testament'. In *Studies in Honor of J. A. Wilson*, 93–98. Studies in Ancient Oriental Civilizations 35. Chicago: The University of Chicago Press.

Wiseman, D. J. 1953, *The Alalakh Tablets*. Occasional Publications 2. London: The British Institute of Archaeology at Ankara.

—, 1958, 'The Vassal-Treaties of Esarhaddon'. *Iraq* 20, 1–99.

—, 1968, 'The Tell al Rimah Tablets 1966'. *Iraq* 30, 175–205.

Wolf, H. 1967, The Apology of Hattusilis Compared with other Political Self-Justifications of the Ancient Near East. PhD Dissertation. Brandeis University.

Xella, P. 1973, 'L'inganno di Ea nel mito di Adapa'. *Oriens Antiquus* 12, 257–66.

—, 1976, *Problemi del mito nel Vicino Oriente antico*. Supplemento n. 7 agli Annali. Naples: Istituto Orientale di Napoli.

—, 1978, 'L'épisode de Dnil et Kothar et Gen. XVIII 1–16'. *Vetus Testamentum* 28, 483–8.

Zaccagnini, C. 1973, *Lo scambio dei doni nel Vicino Oriente durante i secoli XV–XIII*. Orientis Antiqui Collectio 11. Rome: Centro per le Antichità e la Storia dell'Arte del Vicino Oriente.

Zayed, Abd el-Hamid 1964, 'A Free-Standing Stela of the XIXth Dynasty'. *Revue d'Égyptologie* 16, 193–208.

Index

PERSONAL NAMES

DEITIES AND MYTHICAL BEINGS

PLACES AND PEOPLES